TO

FROM

DATE

365 BIBLE ANSWERS for CURIOUS KIDS

An "If I Could Ask God Anything"
Devotional

Kathryn Slattery

An Imprint of Thomas Nelson

Published in Nashville, Tennessee, by Tommy Nelson. Tommy Nelson is an imprint of Thomas Nelson. Thomas Nelson is a registered trademark of HarperCollins Christian Publishing, Inc.

Unless otherwise noted, Scripture quotations are taken from the International Children's Bible®. Copyright © 1986, 1988, 1999, 2015 by Thomas Nelson. Used by permission. All rights reserved.

Scripture quotations marked ESV are from the ESV® Bible (The Holy Bible, English Standard Version®). Copyright © 2001 by Crossway, a publishing ministry of Good News Publishers. Used by permission. All rights reserved.

Scripture quotations marked KJV are from the King James Version. Public domain.

Scripture quotations marked THE MESSAGE are from The Message. Copyright © by Eugene H. Peterson 1993, 1994, 1995, 1996, 2000, 2001, 2002. Used by permission of Tyndale House Publishers, Inc.

Scripture quotations marked NCV are from the New Century Version®. © 2005 by Thomas Nelson. Used by permission. All rights reserved.

Scripture quotations marked NIV are from the Holy Bible, New International Version®, NIV®. Copyright © 1973, 1978, 1984, 2011 by Biblica, Inc.® Used by permission of Zondervan. All rights reserved worldwide. www.Zondervan.com. The "NIV" and "New International Version" are trademarks registered in the United States Patent and Trademark Office by Biblica, Inc.®

Scripture quotations marked NKJV are from the New King James Version®. © 1982 by Thomas Nelson. Used by permission. All rights reserved.

Scripture quotations marked NLT are from the Holy Bible, New Living Translation. © 1996, 2004, 2007, 2013, 2015 by Tyndale House Foundation. Used by permission of Tyndale House Publishers, Inc., Carol Stream, Illinois 60188. All rights reserved.

Scripture quotations marked NRSV are from the New Revised Standard Version Bible. Copyright © 1989 National Council of the Churches of Christ in the United States of America. Used by permission. All rights reserved.

Scripture quotations marked RSV are from the Revised Standard Version of the Bible. Copyright 1946, 1952, and 1971 National Council of the Churches of Christ in the United States of America. Used by permission. All rights reserved.

Scripture quotations marked TLB are from The Living Bible. Copyright © 1971. Used by permission of Tyndale House Publishers, Inc., Carol Stream, Illinois 60188. All rights reserved.

Scripture quotations marked ERV are from the Easy-to-Read Version Copyright © 2006 by Bible League International.

Buzz Aldrin's words are taken from his 1970 article in *Guideposts Magazine*, "Is It True That an Astronaut Celebrated Communion on the Moon?", available online at https://www.guideposts.org/better-living/life-advice/finding-life-purpose/guideposts-classics-buzz-aldrin-on-communion-in-space.

The prayer we said for our dog Max as he was passing away, used in the September 10 devotion, was adapted from a "Blessing for an Animal That Has Died or Is About to Die," published in *I Will See You in Heaven*, by Jack Wintz, Paraclete Press, 2010.

ISBN-13: 978–0–7180–8564–3

Library of Congress Cataloging-in-Publication Data on File

Printed in China

17 18 19 20 21 DSC 5 4 3 2 1

Mfr: DSC / Shenzhen, China / November 2017 / PO #9457099

For Katy and Brinck, and children
of all ages, everywhere . . .

Just for You

Dear Reader,

I am so excited that you have chosen to read this 365-day devotional! Here is why: it is *very* important to understand these three life-changing truths about God.

God is real.

God personally loves and cares for you.

God has a unique purpose for your life on planet Earth.

Why are these three truths so important? Because you were born to really and truly get to know God, understand how much He loves you, and discover His special purpose for your life.

This is good news! And it is the reason I wrote this devotional just for you. In case you are wondering, a *devotional* is a special book you read daily to help you grow closer to God. The word *devotional* includes the idea of being "devoted" or lovingly faithful to God. You may be wondering: *Why, if there are 365 days in the year, are there 366 daily devotions?* Because every four years, on February 29, there is an extra day—a leap day!

In this daily devotional you will learn all about our real, loving Father God; His Son, Jesus; God's Holy Spirit; God's Holy Word, the Bible; Christianity; faith; prayer; the church; Christian seasons, holidays, and traditions; the history of Christianity; what it means to be a Christian in today's world; famous Christians—and much, much more! Day by day, over the course of one year, we'll explore 366 real-life questions and answers to help you deepen your knowledge of the Bible. You will build your faith vocabulary so you can better understand and share the message of God's love with others. Most importantly, you will establish a deep and lasting personal relationship with our living, loving Father God, through faith in His Son, Jesus.

It's a good idea to pick ten or fifteen minutes each day—maybe first thing in the morning or at bedtime before you go to sleep—to read and think about each day's devotional. In addition to a real-life question and answer, each entry begins with a Bible verse and ends with a short prayer. You might want to have your Bible handy in case you want to look up the day's Bible verse and find out more about it. At the back of this devotional you will find a list of all the questions in this book.

If you want to read ahead to the next day or go back and read yesterday's devotion, that's okay. The more you read, the more you will learn! And don't worry if you miss a day . . . or a week . . . or even a month of readings. The good news is that *whenever* you open this book, *whatever day* it might be, God is patiently waiting for you. He is so happy to have your attention and eager to speak to you in a loving, close, deeply personal way. That's just the way God is.

There are, of course, zillions of questions about God and Jesus and Christianity—way more than can ever be answered in a single year. But every day, through the pages of this devotional, I promise that you will begin to understand what you believe about God—and why. And if there's something you read that you don't understand, or if you have more questions, feel free to ask your mom or dad or a grown-up you can trust.

Remember, God loves a curious mind and seeking heart. And God loves *you*. So fasten your seat belt, turn the page to today's date, and get ready to take off on an exciting journey in faith!

Love and Blessings,

Kitty Slattery

P.S. — Even though we haven't met, you are in my most loving prayers each and every day!

Who Invented Time?

There is a time for everything, and a season for
every activity under the heavens.
—ECCLESIASTES 3:1

What a good question for the first day of the year! The answer is simple: God invented time. The Bible says that God is both the beginning and the end (Revelation 21:6). This is because God is *eternal*, which means "forever" or "endless." Because God is eternal, He lives outside time and space. We call this place the kingdom of God, or heaven.

Although we experience time, God in heaven doesn't. For God "a day is like a thousand years, and a thousand years are like a day" (2 Peter 3:8).

Here is good news: God loves us so much that approximately 2,000 years ago He sent His only Son, Jesus, into human history to live, die, and miraculously rise from the dead, so that everyone who believes can live forever too (John 3:16). Isn't that amazing?

In the coming year, we'll discover how knowing God and His Son, Jesus, can make a powerful, positive difference in your life.

> *Thank You, God, for Your gift of time on*
> *Earth and eternal life in heaven!*

? Want to know more? See January 14, "What Is the Kingdom of God?" and February 5, "Who Is Jesus?"

Why Do Christians Celebrate Special Seasons and Holidays?

*"You will announce the Lord's appointed feasts as
holy meetings. These are my special feasts."*
—LEVITICUS 23:1–2

Christians celebrate special seasons and holidays as a way of remembering, honoring, and thanking God throughout the year. The word *holiday* means "holy day," or special day set apart for God. Most Christian seasons and holidays focus on the life and teachings of Jesus. Some Christian holidays, such as Easter and Christmas, include feasting, fun family traditions, and joyful church services with special music. Others, such as Good Friday and the season of Lent, are times for prayer and thoughtful reflection. All these times teach us about God and help us get to know Him better. Here are some special seasons and holidays celebrated by believers around the world that we will learn about:

- Epiphany (January 6)
- The Season of Lent
- Holy Week
- Palm Sunday
- Good Friday

- Easter
- Pentecost
- All Saints' Day (November 1)
- The Season of Advent
- Christmas (December 25)

*Thank You, God, for special seasons and holidays that help me
remember the life and teachings of Jesus and grow closer to You.*

? Want to know more? See May 2, "What Is the Bible?"

Who Is God?

In the beginning God created the heavens and the earth.
—GENESIS 1:1 NIV

God is the Creator of everything, visible and invisible. God created heaven and the angels. He created time and space. From God's fingertips tumbled galaxies, the stars, and our beautiful planet. God loved His creation so much that He didn't stop there. He went on to create the oceans, animals, birds in the sky, and fish in the sea. At the end of each day of creation, God saw that it was good (Genesis 1:10, 12, 18, 21, 25).

As His final act of creation, God created the first human man and woman, Adam and Eve. God was so pleased with them that He could barely contain His joy. Looking at Adam and Eve, God saw that they were not only good but *"very* good" (v. 31)! It is easy to imagine God's eyes sparkling with love and pride.

Guess who else God created?

God created *you*!

God's children include all the people on Earth, people who are living and people who have died. God's children even include people who haven't been born yet (Psalm 139:13–16).

Who is God? God is your loving Creator.

> *Thank You, God, for being my awesome, loving Creator!*

? Want to know more? See July 28 and 29, "Who Are Adam and Eve, and How Did Sin Enter the World? (Parts 1 and 2)."

If God Is My Creator, How Is He Different from My Parents?

The Father has loved us so much! He loved us so much that we are called children of God.

—1 JOHN 3:1

Every child begins life with a biological or earthly mother and father. Unlike God, human moms and dads are not perfect. They make mistakes. They can get tired and grumpy. They can have problems and get divorced. Earthly parents can get hurt or sick or even die.

The good news is that every child also has a spiritual Parent—our Father God in heaven. God loves us perfectly and never gets tired, grumpy, or sick. Best of all, God never dies—or changes. He is the same today as He was yesterday and will be tomorrow (Hebrews 13:8)! You can always count on God.

Know this: *God always has time for you.* Whenever you call God's name, out loud or silently, it is as if you are the only person in the world, and God turns His total attention to you. Why? Because God loves you perfectly. You are *never* inconvenient to your Father God. This is because God's love for you is perfect.

Who is God? He is your Creator and your perfect Parent. What is the best word to describe God? God is *love* (1 John 4:8).

Thank You, God, for being my Creator and my loving, perfect Parent!

? **Want to know more?** See December 3, "How Is It Possible for God to Truly Love Billions of Different People?"

If God Is Invisible, How Can I Know He Is Real?

"You hear the wind blow. But you cannot tell where it comes from or where it is going. It is the same with every person who is from the Spirit."
—John 3:8

We can't see some things with our eyes, yet we know they are real. We can't see gravity, but it is real. How do we know? Because if you let go of this book, it will drop to the floor with a big thud! We can't see electricity, but it powers our lights.

My favorite example is the wind. We can't see it, but we can feel it when it cools our skin on a hot summer day. We can see treetops swaying and clouds racing across the sky. God is like the wind. Even though we can't see God, we can feel His love and hear His loving voice in our hearts.

More than anything, God wants you to know that He is real and that He loves you. You are special! No one is quite like you. And God has a very special purpose for your life!

> *Thank You, God, for being real, even when I can't see You. Help me hear Your voice whispering like the wind in my heart.*

? **Want to know more?** See October 6, "What Does It Mean to Be Born Again?" and October 24, "What Is a Quiet Time?"

What Is Epiphany?

My eyes have seen your salvation, which you have prepared in
the sight of all nations: a light for revelation to the Gentiles.
—LUKE 2:30–32 NIV

Today is Epiphany (Ee-*pi*-fun-ee), when Christians around the world celebrate the visit of the *Magi*, or wise men, who brought gifts to the young child Jesus (Matthew 2:1–11). Epiphany is also known as "King's Day" and the "Twelfth Day" because it takes place twelve days after Christmas. Epiphany reminds us that Jesus truly is God's Son.

The word *epiphany* means to "reveal" or "show." An epiphany is that "*Aha!*" moment when you suddenly understand something. It's like a light bulb coming on!

We remember the Magi at Epiphany because they were among the first people to understand that Jesus was sent to earth by God. Even though Jesus was just a small child, these very wise men recognized that He was divine. The word *divine* means "to come from God." Lots of stories in the Bible tell us about people having epiphanies and realizing that Jesus is God. You can have an epiphany too!

> *Thank You, God, for sending Jesus to earth. Show*
> *me how to recognize, know, and love Him.*

? **Want to know more?** See February 5, "Who Is Jesus?"; December 14, "Who Are the Magi?"; and December 15, "Why Did the Magi Present Jesus with Gifts of Gold, Frankincense, and Myrrh?"

How Can I Know for Sure God Loves Me?

"God even knows how many hairs are on your head."
—MATTHEW 10:30

God sure is busy. He keeps the stars in the sky and our planet Earth spinning in space! You might think He has no time for all His human children. But God is not like us. With His perfect memory, He knows every person's name—including yours! God loves and cares for you a *lot*.

In fact, He knew you even before you were born (Psalm 139:13–16). God even knows exactly how many hairs are on your head! He loves you so much that He watches over you every minute of every day and night—even right now (Psalm 139:1–10).

How else can you know God loves you? The Bible says that even when you can't hear God's voice, He is still watching over and loving you (Psalm 121:4). This is very good news!

Sometimes He speaks to you in your heart. Although God is big and strong, His voice is a gentle whisper (1 Kings 19:12). Close your eyes and listen. Can you hear God's voice calling your name? Can you hear Him whispering, *I love you*?

> *Thank You, God, for loving and watching over me*
> *so carefully. Help me hear Your voice!*

? Want to know more? See December 3, "How Is It Possible for God to Truly Love Billions of People?" and December 28, "Is It Okay to Question and Sometimes Have Doubts About God?"

Who Is the Trinity?

"Go and make followers of all people in the world. Baptize them in the name of the Father and the Son and the Holy Spirit."
—MATTHEW 28:19

Today's question is not *"What* is the Trinity?" but *"Who* is the Trinity?" This is because the Trinity is not a thing. It's a *Person.* And that Person is God!

The Bible teaches that God is made up of three Persons (Matthew 28:19):

1. God
2. God's Son, Jesus
3. God's Holy Spirit

The word *trinity* means "three-in-one." The Trinity is a way to describe God. Even though Jesus didn't use the word *trinity,* He was the first person to speak clearly about it (Matthew 28:19). We have hints of the Trinity even as far back as the very first book in the Bible. Genesis says that when God made the world, He said: "Let *us* make mankind in *our* image, in *our* likeness" (1:26). Isn't that amazing? Although Jesus would not arrive on earth for thousands of years, Jesus and the Holy Spirit *were with and part of God* since before the dawn of time.

Thank You, God, for being three-in-one. And thank You for the Bible, with all its hints and mysteries about who You are!

How Can God Be Three Persons at the Same Time?

"Just as the heavens are higher than the earth, so are my ways higher than your ways. And my thoughts are higher than your thoughts."
—ISAIAH 55:9

No doubt about it, the idea of God being three persons at the same time is hard to understand. That's because God's thoughts and ways are so different and so much higher than ours. We are humans. God is God! He knows everything!

But we can still try to understand how God can be three-in-one. Take an egg, for example. It has three parts: the shell, the white, and the yolk, but they're all part of the same egg. What about your family? You might be a daughter, a niece, and a sister all at the same time. Or think about water. When water is room temperature, it's a flowing liquid. When heated in a teakettle, it becomes steam. When frozen, it becomes ice. But it is always water.

Although these examples are not perfect, they will help you understand how God can be three persons at the same time.

Tomorrow we will discover *why*!

Thank You, God, that even when I don't always understand You, I can always trust You. Help me understand You better every day.

? Want to know more? See January 1, "Who Invented Time?" and January 14, "What Is the Kingdom of God?"

Why Is God Three Persons at the Same Time?

"You can be sure that I will be with you always."
—MATTHEW 28:20

Yesterday we talked about water having three different forms: liquid, ice, and steam or gas. It can be liquid rain, frozen snow, or puffy white clouds in the sky. But it's always water. Water is a little bit like the Trinity in the way different forms serve different purposes.

God, your *Father* in heaven, watches over you as you live your life as His helper here on Earth. He is waiting for you to join Him in heaven one day.

God's *Son*, Jesus, came to show people who God really is and to die for your sins. After Jesus was resurrected, He went up to heaven, and that's where He is right now!

God's Holy *Spirit* is not limited by time or space, which is how God lives in your heart. He guides you and gives you special spiritual gifts, and He whispers God's love to you.

God is three persons in one so He can be with you every minute of every day. Why does God want that? Because He loves you (1 John 3:1).

> *Thank You, God, for Your Son, Jesus, and for Your Holy Spirit, and for how You love me and are always with me.*

? Want to know more? See March 21, "What Is the Resurrection of Jesus?" and April 17, "What Are the Gifts of the Holy Spirit?"

How Do I Know God Has a Special Purpose for My Life?

We are God's masterpiece. He has created us anew in Christ Jesus,
so we can do the good things he planned for us long ago.
—EPHESIANS 2:10 NLT

When God makes snowflakes, each one is different. Some are big. Some are tiny. Some are star-shaped and pointy. Some are lacy and round. If God makes billions of different snowflakes, think how different He makes each one of His children!

You are unique. The word *unique* means "one of a kind." You see, there is no one else on Earth exactly like you. And God has special work for you to do during your life that only *you* can do. It's the reason you were born.

In fact, God knew and loved you even before you were born (Psalm 139:13–16)! You are God's special child, His "masterpiece," created to be His helper. Your mission in life is to discover the good things God wants you to do. Talk about an exciting adventure!

Here's a hint: the good things God has planned for you to do always have to do with *love*. Why? Because "God is love" (1 John 4:8).

Dear God, please show me today the good, kind,
and loving works You created me to do!

? **Want to know more?** See April 29, "How Can I Discover My God-Given Gifts and Talents?"

How Can I Share God's Love?

Serve each other with love.
—Galatians 5:13

God has planned so many wonderful ways for you to share His love with others! It helps to remember that the good things God has planned for you to do always have to do with *love*. Need some ideas? You can discover God's special purposes for your life when you:

- Tell your mom and dad you love them.
- Surprise your mom by unloading the dishwasher or setting the table.
- Hug your grandma and grandpa.
- Write your aunt a letter and tell her how much you love and miss her.
- Thank your teacher for working so hard.
- Invite the new kid in school to sit with you at lunch.
- Tell your friend you're sorry you hurt her feelings.
- Listen to your friend who is sad.
- Pray for your friend who is sick.
- Invite your friend to church or youth group.
- Show God how much you love Him by loving and helping others.

I bet you can come up with lots more good ideas. Have fun!

*Thank You, God, for all the chances I have
to share Your love with others!*

? **Want to know more?** See September 22, "Is It Okay for Me to Invite a Friend to Visit My Church?"

What Does It Mean That I'm Created "in the Image of God"?

*So God created human beings in his image. In the image of
God he created them. He created them male and female.*
—GENESIS 1:27

The Bible says that human beings are created "in the image of God" (Genesis 1:27). Because you are God's child, you are like your heavenly Father in many ways:

- Because God is loving, you can be loving.
- Because God has a sense of humor, you can laugh.
- Because God is joyful, you can be joyful.
- Because God knows sadness, you can cry.
- Because God is eternal, you have a soul that is eternal.
- Because God knows and loves you, it is possible for you to know and love Him (1 John 4:19).

God loves you so much He wants you to live with Him forever! In fact, the Bible says God loves you so much that nothing—not even sickness or death—can separate you from His love (Romans 8:39). Isn't that amazing?

> *Thank You, God, that I am created in Your image, and that
> nothing—nothing!—can separate me from Your love.*

? **Want to know more?** See January 3, "Who Is God?"

What Is the Kingdom of God?

"God's kingdom is within you."
—LUKE 17:21

The "kingdom of God" is another way to say *heaven*. A modern-day scientist might describe heaven as being another dimension. Although we can't see heaven, the Bible tells us that it is real and wonderful! Heaven is home for God, His Son, Jesus, the Holy Spirit, God's angels, and all believers in Jesus. Many theologians believe that heaven "breaks through" to earth every day, in ways large and small. A *theologian* is a person who studies God. The biggest breakthrough happened when God sent Jesus to save and change the world forever! Three days after His death on the cross, Jesus miraculously rose from the dead with a brand-new heavenly body designed to live forever. Forty days later, Jesus *ascended* or "went up" to heaven where He lives and rules as our heavenly King.

Thanks to Jesus, one day we too will receive new bodies and join God and Jesus in heaven. For now, we have the gift of God's Holy Spirit living in our hearts, helping us share God's love with others. That's what Jesus meant when He said, "God's kingdom is within you" (Luke 17:21). This is very good news!

> *Thank You, God, for Your Holy Spirit and
> Your kingdom living in my heart!*

? **Want to know more?** See March 21, "What Is the Resurrection of Jesus?" and November 17, "What Will Happen to Me When I Die?"

How Can I Get to Know God Better?

"Let the little children come to me. Don't stop them. The kingdom of God belongs to people who are like these little children."
—MARK 10:14

Here is good news: when it comes to knowing God, kids are natural-born experts! Here are three good ways to get to know God even better:

- Read your Bible. The Bible is God's love letter to you. The more you read it, the more you will get to know and love God.
- Spend time with God in prayer. Prayer is talking and listening to God. Spend time with Him, and you will get to know Him better! Remember: God always has time for you, and when you pray, God always listens.
- Spend time with friends who believe in God. This way you can share what you know about God and pray for one another. You will be amazed how much fun it is!

Do you know what God thinks about you wanting to get to know Him better? It makes Him *so* happy! Why? Because *God loves you* (1 John 3:1).

Thank you, God, for loving me. Help me read my Bible, pray, and make friends with kids who want to get to know You better too!

? Want to know more? See May 2, "What Is the Bible?"; August 11, "What Is Prayer?"; October 18, "What Is Christian Fellowship?"; and October 24, "What Is a Quiet Time?"

When God Looks at Me, What Does He See?

The Lord knows what is in every person's mind.
He understands everything you think.
—1 Chronicles 28:9

When God looks at you, He sees you busily living your everyday life. He sees you sitting at your desk in school, riding your bike, watching TV, and eating dinner. He sees you sleeping too. This is not surprising, because God is your loving Creator and heavenly Father. But God also sees the *inside* of you (1 Chronicles 18:9; 1 Samuel 16:7). In fact, God is more interested in who you are on the inside than on the outside. That's because what's inside is *eternal*—it lasts forever and ever. Who you are on the inside is called your *soul*. It's made up of your unique personality—all your thoughts, feelings, dreams, hopes, interests, and knowledge. It's made up of the love in your heart. Do you try to be kind? Are you honest? Do you like to laugh? That's what's important to God.

When God looks at you, He loves you completely—inside and out. God loves you so much that He wants you to live forever with Him in heaven (John 3:16)!

Thank You, God, that You see and love me, inside and out!

? **Want to know more?** See January 1, "Who Invented Time?";
October 20, "What Does the Bible Mean When It Says My Body
Is the 'Temple of God?'"; and November 20, "When I Die, Will I
Become an Angel with a Halo and Wings?"

Does God Care What My Body Looks Like?

I praise you because you made me in an amazing and wonderful way.
—Psalm 139:14

God doesn't care whether your eyes are blue or brown. He doesn't care whether your hair is curly or straight, or whether you wear glasses or use a wheelchair. God creates His children in all shapes, sizes, colors, and abilities. God made each of us "in an amazing and wonderful way." Because He made you special, you are one of a kind! No matter what you look like, or how your body works, God loves you just the way you are. God also wants your body and soul to be as healthy as possible (1 Thessalonians 5:23; 3 John v. 2).

For a healthy body, eat nutritious foods, get enough sleep, and try to get lots of sunshine and exercise. For a healthy soul, read your Bible, talk and listen to God in prayer, go to church, and spend time with friends who love God too. Why are a healthy body and soul important? Because God loves you and wants you to be His special helper, sharing His love with others.

> *Thank You for my body, God. Help me take good care of it so I can be Your helper!*

? Want to know more? See October 20, "What Does the Bible Mean When It Says My Body Is the 'Temple of God?'" and November 10, "Who Is Fred Rogers? (Part 2)."

What Do I Have to Do to Get God to Love Me?

Those who are in Christ Jesus are not judged guilty.
—ROMANS 8:1

Here is good news. You don't have to do anything to get God to love you. God loves you just the way you are, because you are His child. It's as simple as that. Although it may be hard to believe, there is nothing you can do, or say, or think that will cause God to love you any more or any less.

God understands that because we are human, we are not perfect. When we mess up, God is slow to anger and overflowing with compassion and love (Psalm 145:8). The good news is that God wants to help us become better, more loving people. He loves it when we grow in our ability to love ourselves and others.

Do you have a temper? Do you sometimes get jealous or impatient? If there is anything you would like God to change, tell Him all about it. You will be surprised how eager He is to help!

> *Thank You, God, for loving me just the way I am and for helping me grow in ways that will make me more like You!*

? Want to know more? See January 20, "What Are Some of God's Promises for Me?"

Does God Ever Sleep?

Lord . . . you know all about me. . . . You know my thoughts
before I think them. . . . You know well everything I do.
—PSALM 139:1–3

Because God loves you, He is always watching out for you. He never gets tired or needs to sleep (Psalm 121:4). Still, God understands how important it is for *us* to rest. The Bible tells us that God worked for six days on His creation. He created the sun, the moon, the stars, Earth, and everything in them. He created the first humans, Adam and Eve. And what did God do after all that creating? The Bible says that on the seventh day God *rested* (Genesis 2:1–3).

The idea of taking time to rest is so important that God made a commandment about it: "Remember the Sabbath day by keeping it holy" (Exodus 20:8). The word *sabbath* means "to rest." Resting is good for our bodies. It is also good for our souls.

When you close your eyes and rest, there is only one thing God wants you to do. God wants you to remember that He loves you (1 John 3:1).

> *Thank you, God, for Your commandment to take*
> *time to rest and remember Your great love!*

? **Want to know more?** See May 30, "What Are the Ten Commandments? (Part 2)" and November 12, "Who Is Eric Liddell?"

What Are Some of God's Promises for Me?

God is faithful.
—1 CORINTHIANS 1:9

Do you ever feel down in the dumps? Lonely? Worried? Guilty? Angry? It's okay. We all have feelings, good and bad, because we are human. Feelings come and go. Some days are sunny and bright. And some days are like a bad storm.

Because God loves and sees you, He knows when you are struggling with bad feelings. He wants to help you feel better (1 Peter 5:7). How? Through His promises in the Bible. Even during a storm of feelings, God's Bible promises can make you feel like you're in a safe, sunny, calm place. God's Bible promises give you hope for a better day.

How can this be? It helps to remember that the Bible is not some old, dry, boring book. It is the *living Word of God!* He uses it to speak to you personally. In fact, the Bible is full of God's promises just for you. And remember: God always keeps His promises (Deuteronomy 7:9; 1 Corinthians 1:9)!

Over the next several days we will have fun discovering God's promises in the Bible . . . promises *just for you!*

> *Thank you, God, for Your Living Word, the Bible,*
> *and for how You always keep Your promises.*

What Are God's Promises for Me When I Am Lonely?

Turn to me and be kind to me. I am lonely and hurting.
—PSALM 25:16

Everyone feels lonely sometimes. It is part of being human. Here are some of God's Bible promises about loneliness, just for you. As you read and think about each verse, remember: God always keeps His promises (1 Corinthians 1:9)!

- "I am with you and will protect you wherever you go." (Genesis 28:15)
- "I will not leave you. . . . I will come back to you." (John 14:18)
- "You can be sure that I will be with you always. I will continue with you until the end of the world." (Matthew 28:20)
- "Nothing can separate us from the love God has for us. Not death, not life . . . nothing now, nothing in the future, no powers, nothing above us, nothing below us, or anything else in the whole world will ever be able to separate us from the love of God." (Romans 8:35, 37–39)

When you are feeling lonely, talk to God in prayer. It can also be helpful to talk to and pray with your mom or dad, or other trusted grown-ups.

Thank You, God, that even when I feel lonely, You are always with me.

What Are God's Promises for Me When I Am Sad?

He heals the brokenhearted.
—PSALM 147:3

Everyone feels sad and brokenhearted sometimes. Try saying a little prayer before reading these verses, asking God to help you with your feelings of sadness. God always keeps His promises.

- "God will wipe away every tear from their eyes." (Revelation 7:17)
- "The LORD is close to the brokenhearted. He saves those whose spirits have been crushed." (Psalm 34:18)
- "I told you these things so that you can have peace in me. In this world you will have trouble. But be brave! I have defeated the world!" (John 16:33)
- "And God's peace will keep your hearts and minds in Christ Jesus. The peace that God gives is so great that we cannot understand it." (Philippians 4:7)

When you are feeling sad, talk to God in prayer. It can also be helpful to talk to and pray with others.

> *Thank You, God, for understanding when I feel sad and for being my loving heavenly Father.*

What Are God's Promises for Me When I Am Worried?

Give all your worries to [God], because he cares about you.
—1 PETER 5:7

Everyone feels worried sometimes. It is part of being human. Take a look at God's Bible promises about worry, just for you. Take your time as you read and think about each verse, and remember that God always keeps His promises.

- "Give your worries to the Lord. He will take care of you." (Psalm 55:22)
- "I leave you peace. My peace I give you. . . . So don't let your hearts be troubled. Don't be afraid." (John 14:27)
- "Don't worry. . . . Look at the birds in the air. They don't plant or harvest or store food in barns. But your heavenly Father feeds the birds. And you know that you are worth much more than the birds. You cannot add any time to your life by worrying about it. . . . Don't worry." (Matthew 6:25–27, 31)

When you are feeling worried and anxious, talk to God in prayer. You can also talk to and pray with friends and family.

> *Thank You, God, for helping me overcome my feelings of worry and anxiety.*

? Want to know more? See September 12, "What Is the Serenity Prayer?"

What Are God's Promises for Me When I Am Afraid?

God did not give us a spirit that makes us afraid. He gave us a spirit of power and love and self-control.

—2 TIMOTHY 1:7

Everyone feels scared sometimes. Sometimes fear is a healthy feeling, in that it is God's way of saying "Watch out! Danger ahead!" If you are feeling seriously frightened about anything, talk to your mom or dad, or another trusted grown-up.

Here are some of God's Bible promises about being afraid:

- "So don't worry, because I am with you. . . . I will make you strong and will help you. I will support you with my right hand that saves you." (Isaiah 41:10)
- "Be strong and courageous. Do not be afraid; do not be discouraged, for the LORD your God will be with you wherever you go." (Joshua 1:9 NIV)
- "I will not be afraid because the Lord is my helper. People can't do anything to me." (Hebrews 13:6)
- "God is love. . . . There is no fear in love. . . . [God's] perfect love drives out fear." (1 John 4:16, 18 NIV)

God, when I am afraid, it is so good to be able to trust that You love me and are watching over me!

What Are God's Promises for Me When I Am Envious or Jealous?

You have jealousy and arguing among you. This shows that you are not spiritual. You are acting like people of the world.
—1 CORINTHIANS 3:3

Everyone feels envy and jealousy sometimes. Envy is when you want some thing, such as a new bike, that belongs to someone else. Jealousy is when you want a relationship, such as being best friends, that belongs to someone else. At the root of both is an upsetting sense of extreme discontent, which is no fun. God wants you to be happy and content! Here are two of God's Bible promises to help you when you are feeling envious or jealous:

- "Be content with what you have, because God has said, 'Never will I leave you; never will I forsake you.'" (Hebrews 13:5 NIV)
- "The thing you should want most is God's kingdom and doing what God wants. Then all these other things you need will be given to you." (Matthew 6:33)

When you are feeling envious or jealous, talk to God in prayer. Talk to and pray with others who love God and love you.

Thank You, God, for helping me overcome envy and jealousy. Show me what true contentment is like!

What Are God's Promises for Me When I Am Angry?

"In your anger do not sin: Do not let the sun go down while you are still angry."
—EPHESIANS 4:26 NIV

Everyone feels angry sometimes. The reason God doesn't want you to "let the sun go down while you are still angry" is so you can enjoy a good night's sleep and have good dreams. It is amazing how better things can look in the morning!

Here are some of God's Bible promises about anger:

- "It is better to be slow-tempered than famous." (Proverbs 16:32 TLB)
- "Always be willing to listen and slow to speak. Do not become angry easily. Anger will not help you live a good life as God wants." (James 1:19–20)
- "Don't get angry. Don't be upset; it only leads to trouble." (Psalm 37:8)
- "A gentle answer will calm a person's anger. But an unkind answer will cause more anger." (Proverbs 15:1)

When you are feeling angry, talk to God in prayer. Talking and praying with others will also help you.

> *Thank You, God, for helping me control my temper, and please help me remember not to go to sleep angry.*

What Are God's Promises for Me When I Am Confused and Need Guidance?

Depend on the Lord. Trust him, and he will take care of you.
—PSALM 37:5

Everyone feels confused and needs guidance at times. It is part of being human. Here are some of God's Bible promises for when you feel confused. Before you read, try saying a little prayer, asking God to open your heart to hear His voice as He guides you.

- "This God is our God forever and ever. He will guide us from now on." (Psalm 48:14)
- "If you go the wrong way . . . you will hear a voice behind you. It will say, 'This is the right way. You should go this way.'" (Isaiah 30:21)
- "If any of you needs wisdom, you should ask God for it. God is generous. He enjoys giving to all people, so God will give you wisdom. But when you ask God, you must believe. Do not doubt God." (James 1:5–6)

When you are feeling confused and need guidance, it can also be helpful to talk with people you know and trust.

> *Thank you, God, that when I am confused, I
> trust that You will show me the way.*

What Are God's Promises for Me When I Need Healing?

"I will bring back your health. And I will heal your injuries."
—JEREMIAH 30:17

Everyone gets sick or injured sometimes. The good news is that healing our bodies is one of God's favorite things to do. When you ask God for healing, all you need is the simplest, most basic faith. A prayer for healing is just like any other prayer. Here are some of God's Bible promises for when you need healing:

- "I will put bandages on those that were hurt. I will make the weak strong." (Ezekiel 34:16)
- "The people who trust the Lord will become strong again. They will be able to rise up as an eagle in the sky." (Isaiah 40:31)
- "The prayer that is said with faith will make the sick person well. The Lord will heal him." (James 5:15)
- "Praise the LORD, my soul, and forget not all his benefits—who forgives all your sins and heals all your diseases." (Psalm 103:2–3 NIV)

When you are sick or hurt, it can also be helpful to pray for God's healing with your mom, dad, or trusted friend.

> *Thank You, God, for Your loving desire and power to heal!*

? Want to know more? See April 21, "What Is the Holy Spirit's Gift of Healing?"; July 3, "What Is the Thorn in Paul's Flesh?"; and December 7, "How Can Anything Good Come Out of Pain and Suffering?"

What Are God's Promises for Me When I Need More Faith?

Faith means being sure of the things we hope for. And faith means knowing that something is real even if we do not see it.
—HEBREWS 11:1

Everyone has doubts about God at times. Sometimes we get so busy we forget to spend time with God, and our faith weakens. The good news is God understands. It's never too late to get back in touch with God! Here are some of God's Bible promises for when you need more faith:

- "We live by what we believe, not by what we can see." (2 Corinthians 5:7)
- "What is impossible with men is possible with God." (Luke 18:27 NIV)
- "If you have faith as small as a mustard seed, you can say to this mountain, 'Move from here to there.' And the mountain will move. All things will be possible for you." (Matthew 17:20)

When you are struggling with faith, talk to God about it in prayer.

> *Thank You, God, for Your patience and love. Help me take time each day to be with You and grow my faith!*

? **Want to know more?** See October 24, "What Is a Quiet Time?" and December 28, "Is It Okay to Question and Sometimes Have Doubts About God?"

What Are God's Promises for Me When I Am Tempted?

"Watch and pray so that you will not fall into temptation."
—MATTHEW 26:41 NIV

We all sometimes feel tempted to do something we know is wrong. But we don't have to *give in* to temptation and sin. To *sin* is to do or say something we know is wrong. Thankfully, God understands how easy it is for us to be tempted. He can give us special power to fight and not give in to sin. Here is one of God's most powerful Bible promises for when you feel tempted: "The only temptations that you have are the temptations that all people have. But you can trust God. He will not let you be tempted more than you can stand. But when you are tempted, God will also give you a way to escape that temptation. Then you will be able to stand it." (1 Corinthians 10:13)

Know this: When you lose a fight with temptation and give in to sin, *God still loves you.* Just tell God what you did and that you are sorry. Your heavenly Father is eager to forgive you and give you a fresh start!

> *Thank You, God, for helping me resist temptation—*
> *and for Your forgiveness when I don't.*

? Want to know more? See July 31, "Why Do I Still Sin, Even When I Don't Want To?" and August 1, "Are There Special Words I Need to Say When I Confess My Sins to God?"

What Are God's Promises for Me When I Feel Guilty?

"I will forgive their sins. I will remember their sins no more."
—JEREMIAH 31:34 NIV

Everyone feels guilty sometimes. The word *guilty* means to feel responsible for having thought, or said, or done something that deep down inside you know is wrong. The Bible says the best way to deal with guilt is to *confess*, or "tell," God about what you've done wrong and ask for His forgiveness. God is in the forgiveness business! You will feel so much better after you tell God you are sorry and ask for His forgiveness. Here are some of God's Bible promises for when you feel guilty:

- "Those who are in Christ Jesus are not judged guilty." (Romans 8:1)
- "Let us come near to God with a sincere heart and a sure faith, because we have been made free from a guilty conscience." (Hebrew 10:22 NCV)
- "He has taken our sins away from us as far as the east is from west." (Psalm 103:12)

When you feel very guilty about something, it can also be helpful to talk to and pray with others.

Thank You, God, for setting me free from guilt when I confess my sins to You!

? Want to know more? See July 31, "Why Do I Still Sin Even When I Don't Want To?" and August 1, "Are There Special Words I Need to Say When I Confess My Sins to God?"

FEBRUARY

What Are God's Promises for Me When I Have Failed?

In everything God works for the good of those who love him.
—ROMANS 8:28

No matter how hard we try, we all sometimes fail. When we fail, we can experience crushing feelings of disappointment and discouragement. But nothing in life goes to waste. God can use our failures to teach us important, unexpected lessons. He can even turn them into something beautiful and good! Here are some of God's Bible promises for when you have tried very hard and failed:

- "The LORD upholds all those who fall and lifts up all who are bowed down." (Psalm 145:14 NIV)
- "The godly may trip seven times, but they will get up again." (Proverbs 24:16 NLT)
- "We have troubles all around us, but we are not defeated. We do not know what to do, but we do not give up. We are persecuted, but God does not leave us. We are hurt sometimes, but we are not destroyed." (2 Corinthians 4:8–9)

> *Thank You, God, that You can turn my failure into something beautiful and good!*

? Want to know more? See December 7, "How Can Anything Good Come Out of Pain and Suffering?" and December 31, "What Does Jesus Mean When He Tells Us to Be Perfect?"

What Are God's Promises for Me When I Need Hope?

"There is surely a future hope for you, and your hope will not be cut off."
—PROVERBS 23:18 NIV

Everyone feels a lack of hope sometimes. When you feel hopeless, it can be helpful to look back and remember an example of when God helped you through a difficult time. You can count on God to help you again (and again!) because the Bible says He is the same today as He was yesterday and as He will be forever and ever (Hebrews 13:8). Here are some of God's Bible promises for when you need more hope:

- "All you who put your hope in the Lord be strong and brave." (Psalm 31:24)
- "I know what I have planned for you," says the Lord. "I have good plans for you. I don't plan to hurt you. I plan to give you hope and a good future." (Jeremiah 29:11)
- "We know that in everything God works for the good of those who love him." (Romans 8:28)

You can pray to God when you have feelings of hopelessness. You can also talk to people you love.

Thank You, God, for filling my heart with hope and for being the same loving God yesterday, today, and tomorrow!

? Want to know more? See August 3, "What Is Christian Hope?"

What Are God's Promises for Me When I Feel Left Out by Others?

If God is for us, who can be against us?
—Romans 8:31 NIV

No doubt about it, one of our most painful feelings is *rejection*, or "being left out." It is helpful to remember that everyone experiences rejection sometimes. Even so, rejection can hurt so badly that it often takes time to get over.

Here are some of God's Bible promises for when you feel left out:

- "He heals the brokenhearted. He bandages their wounds." (Psalm 147:3)
- "I will never leave you; I will never abandon you." (Hebrews 13:5)
- "The Lord loves justice. He will not leave those who worship him." (Psalm 37:28)
- "God even knows how many hairs are on your head. So don't be afraid. You are worth much more than many birds." (Matthew 10:30–31)

When you are feeling left out, talk to God in prayer. He always listens.

Thank You, God, for how You do not reject me but always include me in Your loving thoughts and plans. Help me feel compassion and be kind to others who are left out!

What Are God's Promises for Me When Someone I Love Has Died?

Jesus cried.
—JOHN 11:35

When someone we love has died, this combination of sorrow and loss is called *grief*. Sadly, everyone eventually experiences grief. We feel grief when a beloved pet dies too. God understands, and He feels your pain and wants to comfort you. Here are three of God's Bible promises:

- "God will wipe away every tear from their eyes." (Revelation 7:17)
- "The Lord comforts his people. He will comfort those who suffer." (Isaiah 49:13)
- "There will be no more death, sadness, crying, or pain. All the old ways are gone." (Revelation 21:4)

When you are feeling the pain and sorrow of grief, it can also be helpful to talk to and pray with others.

God, day by day, please heal and comfort my broken heart.
Thank You for Your promise of eternal life in heaven.

? Want to know more? See November 17, "What Will Happen to Me When I Die?"; December 1 and December 2, "What Is Heaven Like? (Parts 1 and 2)"; and September 10, "What Is a Good Prayer for When My Pet Is Close to Death?"

Who Is Jesus?

*The high priest asked Jesus another question: "Are you the Christ,
the Son of the blessed God?" Jesus answered, "I am."*
—MARK 14:61–62

Jesus is God's only Son. He's the most important person who ever lived. Know this: the story of Jesus is not a legend, myth, or fairy tale. It is true. Jesus was a real person. Just like us, Jesus was born, lived, and finally died during His time here on Earth. But unlike anyone else ever, three days after He died, He came back to life with a brand-new body designed to live forever. Why? So that one day after we die, we will get brand-new bodies and live forever with Jesus and God in heaven too!

One of Jesus' best friends, a man named John, wrote: "God loved the world so much that he gave his only Son . . . so that whoever believes in him may not be lost, but have eternal life" (John 3:16).

There is so much more to learn about Jesus! But this is a great start.

> *Thank You, God, for sending Your only Son, Jesus, to die for my sins so that I can live forever with You and Jesus in heaven!*

? Want to know more? See July 23, "Why Do Some Christians Carry Signs That Say 'John 3:16' at Sporting Events?"

When Was Jesus Born?

While Joseph and Mary were in Bethlehem, the
time came for her to have the baby.
—LUKE 2:6

You might expect this question to be asked on December 25 because that is the day we celebrate Christmas. But December 25 is not the actual date of Jesus' birth.

Jesus was born a little more than two thousand years ago in the tiny town of Bethlehem, in the country of Israel. We know this is true. It is not a legend, myth, or fairy tale (Luke 2:1–7).

But because Jesus was born so many years ago, we don't know for sure exactly what year it was. Many *scholars*, or people who study the Bible, think it was between 8 BC and 4 BC. We also don't know the exact address in Bethlehem. Scholars believe that Jesus was probably born in a stable, which is like a small barn where farm animals are kept. That's because after Jesus was born, His mother, Mary, placed the baby Jesus in a *manger*, or wooden feeding box for animals (Luke 2:7).

> *Thank You, God, that Your only Son, Jesus, is not a*
> *myth, legend, or fairy tale. I'm so glad that Jesus really*
> *came to Earth and that He is alive today!*

? Want to know more? See December 16, "Was There Really a Star of Bethlehem?"; December 17, "What Is a Christmas Crèche?"; and December 25, "Is December 25 Really Jesus' Birthday?"

Why Was Jesus Born in a Stable?

*There were no rooms left in the inn. So [Mary] wrapped the baby
with cloths and laid him in a box where animals are fed.*

—LUKE 2:7

At the time of Jesus' birth, a Roman emperor named Caesar Augustus
ordered that all his people be officially counted in a *census*. To be
counted, Mary and Joseph had to travel from their home in Nazareth
to Bethlehem. We don't know for certain how Mary and Joseph traveled, but it probably took them about one week by foot. Because Mary
was expecting a baby, and was probably tired, she might have ridden on
a donkey.

When Mary and Joseph arrived in Bethlehem, the town was very
crowded. There was no room at the village inn. Hospitals hadn't been
invented yet. So Mary and Joseph had to stay in a stable.

When Jesus was born, Mary wrapped Him in *swaddling clothes*, or
strips of soft cloth, to keep Him snug and warm. Then she gently placed
Him in a manger (Luke 2:7).

How happy Mary and Joseph must have been! Welcoming a new
baby can be such a joyful time.

*Thank You, God, for the birth of baby Jesus. Thank You, also,
that Mary and Joseph were such good and loving parents.*

? **Want to know more?** See December 17, "What Is a Christmas
Crèche?"

How Did Jesus Get His Name?

*The angel said to her . . . "You will give birth to
a son, and you will name him Jesus."*
—LUKE 1:30

Names had a very special importance in ancient times, especially for the Jewish people. Names were chosen to describe the person. For example, God named the first person in the Bible Adam, from the Hebrew word *adama*, which means both "man" and "earth," or "ground." God did this because Adam was created from "dust from the ground" (Genesis 2:7).

Likewise, Jesus' name has a special meaning.

Months before Mary knew she was going to have a baby, an angel visited her and her fiancé, Joseph. They were both very surprised!

"You are going to have a son," the angel Gabriel announced. "And His true Father will be God in heaven." He told Mary and Joseph to name the baby Jesus, which means "Savior," or "one who saves the people."

It would be many years before Mary and Joseph would really understand why God wanted His only Son to be named Jesus. But because they loved and trusted God, this is what they did.

> *Thank You, God, for sending Your only Son, Jesus, to be my Savior. What a beautiful name with a beautiful meaning!*

? Want to know more? See June 21, "What Does It Mean When God Changes a Person's Name?"

Is "Christ" Jesus' Last Name?

The first thing Andrew did was to find his brother, Simon. He said to Simon, "We have found the Messiah." ("Messiah" means "Christ.")
—JOHN 1:41

The word *Christ* comes from the Greek translation of the Hebrew word *messiah,* which means "God's anointed one." The word *anointed* means to "be chosen by God." So *Christ* is a description, or title, not a name. "Jesus, *the* Christ" is the more accurate way to refer to Jesus. But over the years, people have combined His name and title together.

In the Old Testament, God promised that He would send a *messiah* to save His people and be their King forever (Psalm 2; Isaiah 4:2). Jesus is that person.

Because people in Israel back then didn't have first and last names like we do today, Jesus was mostly known as "Jesus of Nazareth," which is the town he was from (Luke 24:19). He was also sometimes known as "Jesus of Nazareth, son of Joseph" (John 6:42). That's because even though Jesus' true Father is God in heaven, Joseph was Mary's husband, and he lovingly helped raised Jesus during His growing-up years.

Thank You, God, for sending Your only Son, Jesus, the Christ, into the world, fulfilling Your long-ago and long-awaited promise!

Is It True That the First Person to Recognize Jesus Was an Unborn Baby?

When Elizabeth heard Mary's greeting, the unborn baby inside Elizabeth jumped. . . . She cried out in a loud voice, "God has blessed you more than any other woman. And God has blessed the baby which you will give birth to."
—LUKE 1:41–42

Mary was a very young woman, still in her teens, when the angel Gabriel visited her to tell her she was going to have a baby. She loved God with all her heart, soul, and mind. When she heard she would bear God's Son, Mary could hardly believe her ears. She wasn't even married yet! Gabriel also told Mary that her cousin Elizabeth was pregnant too. *How could this be?* Mary wondered. Elizabeth was very old and unable to have children. But nothing is impossible with God. Mary visited her beloved cousin Elizabeth. When Elizabeth heard the sound of Mary's voice, Elizabeth's unborn baby jumped in her womb! The Holy Spirit told her that both Mary and the baby would be blessed. Elizabeth's baby would grow up to be John the Baptist. He is famous for announcing the arrival of Jesus and for baptizing Jesus (Matthew 3:13).

Thank You, God, that with You nothing is impossible!

? Want to know more? See February 23, "Who Is John the Baptist?"

What Is the *Song of Mary?*

Mary said: "My soul magnifies the Lord."
—LUKE 1:46 NKJV

When Mary's cousin Elizabeth said to Mary, "And blessed is the child you will bear!" Mary remembered what the angel Gabriel had told her (Luke 1:42). She, like Elizabeth, was suddenly filled with God's Holy Spirit.

Mary felt incredibly humbled and honored that God had chosen her, of all women, to be the mother of His only Son, Jesus. She thought her heart would burst with joy.

Mary's beautiful response to Elizabeth is called the *Song of Mary*. It is also called the *Magnificat*, from a Latin word that means "to magnify." This is because in some versions of the Bible, Mary's song begins, "My soul magnifies the Lord."

You can read the whole *Song of Mary* in your Bible in Luke 1:46–55. Here's how Mary's beautiful song begins:

"My soul praises the Lord; my heart rejoices in God my Savior, because he has shown his concern for his humble servant girl. From now on, all people will say that I am blessed, because the Powerful One has done great things for me" (Luke 1:46–49 NCV).

Thank You, God, for Mary's beautiful song and her tender, trusting heart. Help me have a heart like that too!

What Was Jesus like When He Was a Boy?

The little child began to grow up. He became stronger and wiser, and God's blessings were with him.

—LUKE 2:40

Jesus was very smart and brave. Mary and Joseph raised their son to be obedient and to love God. When Jesus was twelve years old, He was separated from His parents while visiting the big city of Jerusalem. Three days later, Mary and Joseph found Jesus talking with the grown-up teachers at the temple, and "all who heard [Jesus] were amazed at his understanding and wise answers" (Luke 2:47). Jesus was calm as could be. But His mother was understandably *very* upset. "Son, why did you do this to us?" Mary asked. "Your father and I were very worried about you" (Luke 2:48).

"Why did you have to look for me?" Jesus asked. "You should have known that I must be where my Father's work is!" (Luke 2:49).

Mary and Joseph didn't understand that Jesus was talking about His Father God in heaven.

Jesus Himself may have been surprised at the words that came out of His mouth. He wasn't being disrespectful. He was only twelve and just beginning to learn who He really was.

> *Help me be patient, God, when I, like Joseph and Mary, do not understand You.*

? Want to know more? See May 31, "What Is the Greatest Commandment?"

Did Jesus Ever Do Anything Wrong?

*Our high priest [Jesus] is able to understand our weaknesses. He
was tempted in every way that we are, but he did not sin.*
—HEBREWS 4:15

We know from the Bible that Jesus was tempted like any other human.
But because Jesus is God's Son, He never gave in to temptation. He never
did anything wrong in God's eyes. Not once!

To be tempted is very stressful. When you are tempted, you feel as if
a giant magnet is pulling you to give in and think, say, or do something
that deep down inside you know is wrong.

Jesus was fully human, so He knows what it feels like to be tempted.
At the same time, Jesus said, "He who has seen me has seen the Father"
(John 14:9). By this, Jesus meant that He and God are one and the same.

When Jesus was tempted to do wrong, He prayed and asked God to
help Him. Jesus loved and trusted God, and God answered His prayers.
Because Jesus suffered when He was tempted, He understands and is
able to help us when we are tempted too (Hebrews 2:18).

> *Thank You, God, for Jesus, who understands
> and helps me when I am tempted.*

? Want to know more? See January 30, "What Are God's Promises
for Me When I Am Tempted?"

Was There Really a Saint Valentine?

Love each other like brothers and sisters. Give your brothers and sisters more honor than you want for yourselves.

—ROMANS 12:10

Happy Valentine's Day! Yes, there once was a Christian named Valentine who lived in Rome. The word *valentine* means "chosen as a sweetheart or special friend." Saint Valentine loved Jesus and refused to worship the Roman gods. Because of his Christian faith, Valentine was thrown into jail and sentenced to death. While he was in jail, Valentine became friends with many children who loved him and passed notes to him through the bars of his jail cell window. Valentine also became friends with the jailer's beautiful daughter.

Valentine was put to death on February 14, AD 269. Before he died, Valentine wrote the jailer's daughter a loving farewell note, signed: "From your Valentine."

Over time, February 14 became known as Valentine's Day. It is a day for exchanging simple expressions of love, such as poems, flowers, cards, and candy. Of course, you don't have to wait for Valentine's Day to share your love. God wants us to love one another every day of the year!

> *Thank You, God, for the love You have poured into my heart. Help me share Your love with others every day.*

? Want to know more? See November 1, "What Is All Saints' Day?"

What Is the Temptation of Christ?

While [Jesus] was in the desert, he was tempted by
Satan. Then angels came and took care of Jesus.
—MARK 1:13

Because Jesus was human, He was tempted. We call the most famous episode the "Temptation of Christ" (Matthew 4:1–11; Mark 1:12–13; Luke 4:1–13). The Spirit sent Jesus into the desert to *fast*, or not eat food, for forty days. Then the devil tried to tempt Jesus to turn stones into bread. Jesus said, "A person does not live only by eating bread. But a person lives by everything the Lord says" (Matthew 4:4). Then Satan tried again. If Jesus were truly God, why not jump off the highest tower in Jerusalem and see if the angels would catch him? Jesus said, "Do not test the Lord your God" (v. 7). Then Satan showed Him all the kingdoms of the world, saying that if Jesus would worship him, He could have everything! Jesus said, "Go away from me, Satan!" Jesus would worship only God (v. 10). Then the devil left Him alone. Jesus didn't live for money, fame, or power. Jesus lived to show the world how much He loves us.

> *God, help me be more like Jesus and live*
> *only to show the world Your love.*

? Want to know more? See January 30, "What Are God's Promises for Me When I Am Tempted?" and November 23 and 24, "Is the Devil Real? (Parts 1 and 2)."

FEBRUARY 16

What Is Lent?

Jesus ate nothing for 40 days and nights. After this, he was very hungry.
—MATTHEW 4:2

Lent is a season of forty days, not counting Sundays, before Easter Sunday. The word *Lent* comes from the Old English words *lencten*, which means "Spring," and *lenctentid*, which means "Springtide," and was also the word for the month of March. Because the date for Easter changes from year to year, the start of Lent changes from year to year too.

Before Jesus began to teach, He spent forty days in the desert. There, Jesus fasted and prayed. To *fast* means to not eat any food. Fasting and praying helped Jesus grow very close to His Father God. When Satan came to tempt Him, He did not give in to sin!

During Lent, many Christians spend extra time with God. They pray and read the Bible. Sometimes they give up something to help others. For example, they give the money they would otherwise spend on candy or video games to help people in need.

Lent is a time to grow closer to God through prayer and to share God's love with others.

> *Dear God, during Lent, help me grow closer to You through prayer.*

? **Want to know more?** See February 15, "What Is the Temptation of Christ?"; March 26, "Why Is Easter Always on a Different Date?" and October 27, "What's the Difference Between Fasting and Dieting?"

What Makes Jesus So Important?

Jesus answered . . . "He who has seen me has seen the Father."
—JOHN 14:9

Jesus is not just any human being. Jesus is the most important person who ever lived in the history of our world. Jesus said that He was God's very own Son (Mark 14:61–62).

Jesus was so close to God that when He prayed, or talked to God, He used the word "Abba" (Mark 14:36). In Jesus' native Aramaic language, the word *abba* means "daddy" or "papa." Imagine that!

Jesus was so close to God that He said, "I and the Father are one" (John 10:30). Jesus is different from all other leaders of a religion who ever lived because three days after He died, He was raised from the dead and received a new body designed to live forever. (We will learn more about this later!)

Jesus is alive today with His Father in heaven. He is alive in our hearts through God's Holy Spirit. Because Jesus is alive, He knows and loves you—and you can know and love Him.

Thank You, God, for being my "Abba" Father in heaven!

Why Did Jesus Come to Earth?

"If you really knew me, then you would know my Father, too."
—JOHN 14:7

Jesus said that God, His Father in heaven, sent Him to earth to show people everywhere once and for all what God is really like (John 14:6–7).

When Jesus was born, it was as though God Himself put skin on and came crashing into human history! Sometimes the birth of Jesus is called the "Incarnation." The word *incarnation* means "God becoming flesh, or human." Until Jesus was born, no one had ever seen God. No one was sure what God was really like. Was God friendly or grumpy? Was God happy or gloomy? Did God cry and laugh? Did God even think about His human children at all? Or was He too busy doing important things like keeping the stars up in the sky?

Jesus said that God cares about each and every one of us—including *you*—a lot.

"For God loved the world so much that he gave his only Son," the Bible says, "so that whoever believes in him may not be lost, but have eternal life" (John 3:16).

> *Thank You, God, for sending Your Son, Jesus,
> to show us what You are really like!*

FEBRUARY 19

Did Jesus Live on Earth Before or After the Dinosaurs?

So God made the wild animals, the tame animals and all the small crawling animals to produce more of their own kind. God saw that this was good.
—GENESIS 1:25

Jesus lived on Earth long after the dinosaurs and approximately two thousand years before the invention of the Internet.

Animals that lived during the days of the Bible and Jesus' life were very much like the animals that live today in the Middle East. The Middle East includes Egypt, which is in northern Africa, and many countries in western Asia. At the heart of the Middle East is Israel, where Jesus was born and lived His life.

Some of the animals that lived during Jesus' life included camels, donkeys, sheep, goats, dogs, cattle, oxen, horses, lions, bears, hyenas, foxes, monkeys, apes, fish, lizards, snakes, cranes, storks, sparrows, peacocks, ostriches, quail, roosters, and chickens. There were also locusts, ants, bees, frogs, flies, fleas, and gnats! *Phew!* In fact, there were so many insects in the Nile Valley in Egypt it was called the "land of whirring wings" (Isaiah 18:1 NIV).

> *Thank You, God, for creating so many different kinds of wonderful animals . . . including insects!*

Did Jesus Have Any Brothers or Sisters?

Jesus, who makes people holy, and those who are made holy are from the same family. So he is not ashamed to call them his brothers.

—HEBREWS 2:11

The words *brother* and *sister* in the Bible can mean a biological or adopted sibling, or can also mean "close friend." Either way, the Bible tells us that Jesus had four brothers: James, Joseph, Simon, and Judas. The Bible also mentions sisters, but we don't know how many (Matthew 13:55).

Jesus' brothers and sisters did not always believe in Him while He was alive (Mark 3:21). But after His resurrection and ascension to heaven, Jesus' brothers (and possibly His sisters) were very active in the early church (Acts 1:14).

Now here is some really big news. The Bible says that because we share the same loving Father in heaven, Jesus is *our* brother too (Matthew 12:50)! Jesus is the best, most caring, and loving brother anyone could ever have. Whenever you need Him, just call His name and Jesus will be with you . . . loving, guiding, and watching over you every minute.

Thank You, Jesus, for being the best, most awesome big brother ever!

? Want to know more? See March 21, "What Is the Resurrection of Jesus?" and April 6, "What Is the Ascension of Christ?"

FEBRUARY 21

What Did Jesus Look Like?

Isn't this the carpenter?
—MARK 6:3 NIV

Because there were no photographs or videos when Jesus walked and talked on Earth, we don't know for sure what He looked or sounded like. But we can guess about several of His physical features.

Because Jesus was from the Middle Eastern country of Israel, He probably had dark hair and brown eyes. We do not know if His hair was curly, straight, or wavy. Jesus probably had a dark, uncut beard and wore His hair long and shoulder-length.

Because the Bible says Jesus worked as a carpenter, He probably had strong, muscular arms. Because people enjoyed being with Jesus, we can assume He smiled and laughed a lot. Because Jesus loved people, He must have had very kind eyes.

When you close your eyes and picture Jesus, whom do you see?

The good news is that even though we cannot see Jesus with our eyes, the Bible says He lives in our hearts through God's Holy Spirit.

Listen carefully. Can you hear Jesus' voice speaking to you in your heart?

Thank You, God, that Jesus is not make-believe, but a real-life Person. Thank You, God, for how Jesus lives and speaks to me in my heart!

What Did Jesus Wear?

He is the One who comes after me. I am not good
enough to untie the strings of his sandals.
—JOHN 1:27

We know from the Bible that Jesus wore a *tunic*, or undergarment, that was one long piece without a seam (John 19:23). In Jesus' day, a tunic was typically sleeveless and loose fitting, falling to the knees. Over His tunic, Jesus wore a loose, flowing *mantle*, or coat, for warmth. It was most likely plain blue, or it may have been white with brown stripes. At the four corners of Jesus' mantle there may have been tassels or fringe.

Around His waist, Jesus wore a *girdle*, or tie. Most girdles were made of leather, about six inches wide, with clasps. The girdle also served as a pouch to carry coins, keys, and other small objects.

It is unlikely Jesus wore any jewelry. He may have carried a cane, staff, or walking stick with some decoration on top made of carved wood or hammered metal. Since most people during Jesus' time wore leather sandals with straps, we can assume He did too (Matthew 10:10).

Thank You, God, for how Jesus knows what it feels like to
wake up in the morning and get dressed—just like me!

Who Is John the Baptist?

John the Baptist came preaching in the wilderness of Judea and saying, "Repent, for the kingdom of heaven has come near."
—Matthew 3:1–2 NIV

John the Baptist was Jesus' cousin. He was a prophet of God—a person who speaks the true word of God to people. God's purpose for John's life was to announce that Jesus truly was God's Son (John 1:15). It's the reason John was born.

When John grew up, he told people to repent, or turn away from their sins. The word *repent* means to "turn around." He told them to prepare their hearts to recognize and welcome Jesus, who was coming soon.

He lived in the wilderness and "wore clothes made from camel's hair and had a leather belt around his waist. He ate locusts and wild honey" (Mark 1:6). Some people thought John was crazy, but many believed him and repented.

People asked John to *baptize* or dip them in the Jordan River. The word *baptize* means "to dip." The water symbolized the washing away of their sins. This is why he is known as "John the Baptist."

> *Thank You, God, for sending John the Baptist to announce Jesus' arrival. And thank You for washing away my sins!*

? Want to know more? See February 10, "Is It True That the First Person to Recognize Jesus Was an Unborn Baby?"

Who Is the Most Important Person Baptized by John the Baptist?

Then Jesus came from Galilee to the Jordan to be baptized by John.
—MATTHEW 3:13 NIV

The most important person John baptized was Jesus. Picture Jesus stepping out from the crowd lining the banks of the Jordan River. He wades into the river's cool waters, where John stands waiting.

The Bible says that after John baptized Jesus, God's Holy Spirit came down from heaven as a dove and hovered over Jesus' head. Then, in a voice so loud that everyone could hear, God said about Jesus, "This is my Son and I love him. I am very pleased with him" (Matthew 3:17). Can you imagine how surprised everyone must have been to hear God's voice?

Jesus' baptism marked the beginning of His mission on earth. For the next three years, Jesus would preach, teach, and share the message of God's great love for people. It is the reason Jesus was born.

You may be wondering, "Why would Jesus, who never sinned, need to be baptized?" He wanted to set an example for us. To this day, Christians around the world get baptized.

Thank You, God, for Jesus' example. I want to be like Him!

? Want to know more? See September 23 and September 24, "What Is Baptism? (Parts 1 and 2)."

FEBRUARY 25

Who Did Jesus Say He Was?

Then Jesus asked, "Who do you say that I am?"
—MARK 8:29

The apostle John was one of Jesus' best friends. John walked, talked, ate, laughed, and cried with Jesus. In other words, John knew Jesus very well.

In his Gospel, John wrote what has come to be known as the seven great "I Am" sayings of Jesus. John wanted to make sure everyone knew who Jesus was.

Here is the list of the seven great "I Am" sayings of Jesus:

- "I am the bread that gives life." (John 6:35)
- "I am the light of the world." (John 8:12)
- "I am the door for the sheep." (John 10:7)
- "I am the good shepherd." (John 10:11)
- "I am the resurrection and the life." (John 11:25)
- "I am the way. And I am the truth and the life." (John 14:6)
- "I am the true vine." (John 15:1)

Why did God send His only Son, Jesus, to be the "bread that gives life" and the "light of the world?" Because God loves the world and all the people in it.

> *Thank You, God, for loving the world and all the people in it—including me!*

Why Did Jesus Do Miracles?

But these [stories of miracles] are written so that you can
believe that Jesus is the Christ, the Son of God. Then, by
believing, you can have life through his name.
—John 20:31

A *miracle* is something wonderful that cannot be explained by natural or scientific laws. Miracles are from our good and loving God. Miracles are not magic. Miracles are real.

Jesus did only loving, kindhearted miracles. He made many sick people well (Mark 5:21–42). He made lame people walk (John 5:2–9). He made blind people see (Matthew 9:27–30). He made deaf people hear (Mark 7:31–37). He even brought His friend, Lazarus, who had died, back to life (John 11:1–34)! In fact, the Bible records at least thirty-seven detailed, true, eye-witnessed miracles of Jesus. His friend John said there were more! "If every one of them were written down," John wrote, "I think the whole world would not be big enough for all the books that would be written" (John 21:25).

Remember: Jesus did not do miracles for money or to show off. Jesus did miracles so people would believe that He is God's Son and to show how much God loves and cares for His children—including *you*!

Thank You, God, for using real-life miracles to show us Your great love!

? Want to know more? See April 22, "What Is the Holy Spirit's Gift of Miraculous Powers?" and September 6, "Do Miraculous Answers to Prayer Still Happen Today?"

Did Jesus Really Feed Five Thousand People with Five Loaves of Bread and Two Fish?

[Jesus] took the five loaves of bread and the two fish. Then he looked to heaven and thanked God for the food. Jesus divided the loaves of bread. He gave them to his followers, and they gave the bread to the people. All the people ate and were satisfied. After they finished eating, the followers filled 12 baskets with the pieces of food that were not eaten. There were about 5,000 men there who ate, as well as women and children.

—MATTHEW 14:19–21

Yes, Jesus really did feed five thousand men, plus women and children, with only five loaves of bread and two fish. Isn't that amazing? It is easy to understand why this is one of Jesus' most famous and best-loved miracles. To this day, it is commonly known as the "miracle of the loaves and the fishes."

Why did Jesus do this miracle? Because the people following Him were hungry. Jesus also did it to teach His disciples to trust God to meet their needs, even in situations that seemed impossible.

> *Thank You, God, that even though You may not always give me what I want, You will always give me what I need.*

Did Jesus Really Walk on Water?

Peter said, "Lord, if that is really you, then tell me to come to you on the water." Jesus said, "Come." And Peter left the boat and walked on the water to Jesus. But when Peter saw the wind and the waves, he became afraid and began to sink. He shouted, "Lord, save me!" Then Jesus reached out his hand and caught Peter. Jesus said, "Your faith is small. Why did you doubt?"
—MATTHEW 14:28–31

Yes, Jesus really did walk on water. The Bible tells us that Jesus performed this miracle on the same day as the miracle of the loaves and fishes! Isn't that amazing?

Jesus did not walk on water to show off. He wanted to show Peter how important it is to keep your eyes on Jesus. When Peter took his eyes off Jesus, he lost his faith and sank. You might think that after seeing Jesus do so many awesome miracles, Peter and the disciples would have had lots of faith. Sometimes they did. But sometimes they didn't. That's because Peter and the disciples were regular people, just like you and me.

> *God, help me keep my eyes on Jesus. Take my faith and make it stronger!*

? **Want to know more?** See January 29, "What Are God's Promises for Me When I Need More Faith?"

What Is Leap Day?

This is the day that the Lord has made. Let us rejoice and be glad today!
—PSALM 118:24

Every four years we add an extra day to the calendar: February 29, known as leap day. While our calendar contains 365 days, the Earth actually takes more time to orbit the sun—about 365.2421 days. Adding a leap day helps make up for that and gets our calendar back in sync with the heavens.

So why do we use the word *leap*? Good question! Normally, a date like your birthday would advance one day every year. So if your birthday were on a Monday, the next year it would be on a Tuesday, and so on. But on a leap year—it *leaps* over two days instead of one!

Leap day is a reminder that humans didn't invent time. God, who lives outside our time and space, invented time. God is perfect. Human beings are not. Even though we've tried to invent a perfect system to mark the passage of time, we cannot.

> *Thank You, God, for the gift of time and for this special leap day. Help me rejoice and be glad for it!*

? **Want to know more?** See January 1, "Who Invented Time?"

MARCH

What Other Things Besides Miracles Did Jesus Do to Show Us What God Is Like?

"Greater love has no one than this: to lay down one's life for one's friends."
—JOHN 15:13 NIV

The Bible teaches us that God is not only loving but that God actually *is* love (1 John 4:8). Because God is love, Jesus used every moment of His life on earth to show us how much God loves us. It is the reason He was born. Jesus demonstrated God's loving nature in many ways:

- When people were sad, Jesus cried with them (John 11:35).
- When people were happy, Jesus shared their joy (John 2:1–2).
- When people were slow to understand Him, Jesus was very patient (John 20:24–29).
- When Jesus made a promise, He kept it (Matthew 17:22–23).
- When people made mistakes, Jesus forgave them (Luke 23:34).
- Jesus prayed for us (John 17:20–23).
- Jesus gave up His life for us, for the forgiveness of our sins so we can live forever with Him and God in heaven (John 3:16).

Jesus did all these things to show how much God loves and cares for us.

> *Thank You, God, for the ways Jesus shows us how much You love us. Help me live a life of love too!*

Who Are the Original Twelve Apostles?

Christ gave gifts to men—he made some to be apostles, some to be prophets, some to go and tell the Good News, and some to have the work of caring for and teaching God's people.

—EPHESIANS 4:11

The twelve apostles are the twelve men Jesus chose to be His *disciples*, or students, while He walked and talked on earth. The word *apostle* means "one who is sent out."

They are Simon (who Jesus called Peter) and his brother, Andrew; James and his brother, John; Philip; Bartholomew; Matthew; Thomas; James the son of Alphaeus; Thaddaeus (or Jude); Simon the Zealot; and Judas Iscariot.

The twelve apostles were ordinary people, just like you and me. They were not educated, rich, or powerful. But through knowing and loving Jesus, they became extraordinary people. Filled with God's Holy Spirit, they traveled all over, risking their lives to share the story of Jesus with everyone they met. Preaching the good news about Jesus, they changed the world forever.

Over the next three days, we will learn more about these twelve fascinating people.

Thank You, God, for how Jesus knows just the right people to choose to share the good news of Your love.

Who Are the Apostles: Simon Peter, Andrew, James, and John?

These are the 12 men he chose: Simon (Jesus gave him the name Peter); James and John, the sons of Zebedee (Jesus gave them the name . . . "Sons of Thunder"); Andrew . . .
—Mark 3:16–18

Jesus gave the apostle Simon the name *Peter*, which means "stone" or "rock" because bighearted Peter was "the rock" upon which Jesus promised to build His church (Matthew 16:18). Sometimes Peter got into trouble by speaking or acting too quickly before thinking. *Andrew* was Peter's brother, and both were fishermen on the Sea of Galilee. The name Andrew means "manly." Andrew was very good at introducing people to Jesus—including his brother, Simon Peter.

James was the older brother of John. His name means "holder of the heel" or "one who overthrows." James was also a fisherman. James, Peter, and John were among Jesus' best friends. *John* was the younger brother of James. His name means "God is gracious." Jesus' nickname for John and James was "Sons of Thunder" because they had very loud voices and big, bold personalities. John and Jesus were very close. Some scholars say that John was Jesus' best friend (John 21:7–20).

> *Thank You, God, for the gift of friends. Thank you for Peter, Andrew, James, and John!*

? Want to know more? See March 18, "What Are the Seven Sayings of Jesus on the Cross?"

Who Are the Apostles: Philip, Bartholomew, Thomas, and Matthew?

These are the 12 men he chose . . . Philip, Bartholomew, Matthew, Thomas . . .
—MATTHEW 10:2–4

Philip was from the same town as Peter and Andrew (John 1:44). The name *Philip* means "lover of horses." We do not know if Philip loved horses, but it is nice to think he did. *Bartholomew* means "son of a farmer." Bartholomew was also one of the eleven apostles who witnessed Jesus' ascension to heaven (Acts 1:1–13).

Thomas became known as "Doubting Thomas," because he wouldn't believe that Jesus had been raised from the dead until he could see Him with his own eyes. When Thomas finally touched Jesus' scars, he was so happy! Then Jesus said, "You believe because you see me. Those who believe without seeing me will be truly happy" (John 20:28–29).

Matthew was a tax collector. His name means "gift of God." Because he collected money for the Romans, he was considered a traitor by the Jews and nobody liked him! When Matthew met Jesus, he stopped being a tax collector and instead followed Jesus everywhere. He learned to love God and soon had many friends.

> *God, please touch my heart and transform my life.*

? **Want to know more?** See March 23 and 24, "How Can I Know for Sure That Jesus Really Was Resurrected? (Parts 1 and 2)."

Who Are the Apostles: James, Thaddaeus, Simon the Zealot, and Judas Iscariot?

Jesus called his followers to him. . . . They were . . . James son of Alphaeus, and Simon (called the Zealot), Judas son of James and Judas Iscariot.
—LUKE 6:13–16

James was the son of Alphaeus. There were two apostles named James—it was a very popular name! He was also known as "James the Less," possibly because he was younger or smaller than James the brother of John. *Thaddaeus* was more commonly known as Jude or "Judas son of James." His name means "courageous heart." John refers to Thaddaeus as "Judas," *not* "Judas Iscariot" (John 14:22), who was another apostle.

Simon the Zealot had strong political views. To be *zealous* is to be "fervently passionate." In Jesus' day, the Zealots were a group of Jews who hoped for an earthly king to restore Israel to its former glory. The name *Judas* means "praised one" but has also come to mean "betrayer" or "double-crosser." This is because Judas Iscariot was the disciple who betrayed Jesus, which led to His death on the cross (Matthew 26:14–16). Even though Judas did a terrible thing, God turned it into something beautiful and good for the whole world.

God, help me be a good friend like Jesus.

? Want to know more? See March 12, "What Did Judas Iscariot Do That Was So Bad?"

What's the Difference Between a Disciple and an Apostle?

*"Whoever helps one of these little ones because they are my
followers will truly get his reward. He will get his reward
even if he only gave my follower a cup of cold water."*
—MATTHEW 10:42

The word *disciple* means "pupil" or "student." Everyone who is a student or follower of Jesus is a disciple. Because you are learning about Jesus, *you* are a disciple! Isn't that exciting?

The word *apostle* means "one who is sent out." Jesus selected His twelve apostles for a special purpose. He taught them about God and then sent them out to spread the good news about God's love all over the world (Matthew 28:16–20). More than two thousand years later, the story of Jesus is still being told—so the apostles did a very good job!

Remember, the disciples and apostles in Jesus' day were ordinary people like you and me. Because they were human, they sometimes didn't understand what Jesus was talking about. As a friend of mine likes to say, "That's why they are called the '*duh*-sciples'!"

> Thank You, God, that I am a modern-day disciple of Jesus! I love to learn more about You and get to know and love You better.

? Want to know more? See March 2, "Who Are the Original Twelve Apostles?"

What Is the Transfiguration of Jesus?

While Peter was talking, a bright cloud covered them. A voice came from the cloud. The voice said, "This is my Son and I love him. I am very pleased with him. Obey him!"

—MATTHEW 17:5

One day Jesus took His disciples Peter, James, and John up on a high mountain. Suddenly, Jesus' clothes became glistening white. His face shone like the sun. The Bible says Jesus was *transfigured*, which means "changed." It was amazing! Then the Jewish prophets Moses and Elijah miraculously appeared, even though they lived hundreds of years before.

Suddenly, a bright cloud covered them, and God's voice said, "This is my Son and I love him. I am very pleased with him. Obey him!" When the disciples heard this, they fell on their faces, terrified. Jesus comforted them, saying, "Stand up. Don't be afraid" (Matthew 17:7). When they looked up, Moses and Elijah were gone. Jesus told them to wait until He had been raised from the dead before telling anyone what they had seen. The event made a big impression on them! Later, Peter wrote all about it (2 Peter 1:16–18).

Thank You, God, for showing us that Jesus is Your amazing Son.

? Want to know more? See May 25, "Is It True That God Spoke to Moses in a Burning Bush?'; May 29 and May 30, "What Are the Ten Commandments? (Parts 1 and 2)"; and June 15, "Who Is the Prophet Elijah?"

Why Does Jesus Love Children So Much?

"I tell you the truth. You must accept the kingdom of God as a little child accepts things, or you will never enter it."
—MARK 10:15

Though Jesus never got married or had children of His own, He deeply loved all the kids He met. And they loved Him back. Grown-ups, Jesus said, could learn a lot from children. This is because they have a simple faith that pleases God. Kids are natural-born experts at believing in and trusting God!

One day, people were bringing their children to Jesus to have Him bless them. The word *bless* means to "impart happiness and goodwill." The disciples thought this was silly and told the people to go away.

Jesus became *very* upset! He told the disciples to let the children come to Him. Then, to everyone's surprise, Jesus lovingly gathered the children in His big, strong arms and blessed them. How happy the children were when He did this!

Even today it is possible to feel the love of Jesus. Close your eyes. Can you feel Jesus hugging you in your heart?

> *Thank You, God, that I came into the world with Your gift of faith already planted in my heart.*

? Want to know more? See July 26, "What Is Faith?"

Why Are There So Many Women Named Mary in Jesus' Life?

Jesus' mother stood near his cross. His mother's sister was also standing there, with Mary the wife of Clopas, and Mary Magdalene.
—JOHN 19:25

In Jesus' day, the name *Mary*, which means "bitter," was *very* popular. There were so many women in Jesus' life named Mary that it can sometimes be confusing! On the terrible day when Jesus was dying on the cross, three Marys were there: Mary, Jesus' beloved mother (Matthew 1:16); Mary Magdalene, whom Jesus healed—and who became His faithful follower and friend (Luke 8:2; Matthew 27:56); and Mary, the wife of a man named Clopas (John 19:25).

Three days after Jesus' death on the cross, three women visited Jesus' tomb: Mary Magdalene (Luke 24:10); Mary, the mother of the apostle James (Luke 24:10); and Salome, a follower of Jesus, whose name is not actually Mary (Mark 16:1)!

There are even more Marys in the New Testament: Mary, the sister of Martha and Lazarus (John 11:1); Mary, the mother of John Mark (Acts 12:12); and Mary, a disciple in Rome (Romans 16:6). In Jesus' day, women were not always treated with respect. But Jesus loved and respected every woman He met. Many faithful women later became leaders in the early church.

Thank You, God, for how Jesus loves and respects everyone. Help me be loving and respectful too.

Who Is Lazarus, and How Is His Resurrection Different from Jesus' Resurrection?

[Jesus] cried out in a loud voice, "Lazarus, come out!" The dead man came out.
—JOHN 11:43–44

Lazarus was a dear friend and follower of Jesus who lived with his two sisters, Mary and Martha. The name *Lazarus* means "my God has helped." When Lazarus died, Jesus was so heartbroken He wept (John 11:35 NIV). But then Jesus prayed to God, thanking Him (in advance!) for the miracle He was about to do. With a big shout—"Lazarus, come out!"—Jesus brought Lazarus back to life! When Lazarus walked out of his tomb, everyone was so happy! The story of Lazarus is true. But the resurrection of Lazarus is different from the resurrection of Jesus. Lazarus would die again, as all humans must. Jesus' resurrection body is one that never dies! Jesus is now in heaven in His resurrection body. Through God's Holy Spirit, He also lives in our hearts. One day Lazarus will receive his heavenly resurrection body—and so will all believers, including you!

Thank You, God, for the amazing true story of Lazarus.

? **Want to know more?** See March 21, "What Is the Resurrection of Jesus?"; April 2, "Why Is Easter So Important?"; April 6, "What Is the Ascension of Christ?"; and March 25, "How Is Jesus' Resurrection Body Different from My Body?"

What Is the Difference Between the Pharisees and the Sadducees?

The Pharisees and Sadducees came to Jesus and tested him
by asking him to show them a sign from heaven.
—MATTHEW 16:1 NIV

The Sadducees and the Pharisees were the two major Jewish religious groups in Jesus' day. Neither of them got along with Jesus.

The Sadducees were priests and *aristocrats*, or noblemen. They believed in only part of the Old Testament. The Sadducees did not believe in angels, demons, miracles, or life after death (Matthew 22:23; Acts 23:8)! The Pharisees were not priests, but a Jewish religious party popular with everyday people. The Pharisees (and Jesus) believed in the entire Old Testament. But the Pharisees were extremely caught up in Jewish laws. Over the years they made up hundreds of new, complicated laws not found in the Bible. Both the Sadducees and Pharisees believed in God. But their faith was not simple and trusting. Here is a fun way to remember the difference between the two: The Sadducees didn't believe in life after death, and that's why they were "*sad, you see*"!

> *Thank You, God, for sending Jesus to prove that Your kingdom and the promise of living with You forever is real.*

? **Want to know more:** See March 8, "Why Does Jesus Love Children So Much?"

What Did Judas Iscariot Do That Was So Bad?

[Judas told the chief priests,] "I will give Jesus to you. What will you pay me for doing this?" The priests gave Judas 30 silver coins. After that, Judas waited for the best time to give Jesus to the priests.
—MATTHEW 26:14–16

Judas Iscariot was one of Jesus' twelve original apostles. Judas was looking for a powerful earthly king for God's people. But Jesus came to tell the world about the kingdom of God. Judas was bitterly disappointed.

Judas's heart turned evil. Late one night, Judas led the crowd of priests and soldiers to Jesus and His disciples. Judas had told them that he would let them know who Jesus was by giving Him a kiss. But Jesus knew all along that Judas would betray Him (John 6:64, 70–71). And here is the awful part: Immediately, after betraying Jesus, Judas knew he had made a terrible mistake. He tried to give the money back to the priests, but it was too late. Judas felt so guilty that he hanged himself (Matthew 27:3–10). Because of Judas's betrayal, Jesus died on the cross. But here is good news: Because of Jesus' death, our sins are forgiven. Because Jesus was raised from the dead, one day we will be too.

> *Thank You, God, that You can turn the most terrible mistake into something beautiful and good.*

? Want to know more? See March 5, "Who Are the Apostles: James, Thaddaeus, Simon the Zealot, and Judas Iscariot?"

Who Is Pontius Pilate, and What Makes Him So Important?

Pilate saw that he could do nothing about this, and a riot was starting. So he took some water and washed his hands in front of the crowd. Then he said, "I am not guilty of this man's death. You are the ones who are causing it!"
—MATTHEW 27:24

Pontius Pilate was the Roman governor in charge of Judea from AD 26 to 36. After the priests and soldiers arrested Jesus, they brought Him to Pontius Pilate for sentencing. But Pilate sensed in his heart that Jesus had done nothing wrong. A criminal named Barabbas was also waiting to be sentenced. Because it was the Jewish festival of Passover, one criminal could be let go. Pontius Pilate couldn't make up his mind. He asked the crowd: "Whom shall I set free? Jesus or Barabbas?"

"Barabbas!"

"But what about Jesus?"

"Crucify Him!" the crowd roared (Matthew 27:15–23).

Pontius Pilate was not happy, but he handed over Jesus. He showed his displeasure by washing his hands and saying, "I am not guilty of this man's death."

Pontius Pilate reminds us that the story of Jesus is real. Pontius Pilate was a historical person. So is Jesus.

Thank You, God, that the story of Jesus—all of it—is true!

? Want to know more? See May 27, "What Is Passover?" and July 24, "What Is the Apostles' Creed?"

Why Did Jesus Have to Die?

When he was living as a man, he humbled himself and was fully obedient to God. He obeyed even when that caused his death—death on a cross.
—PHILIPPIANS 2:8

Many people understood and believed that Jesus truly was God's Son. They witnessed Jesus' love, forgiveness, and healing miracles. They liked what Jesus taught about God's great love for His children. But many other people did not.

Some people thought Jesus was crazy.

Others thought Jesus was lying.

Still others said it was against the law for Jesus to say that God was His Father (John 10:36).

So when Jesus was still a young man, just thirty-three years old, He was killed. Jesus was crucified, or put to death by hanging on a wooden cross on a sad, lonely hill called *Golgotha,* or "the place of the skull" (John 19:17). The word *crucify* means "to attach to a cross." It was a terrible, painful way to die.

Jesus was killed by fearful, angry people who couldn't find it in their hearts to have faith in Him and in His Father God.

Thank You, Father, that I came into the world with Your gift of faith. With every heartbeat, please grow my faith in Jesus!

? Want to know more? See October 10, "Why Do Some Crosses Have Jesus on Them and Others Don't?"

Did Jesus Know Ahead of Time That He Was Going to Die?

[Jesus said to the disciples,] "We are going up to Jerusalem, and the Son of Man will be delivered over to the chief priests and the teachers of the law. They will condemn him to death and will hand him over to the Gentiles to be mocked and flogged and crucified. On the third day he will be raised to life!"
—MATTHEW 20:17–19 NIV

Several times Jesus told His disciples that He was going to die. But each time He mentioned His death, the disciples cried, "No! Don't say such a thing!" Such talk made them very sad. Jesus also told His disciples that three days after His death, He was going to rise from the dead and overcome death forever (Matthew 17:22–23).

Because no one had ever risen from the dead this way, this was impossible for the disciples to understand. It didn't make sense. It was so strange that the disciples were afraid to ask Jesus about it.

Jesus told His disciples ahead of time about his death and resurrection for a special reason. When these things happened, the disciples would remember His words, and they would believe (Luke 24:8).

Thank You, God, that even when I don't understand and am afraid, I can trust that You are in charge.

? Want to know more? See February 2, "What Are God's Promises for Me When I Need Hope?"; March 10, "Who Is Lazarus, and How Is His Resurrection Different from Jesus' Resurrection?"; and August 3, "What Is Christian Hope?"

If Jesus Is God's Son, Why Didn't He Save Himself from Being Killed?

Then Jesus went with his followers to a place called Gethsemane.
He said to them, "Sit here while I go over there and pray." . . .
Then Jesus began to be very sad and troubled.
—MATTHEW 26:36–37

Since Jesus is God's Son, He could have stopped the people from killing Him, but He didn't. Why? Jesus wanted to be obedient to His Father God in heaven. Even so, Jesus was human—and it's sometimes hard for humans to do what is right.

Jesus was very sad and troubled because He loved life. He didn't want to die. He cried out to God: "Abba, Father! You can do all things. Let me not have this cup of suffering. But do what you want, not what I want" (Mark 14:36). When Jesus said "Abba," He meant Daddy. By "cup of suffering," He meant that dying would be like drinking a cup of poison.

Choosing to give up His life, Jesus took upon Himself the punishment for all the bad things people think, say, and do (1 John 2:2). That's why He is called our Savior.

> *God, help me do the right thing when I face hard choices.*

? **Want to know more?** See February 17, "What Makes Jesus So Important?"

Was There Really a Saint Patrick?

The grace of the Lord Jesus Christ, and the love of God, and the fellowship of the Holy Spirit be with you all.
—2 CORINTHIANS 13:14

Yes, there really was a Saint Patrick, and the story of his love for Jesus is amazing! He was born with the name Maewyn Succat in Britain, around AD 389. At age sixteen, Maewyn was captured by pirates and sold into slavery in Northern Ireland, where he served as a shepherd. While he watched the sheep, Maewyn prayed and grew close to God. Six years later he escaped and fled home. Maewyn loved Jesus with all his heart. He dreamed of returning to Ireland to share God's love with his captors. So Maewyn studied to be a priest. When he finally became one, he took the Christian name *Patrick*, which means "noble." Saint Patrick converted many thousands of people in Ireland to Christianity. According to legend, he used a *shamrock*, a kind of three-leafed clover, to explain the idea of the Holy Trinity to the Irish: one leaf for the Father, one for the Son, and one for the Holy Ghost. Three parts, but one leaf!

Thank You, God, for your faithful servant Saint Patrick and for his amazing true story.

? Want to know more? See January 8, "Who Is the Trinity?";
January 9, "How Can God Be Three Persons at the Same
Time?"; November 1, "What Is All Saints' Day?"; and
September 14, "What Is Saint Patrick's Breastplate Prayer?"

What Are the Seven Sayings of Jesus on the Cross? (Part 1)

Jesus said, "Father, forgive them. They don't know what they are doing."
—LUKE 23:34

When Jesus was on the cross, He said seven statements before He died. These words reveal to us His great love for everyone in the world—including you! We call these words the Seven Sayings of Jesus on the Cross. Today we will learn about the first three:

1. "Father, forgive them. They do not know what they are doing" (Luke 23:34). Jesus was praying for the Roman soldiers who hurt Him. Even on the cross, Jesus offered His love and forgiveness to others, even strangers.
2. "Listen! What I say is true: Today you will be with me in paradise!" (Luke 23:43). Jesus said this to a criminal hanging on the cross next to Him, who had recognized Jesus as God's Son. Jesus forgave his sins and promised that he'd soon be in *paradise*, or heaven.
3. "Dear woman, here is your son." Then he said to the follower, "Here is your mother" (John 19:26–27). Jesus loved His mother, Mary, and asked His disciple and close friend John to take care of her. John took Mary to live with him.

Thank You, God, for Jesus' loving words on the cross.

What Are the Seven Sayings of Jesus on the Cross? (Part 2)

[Jesus] said, "It is finished." He bowed his head and died.
—JOHN 19:30

Today we will learn about the final four of the Seven Sayings of Jesus on the Cross.

1. "My God, my God, why have you left me alone?" (Mark 15:34). Jesus said this when He was taking all the sins of the world upon Himself. He felt abandoned, and He was sad, but He never lost His faith. He kept talking to God.

2. "I am thirsty" (John 19:28). Jesus was God's Son, but He was also human. The cross was a terrible way to die.

3. "Father, into your hands I commit my spirit" (Luke 23:46 NIV). Jesus said this in a loud voice. It must have taken a lot of strength. Because Jesus believed in His Father's love, Jesus willingly gave God His life.

4. "It is finished" (John 19:30). Jesus died knowing that He had been obedient to God. With these three words Jesus completed His mission.

> *Thank You, God, for how I can trust that nothing can separate me from Your love.*

? Want to know more? See December 28, "Is It Okay to Question and Sometimes Have Doubts About God?"

What Happened to Jesus' Body After He Died?

Joseph [of Arimathea] went to Pilate and asked to have Jesus' body. Pilate gave orders for the soldiers to give it to Joseph.
—MATTHEW 27:57–58

One of Jesus' disciples was a rich man named Joseph of Arimathea. After Jesus was crucified, Joseph got permission to take and bury the body of Jesus.

Joseph and his friend Nicodemus wrapped Jesus' body in clean linen cloth with good-smelling spices and gently laid it in a tomb (John 19:38–42). Back then, a *tomb* was a cave-like, small, dark room with a dirt floor, carved into the earth.

Jesus' mother, Mary, was there. So was Jesus' friend Mary Magdalene. After they laid Jesus' body in the tomb, Joseph of Arimathea rolled a big stone over the opening (Matthew 27:57–61). And then with their hearts breaking, they all walked away.

How shocked and sad people were on the day Jesus died! They cried and cried. *If only Jesus could somehow come back and be with us*, they thought. But that was impossible.

Or so they thought . . .

Thank You, God, for happy surprises!

What Is the Resurrection of Jesus?

The angel said to the women, "Don't be afraid. I know that you are looking for Jesus, the one who was killed on the cross. But he is not here. He has risen from death as he said he would."
—MATTHEW 28:5–6

Three days after Jesus died, early in the morning, Jesus' mother, Mary, and His friend Mary Magdalene went to visit the tomb where Jesus' body had been laid. But when they arrived, the big stone that covered the opening to the tomb had been rolled away. And that wasn't all.

The tomb was empty! *Who took the body of our dear Jesus?* the women wondered. Moments later, they made an extraordinary discovery: Jesus was alive! He had *come back to life!* The word *resurrect* means "to bring back to life." So, as fast as their legs could carry them, the women ran to tell the disciples the good news.

Each of the four Gospels reports different, exciting eyewitness details about Jesus' resurrection, which is the most important event in human history! To get the full story, read all four Gospel reports (Matthew 28:1–10; Mark 16:1; Luke 24:1–12; John 20:1–18).

Thank You, God, for Your amazing love and power to do the impossible!

? Want to know more? See March 10, "Who Is Lazarus, and How Is His Resurrection Different from Jesus' Resurrection?" and March 25, "How Is Jesus' Resurrection Body Different from My Body?"

Why Is the Resurrection of Jesus So Important?

Jesus said to her, "I am the resurrection and the life. He who believes in me will have life even if he dies."

—JOHN 11:25

After Jesus' resurrection, He explained that soon He would be going back to heaven to live with His Father God. But before He left, He had some very good news.

"The good news," said Jesus, "is that because I have come back to life, you can too. After you die, you can live forever with My Father God and Me in heaven. God loves you so much He wants this for you. God wants you to believe in Him and Me. God wants to forgive Your sins. He wants you to live in His kingdom forever" (John 3:16, paraphrased).

What a happy place God's kingdom is! That's because everyone in heaven is happy and healthy. Everyone in heaven has new bodies that live forever, and there is no more death or sadness or crying or pain (Revelation 7:17). The resurrection of Jesus means our sins can be forgiven. Because you believe in Jesus, you can live forever with God and Jesus in heaven.

Thank You, God, for Your promise that one day I will live forever with You and Jesus in heaven!

? **Want to know more?** See December 1 and 2, "What Is Heaven Like? (Parts 1 and 2)."

How Can I Know for Sure That Jesus Really Was Resurrected? (Part 1)

Jesus' followers were together. The doors were locked, because they were afraid of the Jews. Then Jesus came and stood among them. He said, "Peace be with you!"
—JOHN 20:19

The resurrection of Jesus is a true historical fact. It is also at the very heart of our Christian faith. Jesus lived on Earth in His resurrected body for about forty days. He appeared to eyewitnesses more than ten times. Let's look at four:

1. The first people to see the resurrected Jesus were His friend Mary Magdalene; His mother, Mary; and other women (Matthew 28:1–9).
2. Jesus appeared to two disciples walking on the road (Mark 16:12). At first they didn't recognize Jesus. Later, while eating with Jesus, they did. Then Jesus disappeared (Luke 24:13–31).
3. Jesus appeared to Peter in Jerusalem (Luke 24:34).
4. Jesus appeared to ten disciples, excluding Thomas, in the Upper Room in Jerusalem (John 20:19). Even though the doors were locked, Jesus appeared.

Help me, God, to recognize Your surprising presence in my life!

How Can I Know for Sure That Jesus Really Was Resurrected? (Part 2)

Thomas said to him, "My Lord and my God!"
—JOHN 20:28

Yesterday we learned that Jesus appeared to people after His resurrection. Let's look at six more eyewitness reports:

1. A week after Jesus first appeared to the disciples, He suddenly appeared *again* in the Upper Room. This time, Thomas saw Jesus with his own eyes, and he believed (John 20:24–29)!
2. Jesus appeared to seven disciples at the Sea of Tiberias (John 21:1–4).
3. Jesus appeared to the eleven disciples on a mountain in Galilee (Matthew 28:16–20).
4. Jesus appeared to five hundred other eyewitnesses (1 Corinthians 15:6).
5. Jesus appeared to the disciple James (1 Corinthians 15:7).
6. Jesus appeared to all those who witnessed His ascension into heaven (Mark 16:19).

> *Thank You, God, that even though I might not be able to see Jesus with my eyes, I am blessed that He lives in my heart.*

How Is Jesus' Resurrection Body Different from My Body?

Jesus said to them, "Come and have breakfast." None of the followers dared ask him, "Who are you?" They knew it was the Lord.

—JOHN 21:12 NIV

Jesus' resurrection body is special. It's a physical body created by God to live forever, and it will never get injured or diseased—or die. Jesus was the first human being to receive this very special body. One day we will receive resurrection bodies too! Jesus' resurrection body is not "perfect" but has scars from when He was nailed on the cross. Jesus showed these scars to Thomas to prove that He truly was alive (John 20:24–29). Jesus lived on earth in His resurrection body for about forty days. Sometimes His disciples did not immediately recognize Him (John 20:14). Jesus' resurrection body can appear and vanish in a most unusual way! He surprised the disciples by suddenly appearing to them and disappearing, even when the doors were locked (John 20:26–29). The resurrected Jesus also invited the disciples to join Him for breakfast on the beach, where they all ate bread and fish (John 21:12). Maybe this means we will eat and drink when we live together in God's kingdom!

Thank You, God, for creating Jesus' amazing resurrection body and for hinting at what heaven will be like.

? Want to know more? See October 20, "What Does the Bible Mean When It Says That My Body Is the 'Temple of God'?"

Why Is Easter Always on a Different Date?

Jesus rose from death early on the first day of the week.
—MARK 16:9

Perhaps you've heard people say, "Easter is early this year." Or "Easter is late." Did you ever wonder why Easter (unlike Christmas) falls on a different date each year?

It is because there is an ancient formula for deciding when Easter will take place. Get out your calendar and sharpen your pencil, and see if you can figure out when Easter will be this year!

In most Christian churches, Easter *is the first Sunday after the first full moon on or after the first day of spring, which is March 21.** This full moon may happen on any date between March 21 and April 18, including those days. If the full moon falls on a Sunday, Easter is the Sunday following. Easter is always on a Sunday, but it cannot be earlier than March 22 or later than April 25.

Phew!

Of all the Christian holidays, Easter is considered to be the most important. We will discover why in the next few days.

Thank You, God, for Easter!

---

*Because Eastern Orthodox Christians use a different method for figuring out Easter's date, they sometimes celebrate Easter on a different day.

What Is Holy Week?

This is how we know what real love is: Jesus gave his life for us.
—1 JOHN 3:16

Holy Week is the final week of Lent and the week before Easter. It's a time when Christians around the world remember the week leading up to Jesus' death and resurrection.

The two best-known days of Holy Week are Palm Sunday and Good Friday.

Palm Sunday is the first day of Holy Week. Good Friday is the Friday before Easter Sunday. Holy Week is a time to think and pray about God's great love for us as we prepare our hearts for Easter.

Of all the Christian holidays, Easter is the most important. Why? Because the story of Easter shows us the incredible goodness and love of God. Through Jesus' life, we see God's desire to forgive and heal us. Through Jesus' death on the cross, we see God's deep desire to save us from our sins. Through Jesus' resurrection, we see how much God loves life—so much that He wants us to live with Him forever in heaven!

> *Thank You, God, for Your great love for me. Help me use each day of Holy Week to prepare my heart for Easter.*

? Want to know more? See February 16, "What Is Lent?" and April 2, "Why Is Easter So Important?"

What Is Palm Sunday?

*Don't be afraid, people of Jerusalem! Your king is
coming. He is sitting on the colt of a donkey.*
—JOHN 12:15

Palm Sunday is the first day of Holy Week, leading up to Easter Sunday. It's a time when Christians remember when Jesus rode into Jerusalem on a young donkey.

The week before His death, Jesus traveled to Jerusalem to celebrate the Passover meal with His disciples. Crowds of people threw their *cloaks*, or capes, on the road. They waved palm branches in the air to celebrate. "Hosanna!" they cried. "Blessed is he who comes in the name of the Lord!" (Matthew 21:1–11 NIV). The word *hosanna* or *hosannah* means "save us, I pray."

The people in the crowd loved Jesus. They had no idea that in less than a week, He would die on the cross—and that three days later He would rise from the dead. But they were happy to welcome Him.

On Palm Sunday, some churches today pass out freshly cut palm branches. They might wave them in the aisles or weave them into the shape of a cross. The palm branches remind us of when Jesus rode into Jerusalem on a donkey.

Thank You, God, for Palm Sunday. Hosanna! Save us, I pray!

? Want to know more? See May 27, "What Is Passover?"

What Is the Passion of Christ?

[Jesus] explained that the Jewish elders, the leading priests, and the teachers of the law would make him suffer many things. And he told them that he must be killed. Then, on the third day, he would be raised from death.
—MATTHEW 16:21

The word *passion* comes from an old Latin word that means "suffering" or "enduring." For Christians, the Passion of Christ refers to the final days in Jesus' life beginning when He rode into Jerusalem on a donkey and ending with His crucifixion and death on the cross.

During Holy Week, many Christian churches read the Passion story from the Bible aloud, in a dramatic fashion, with church leaders and members taking part. Reading the Passion story this way can be a very moving experience. In the Bible, there are four versions of the Passion of Christ, each with different details.

- Matthew 21:1–11; 26; 27
- Mark 11:1–11; 14; 15
- Luke 19:29–38; 22; 23
- John 12:12–19; 18; 19

You don't have to be in church to read the Passion stories aloud. You can read these true, amazing stories any time of the year, on your own or with family and friends.

Dear God, help me better understand what the story of Jesus' Passion means for me.

What Is the Last Supper?

Taking a towel, [Jesus] wrapped it around his waist. Then he
poured water into a bowl and began to wash the followers' feet.
—JOHN 13:4–5

On the night before Jesus died, He shared a special Passover meal
with His disciples. Today we call this meal the Last Supper (Luke 22:7–
30). Jesus knew He was going to die. To show the disciples how much He
loved them, Jesus washed their feet (John 13:1–17). This was shocking!
The roads in Israel were dusty and dirty. So were the disciples' feet. Jesus
was their *rabbi*, or teacher. In Jesus' day, to wash His students' dirty feet
is something a rabbi would *never* do! But Jesus saw things differently.

"I, your Lord and Teacher, have washed your feet," said Jesus. "So
you also should wash each other's feet" (John 13:14). This was Jesus' way
of saying that no one is greater than anyone else, and that they (and we!)
should lovingly and humbly serve one another.

During Holy Week, on the Thursday before Easter, many churches
remember this event with a special Holy Thursday service where the
church leaders and members wash one another's feet, just as Jesus did
with His disciples.

> *Help me, God, to follow Jesus' example and*
> *treat people with love and respect.*

? Want to know more? See May 27, "What Is Passover?" and
September 25 and 26, "What Is Communion? (Parts 1 and 2)."

What Is Good Friday?

Then Jesus cried in a loud voice and died.
—MARK 15:37

Good Friday is the Friday before Easter. It is the day during Holy Week when Christians remember the day Jesus died (Luke 23:26–56). Many churches hold special services to remember the time when Jesus suffered on the cross.

The Good Friday church service is very somber and quiet. It is a time to pray and to remember that God loves us so much He was willing to give up His only Son, Jesus, to die for us (John 3:16). We also remember that Jesus loves us so much He was willing to die for us (John 15:9). There is no greater love than this (John 15:13).

At first glance, Good Friday might not seem "good" at all. Jesus suffered terribly and died. But because of Good Friday, there is much good news.

Because of Good Friday, we can thank God for Easter—for Jesus' resurrection and for forgiving our sins. We can thank God that we will join Jesus and live forever with Him and God in heaven!

On Good Friday, we remember that nothing, not even death, can separate us from God's love (Romans 8:38–39).

> *Thank You, God, that not even death can*
> *separate me from Your amazing love!*

APRIL

APRIL 1

Why Do We Light Candles on Easter?

"I am the light of the world. The person who follows me will never live in darkness. He will have the light that gives life."
—JOHN 8:12

Candlelight is a symbol of Jesus' victory over the darkness of evil, sin, and death. Lighting candles in church reminds us of Jesus' love, which lives and shines in our hearts. Jesus described Himself as "the light of the world." Jesus told His disciples that they are "the light of the world" too (Matthew 5:14 NIV)! He went on to explain, "Let your light shine before others, that they may see your good deeds and glorify your Father in heaven" (Matthew 5:16 NIV). We can do the same! The day before Easter is known as Holy Saturday or Easter Eve. Many churches celebrate it with a nighttime vigil service. A *vigil is* a special time for prayer. On Easter Eve, some churches turn out all the lights until the stroke of midnight, when the leader lights a tall white *paschal*, or Easter candle. Everyone else lights the smaller candles from it, until the church is filled with light, and it's Easter morning! The light-filled church is a symbol of the risen Jesus, the "light of the world."

Thank You, God, that because Jesus lives in my heart, His love shines in me too!

? Want to know more? See February 25, "Who Did Jesus Say He Was?" and November 30, "What Is an Advent Wreath?"

Why Is Easter So Important?

The Lord really has risen from death!
—LUKE 24:34

Easter is the most important Christian holy day of the year. It is also the most important day in human history. On Easter Sunday, Christians around the world gather to remember and celebrate the fact that Jesus rose from the dead, completing God's mission for Him to save the world and all the people in it (Mark 16:1–8). They celebrate with joyful prayers and singing. In America, many churches have special sunrise services and meet in the early morning darkness. On hillsides and beaches, they wait for the Easter morning sunrise. As the day dawns, they celebrate the fact that Jesus is not dead, but truly alive! The rising sun symbolizes the light of God's risen Son, Jesus.

Because Jesus rose from the dead, the dark power of evil, sin, and death is forever broken. How surprised and happy everyone was to see Jesus alive! Not even Jesus' family and closest friends ever expected such a miracle. Because Jesus is alive, and we believe in Him, we can live forever with Him and God in heaven.

Thank You, God, for how You totally surprised everyone when You raised Jesus from the dead. Thank You for Easter!

? Want to know more? See March 21, "What Is the Resurrection of Jesus?" and December 1 and 2, "What Is Heaven Like? (Parts 1 and 2)."

Is It True That Jesus Knows My Name?

Jesus said to her, "Mary."
—John 20:16

Yes, it is true: Jesus knows your name. Jesus knows and loves everything about you, including your name! My favorite Easter story shows how Jesus personally knows and loves each one of us.

Early on Easter morning, Mary Magdalene went to visit Jesus' tomb. But the stone was rolled away and Jesus' body wasn't there! There was nothing left but His *grave clothes*, or linen strips of cloth, that they had wrapped Him in.

Mary was *so* upset! How could someone do this? She cried and cried—until she looked into the tomb and saw two angels! "Woman, why are you crying?" they asked. After she told them, she turned around and saw a mysterious man. He, too, asked her why she was so sad. At first, she thought the man was a gardener . . . until He said her name—"Mary." At once she recognized the voice. It was Jesus! He was alive (John 20:10–18)!

Just as Jesus knew Mary's name, He knows your name. You can recognize His voice too.

Thank You, Jesus, that You know my name. Help me hear Your voice when You speak to me in my heart!

? Want to know more? See April 13, "Who Is the Holy Spirit?"

Why Do We Say "Alleluia!" at Easter?

Hallelujah! Our Lord God rules.
—REVELATION 19:6

At Easter, the word *alleluia* (al-lay-*lew*-ya) is used in many prayers and hymns. The word *alleluia* is a Latin version of the Hebrew word *hallelujah*, which means "Praise the Lord." So when you say and sing "Alleluia!" at Easter, you are praising the Lord.

To *praise* the Lord means to express heartfelt approval of God. It means to acknowledge, privately and publicly, the greatness and goodness of God.

Praising the Lord is a good thing to do! God loves it when His children speak and sing His praises—not only in church on Easter but everywhere, every day of the year. The Bible says, "Praise the Lord, because he is good. Sing praises to him, because it is pleasant" (Psalm 135:3). It's fun to praise the Lord!

> *I love You, Lord—Alleluia!*

Why Do We Celebrate Easter in Springtime with the Easter Bunny and Painted Eggs?

Jesus' followers came to him. They said, "We will go and prepare everything for the Passover Feast."

—MARK 14:12

Springtime is the season for celebrating new life and growth. Plants that looked dead during winter grow tender, new leaves. Baby chicks and bunnies are signs of new life. The egg has long been a symbol of new birth, and even today we paint eggs and give them as gifts. In the days of the early church, many cultures already had springtime festivals, and Christians attached Easter to these established celebrations. Easter is also linked to Passover, a Jewish holiday that celebrates the Israelites' escape from Egypt. The night before Jesus died, He celebrated the Passover meal with His disciples. Passover and Easter are both celebrated in the spring.

The Easter Bunny is a legendary character brought to America by German settlers. But sometimes we get so excited about the Easter Bunny, we almost forget about Jesus. Easter celebrates the most important day in history—the day Jesus rose from the dead to live forever!

> *Thank You, God, for helping me remember that Jesus is the reason for Easter.*

What Is the Ascension of Christ?

After the Lord Jesus said these things to the followers, he was carried up into heaven. There, Jesus sat at the right side of God.

—MARK 16:19

Jesus walked and talked on earth in His resurrected body for forty days. Then He gathered His disciples on the Mount of Olives. It was time for Jesus to join His Father God in heaven. Before Jesus left, He told the disciples to preach the good news of God's love everywhere. He also told them to stay in Jerusalem until the Holy Spirit came to them. Suddenly, to everyone's amazement, Jesus was "taken up into heaven" (NIV). The word *ascension* means "the act of going up." Witnesses said it was as though a cloud took Jesus from the disciples' sight (Acts 1:8–9).

Many Christians celebrate this historic event with a special Ascension Day service, thirty-nine days after Easter Sunday. At the service they read aloud the Bible story of Jesus' return to heaven. The Bible says Jesus will one day return to earth "in the same way" He left (Acts 1:10–11). What an exciting day that will be!

> *How wonderful, God, that Jesus ascended to heaven! Thank You for looking after me.*

? Want to know more? See April 8, "Why Couldn't Jesus Stay on Earth Forever?" and September 4, "Is It True That Jesus Is Praying for Me Now in Heaven?"

What Is the Great Commission?

Jesus said to the followers, "Go everywhere in the world. Tell the Good News to everyone."
—MARK 16:15

These are among the last words Jesus told His disciples before ascending to heaven: "All power in heaven and on earth is given to me. So go and make followers of all people in the world. Baptize them in the name of the Father and the Son and the Holy Spirit. Teach them to obey everything that I have told you. You can be sure that I will be with you always. I will continue with you until the end of the world." (Matthew 28:18–20)

Over the years, this powerful command has become known as the Great Commission. The word *commission* means "a request or order for someone to do something."

Jesus' last words on earth granted authority to the disciples to go out and tell the whole world the good news about God's love through Jesus. This is our commission too. Jesus wants us, each in our own way, to let the world know about God's reality and love.

Teach me, God, to share the good news of your love with others— not only with words but also with kind and loving actions!

? **Want to know more?** See October 5, "Is It True to Be a Missionary You Have to Travel Far from Home?"

Why Couldn't Jesus Just Stay on Earth Forever?

"I tell you the truth, it is better for you that I go away. When I go away, I will send the Helper to you. If I do not go away, the Helper will not come."
—JOHN 16:7 NCV

Before Jesus' ascension to heaven, He explained to His family and friends that although He could no longer stay with them on earth, there was a special way that He could live with them in their hearts.

"It is for your good that I am going away," said Jesus. "When I go, God will send you His Holy Spirit. The Holy Spirit will live in your hearts and guide you. He will comfort you. He will lead you to truth. He will help you remember everything I have taught you. He will give you the power to love others the way I have loved you" (John 14:15–26; 16:7–15, paraphrased).

Through the Holy Spirit, Jesus can live in the hearts of all believers in all places. Another name for God's Holy Spirit is the "Helper." The Holy Spirit helps us know and love God. He helps us change in good and beautiful ways to be more like Jesus.

In coming days, we will learn much more about the Holy Spirit.

Thank You, God, for sending Your Holy Spirit to live in my heart.

? **Want to know more?** See April 13, "Who Is the Holy Spirit?" and April 14, "What Is Pentecost?"

What Is the Second Coming of Christ?

"Then people will see the Son of Man coming in clouds with great power and glory."
—Mark 13:26

While the disciples were gazing up in wonder at Jesus' ascension into heaven, two angels in white robes appeared. "Men of Galilee," they said, "why are you standing here looking into the sky? You saw Jesus taken away from you into heaven. He will come back in the same way you saw him go" (Acts 1:10–11).

Jesus will return to earth again someday. When Jesus comes back, everyone will recognize that He is God's Son. There will be no confusion or mistaking His identity. The Bible says that Jesus will come "in clouds," with God's holy angels (Mark 8:38). For people who believe in Jesus, this will be the happiest day in human history (Hebrews 9:28). Jesus will gather us all in His big, strong arms, and our hearts will be filled with joy as we've never known!

This big event has become known as the Second Coming of Christ.

This promise of Jesus' return to earth is so important that early Christians greeted one another with the Aramaic language word *"Maranatha!"* which means "The Lord is coming!" or "Come, O Lord!"

Maranatha! Come, Lord Jesus!

When Will the Second Coming of Christ Happen?

"No one knows when that day or time will be. The Son and the angels in heaven don't know. Only the Father knows. Be careful! Always be ready!"
—MARK 13:32–33

Oh, what a big question! For such a big question, the answer is surprisingly simple. No one knows for sure when Jesus will return. Not even the angels. In fact, Jesus says that only His Father God in heaven knows for sure (Mark 13:32–37)!

How should we prepare for the second coming of Jesus? Jesus answered this key question with two words: "Be ready!" (Mark 13:37). While we watch and wait, Jesus wants us to live our lives as though He were coming back today. That's because He can come at any time. He could come this very hour. He could come before you finish reading this devotion! The important thing is that He wants us to be ready for His arrival. What can we do to be ready for Jesus? Love God and love each one another. Love is the key. Here is what we do know for sure: Jesus promises He will return—and He always keeps His promises (Deuteronomy 7:9).

God, help me live a life of love and be ready to greet Jesus when He returns!

? **Want to know more?** See January 12, "How Can I Share God's Love?"

Can Anyone Believe in Jesus?

Anyone who asks the Lord for help will be saved.
—ACTS 2:21

Yes, anyone can believe in Jesus. God loves all His children and wants them all to believe in Him and in His Son, Jesus.

But God does not force His children to love Him. It is up to every person, each on his own, to have faith in His Son, Jesus.

There is an old saying that "Jesus is a gentleman." That is, Jesus will not force His way into your heart. Instead, the Bible says, He stands at the door and knocks (Revelation 3:20). He enters and lives in your heart when He is invited.

The good news is that it's never too late to believe in God and in His Son, Jesus. You can be ten years old or one hundred years old. God is very patient and forgiving. God is always waiting with open arms for His children to come to Him (Luke 15:11–20).

Why is God always waiting for you with open arms?

Because God loves you (1 John 3:1).

> *When I hear Jesus knocking on the door of my heart, God, help me not waste one second and invite Him in!*

? Want to know more? See September 16, "What Is the Most Important Prayer in the World?"; December 8, "Is It True That Knowing Jesus Is the Only Way to Know God?"; and December 9, "Do People Who Never Have Heard of Jesus Go to Heaven Too?"

How Do I Get to Know Jesus?

"I loved you as the Father loved me. Now remain in my love."
—JOHN 15:9

The best way to get to know Jesus is to talk to Him. Tell Him that you want to get to know Him better. Jesus is always eager and ready to hear your prayers.

Just pray: "Jesus, I really want to know You. I believe You are the Son of God. I believe that You died on the cross for my sins. Thank You for loving me so much. Now please come into my heart and live in me."

When Jesus lives in your heart, He will help you tell right from wrong. He'll forgive you when you make mistakes (1 John 1:9). He'll comfort you when you're feeling down. He'll be your very best friend—the best you ever had (John 15:15)!

How can you be sure Jesus will come into your heart if you ask Him? Because Jesus said He would, and He always, always keeps His promises (1 Thessalonians 5:24; Hebrews 10:23).

Why does Jesus want to do all this for you? Because Jesus loves you. It's as simple as that.

> *Thank You, Jesus, for coming into my heart.*
> *I am so excited to know You!*

? Want to know more? See September 16, "What Is the Most Important Prayer in the World?"; October 24, "What Is a Quiet Time?"; and October 25, "How Can I Make the Most of My Quiet Times with God?"

Who Is the Holy Spirit?

"But when the Spirit of truth comes he will lead you into all truth."
—JOHN 16:13

Did you notice that today's question does *not* begin with "What" but rather "*Who* Is the Holy Spirit?" This is because the Holy Spirit is not just a vague, floaty idea. The Holy Spirit is a powerful, living person!

As Christians we understand God to be made up of three living persons: God the Father; God's Son, Jesus; and God's Holy Spirit. We call this the Holy Trinity. The Holy Spirit is the third person of the Holy Trinity. But He is no less important! Like God and Jesus, the Holy Spirit *is love*.

The Holy Spirit is the way God lives in the hearts of human beings— the way God lives in our hearts! The Bible describes the Holy Spirit as God's love poured into our hearts (Romans 5:5).

The Holy Spirit helps us grow to be more like Jesus. He opens our minds to understanding God's Word in the Bible. He allows God to use our lives to accomplish His work on earth.

How loving God is to fill us with His Holy Spirit!

Thank You, God, for Your Holy Spirit. Fill my heart to overflowing!

? **Want to know more?** See January 8, "Who Is the Trinity?" and February 5, "Who Is Jesus?"

APRIL 14

What Is Pentecost?

*They were all filled with the Holy Spirit, and they began
to speak different languages. The Holy Spirit was giving
them the power to speak these languages.*

—ACTS 2:4

Pentecost is the name of an ancient Jewish festival that takes place fifty days after Passover. The word *Pentecost* means "fiftieth day." After Jesus ascended into heaven, the disciples gathered in Jerusalem with Jews from many nations to celebrate Pentecost. Just as Jesus promised, God's Holy Spirit suddenly arrived and set their hearts afire with His love and power. The disciples found themselves speaking about God's love in languages they didn't know but were understood by others!

It was truly a miracle, and the crowd was amazed. On that miraculous day, many new people came to believe in Jesus. Over time, the arrival of God's Holy Spirit at Pentecost has become known as the historic beginning of the Christian church. Christians celebrate Pentecost on the seventh Sunday after Easter. It's a day for celebrating the arrival of God's Holy Spirit and the birth of the Christian church. Some churches celebrate Pentecost with a birthday cake!

> *Thank You, God, for sending Your Holy Spirit to live
> in the hearts of all believers—including me!*

? Want to know more? See April 25 and April 26, "What Are the Holy Spirit's Gifts of Speaking in and Interpreting Different Kinds of Tongues? (Parts 1 and 2)."

How Does the Holy Spirit Help Me?

"But the Helper will teach you everything."
—John 14:26

The Holy Spirit gives you God's special power to love (Romans 5:5). The Holy Spirit is like a battery in a flashlight. Without a battery, a flashlight looks just fine on the outside. But when it's dark and you need to use it, it is of no help. A flashlight *with* a battery looks the same on the outside as the flashlight without a battery. But when it's dark and you need to use it, it works. It shines the light into the darkness and keeps you from stumbling. God's Holy Spirit living in your heart is like your spiritual battery.

Another name used for God's Holy Spirit is "the Helper." That's because the Holy Spirit helps you in many ways. He gives you the power to tell right from wrong, to care more about other people, and to think, speak, and act more like Jesus. He gives you special gifts from God. God's Holy Spirit gives you the power to shine the light of God's love in a world that can sometimes be dark and scary.

> *God, help me be Your flashlight in today's world, shining the light of Your love!*

? Want to know more? See April 17, "What Are the Gifts of the Holy Spirit?"; April 27, "What Is the Most Important Gift of the Holy Spirit?"; and April 28, "How Are God's Gifts of the Holy Spirit Different from Natural God-Given Gifts?"

Is the Holy Ghost Really a Ghost?

[Jesus] breathed on them, and saith unto them, "Receive ye the Holy Ghost."
—JOHN 20:22 KJV

No, the Holy Ghost is *not* a ghost! *Holy Ghost* is simply an old-fashioned name for the *Holy Spirit.*

The word *spirit* means "breath." When God's Holy Spirit lives in your heart, He allows God to breathe through you. The word *ghost* also means "spirit," but today we often think of a ghost as the so-called spirit of a dead person. God is *not* a dead person! God is your living, loving Creator and heavenly Father!

The name "Holy Ghost" comes from an English translation of the Bible called the King James Version. It was published more than four hundred years ago, in 1611, when King James ruled England. Some people think it is one of the most beautiful books ever written.

Today there are other translations of the Bible that are easier to understand, but some Christians still use the King James Version and prefer to call the Holy Spirit the Holy Ghost.

> *God, I am so glad You are not a ghost—and that You are alive and real!*

? **Want to know more?** See January 3, "Who Is God?" and
January 4, "If God Is My Creator, How Is He Different from My Parents?"

What Are the Gifts of the Holy Spirit?

But the Holy Spirit will come to you. Then you will receive power.
—ACTS 1:8

God's Holy Spirit gives you the power to think, speak, and act like Jesus. The gifts of the Holy Spirit are supernatural. That is, they often defy the laws of nature. What do they do? They help us love and help one another—just as Jesus did during His time on earth.

The gifts of the Holy Spirit are listed three times in the Bible by the apostle Paul (Romans 12:6–8; 1 Corinthians 12:4–11; 1 Corinthians 12:28). They are: wisdom, knowledge, faith, healing, doing miracles, prophesying, knowing the difference between good and evil, and speaking in and interpreting unknown languages. Paul said, "One Spirit, the same Spirit, does all these things. The Spirit decides what to give each person" (1 Corinthians 12:11). In coming days, we'll learn more about each gift.

When the Holy Spirit lives in your heart, others can tell. That's because the Holy Spirit changes you to be more like Jesus. He helps you be God's loving helper here.

These special gifts were not only for Jesus and His followers thousands of years ago. They are for believers today—including *you!*

Thank You, God, for the amazing, awesome gifts of Your Holy Spirit!

What Is the Holy Spirit's Gift of Wisdom?

The wisdom that comes from God is like this: First, it is pure. Then it is also peaceful, gentle, and easy to please . . . always ready to help those who are troubled and to do good for others.

—JAMES 3:17

The gifts of the Holy Spirit are supernatural. They operate outside the laws of nature and typical human experience. When gifts of the Holy Spirit are *manifested*, or take place, they are very special moments when the kingdom of God breaks through on earth.

For us, gaining wisdom takes time. Wisdom is earned through years of experience, knowledge, and common sense. Even so, human wisdom can't compare to God's perfect wisdom. That's because God sees and knows everything. God *is* wisdom!

Sometimes God's Holy Spirit gives a believer an overwhelming sense to share "a word of wisdom" from God. It is not her own thought, but God's thought—God's wisdom. The message can be for a single person or for the church. It may be a word of warning or encouragement. But it is always rooted in the love of God for His children. It always serves to *edify*, or build us up. Isn't that beautiful?

Thank You, God, for Your Holy Spirit's supernatural gift of wisdom!

? Would you like to know more? See January 14, "What Is the Kingdom of God?"

What Is the Holy Spirit's Gift of Knowledge?

Knowledge begins with respect for the Lord.
—PROVERBS 1:7

The gifts of the Holy Spirit are meant to *edify* or "build up" the church, or community of believers, for the common good (1 Corinthians 12:7).

The word *knowledge* comes from a Middle English word that means "to recognize or know a subject, situation, or person." Knowledge of God includes not just knowing *about* Him but actually knowing *Him* personally. Compared to God, our knowledge is small. God knows about every subject, situation, and person on earth!

Sometimes God's Holy Spirit gives a believer an overwhelming sense to share "a word of knowledge" from God. It is not his own knowledge, but God's. These words often have to do with healing. For example, when a Christian prays for healing, she may receive a "word of knowledge" about the person God is about to heal, the person's name, and a very specific description of the illness. The *manifestation*, or demonstration, of the Holy Spirit's gift of knowledge is a good and beautiful thing. It's an example of heaven breaking through to accomplish God's will on earth.

Thank You, God, for Your Holy Spirit's supernatural gift of knowledge!

? Want to know more? See April 21, "What Is the Holy Spirit's Gift of Healing?"

What Is the Holy Spirit's Gift of Faith?

It was by faith Noah heard God's warnings about things that he could not yet see.

—Hebrews 11:7

Having faith is knowing that something is real even if we can't see it. For Christians, having faith means both to *believe* in and *trust* God. We can trust God because the Bible says that God is good and He loves us.

All believers in Jesus have been given what is known as "saving" faith from God. Paul writes, "For it is by grace you have been saved, through faith—and this is not from yourselves, it is the gift of God" (Ephesians 2:8 NIV). What a wonderful gift! So how is the Holy Spirit's gift of faith different from God's gift of saving faith? Remember: when true gifts of the Holy Spirit are *manifested*, or take place, they are very special moments when the kingdom of God breaks through, sometimes in a dramatic, life-changing way.

The Holy Spirit's gift of faith takes place when a believer has an extraordinarily strong confidence in God's Word and His promises. It is a supernatural, deep-down knowing that God will do what He says, even if it seems impossible. It is faith that never gives up. With faith, "all things are possible" (Mark 9:23)!

Thank You, God, for Your Holy Spirit's supernatural gift of faith!

? Want to know more? See May 10, "Was There Really a Flood in the Time of Noah?"

What Is the Holy Spirit's Gift of Healing?

When Jesus arrived, he saw a large crowd. He felt sorry
for them and healed those who were sick.
—MATTHEW 14:14

It's amazing the way God created our human bodies to heal naturally. When you cut your finger, a scab forms and the wound heals. When you get a cold, you eventually get better. At the same time, because our human bodies are mortal and will one day die, we sometimes suffer illnesses and injuries that cannot be healed so easily. The good news is that through the gift of God's Holy Spirit, we can pray for supernatural healing, just as Jesus and His disciples did. In fact, the Bible contains at least 139 stories about the healing power of God's love! Just as in Jesus' day, healing comes from God alone. When healing takes place, it is a beautiful example of heaven breaking through to accomplish God's will on earth. Praise God for His loving power and desire to heal!

Thank You, God, for Your Holy Spirit's supernatural gift of healing!

? Want to know more? See February 26, "Why Did Jesus Do Miracles?" and September 6, "Do Miraculous Answers to Prayer Still Happen Today?"

What Is the Holy Spirit's Gift of Miraculous Powers?

[Jesus] taught the people in the synagogue, and they were amazed. They said, "Where did this man get this wisdom and this power to do miracles?"
—MATTHEW 13:54

A miracle is something wonderful that cannot be explained by natural or scientific laws. Miracles are not magic. Miracles are real. They are loving, powerful demonstrations of God's will being done on earth. The Bible records at least thirty-seven true, eyewitnessed miracles of Jesus! He commanded His disciples to do the same: "He who believes in me will do the same things that I do. He will do even greater things than these" (John 14:12).

Miracles come through Holy Spirit-inspired prayer. They can happen suddenly or over time. They can be large or small. When a miracle takes place, it is important to thank God and give Him all the credit and glory. God touches our lives with miracles because He loves us. Here is a fun experiment: Ask a grown-up you love if he has ever experienced a miracle. You may be surprised at the answer!

> *Thank You, God, for Your Holy Spirit's supernatural gift of miraculous powers!*

? Want to know more? See February 26, "Why Did Jesus Do Miracles?" and September 6, "Do Miraculous Answers to Prayer Still Happen Today?"

APRIL 23

What Is the Holy Spirit's Gift of Prophecy?

Follow the way of love and eagerly desire gifts
of the Spirit, especially prophecy.
—1 CORINTHIANS 14:1 NIV

The word *prophecy* means "to divinely foretell the future." *Divinely* means "coming from God." The Holy Spirit's gift of prophecy is *not* to be confused with human fortune-telling of any kind. Palm-reading and tarot cards *don't* come from God. In fact, the Bible says God hates fortune-telling. It's against His holy laws (Deuteronomy 18:10–12)! Jesus and His disciples never used God's gift of prophecy to show off or to entertain people. They used it to demonstrate God's great love and care for His children. The Old Testament records many examples of prophecy, including books written by true-life prophets. A prophecy may not make sense until later. Jesus' birth was foretold hundreds of years before it happened!

Even today God's Holy Spirit inspires some believers to share a prophetic word. These thoughts are not their own, but God's. Prophecies are always rooted in God's love for His children—and that includes *you*! How do we know if a prophecy is of God? It always comes true.

Thank You, God, for Your Holy Spirit's supernatural gift of prophecy!

? **Want to know more?** See June 22, "Does the Old Testament Have Anything to Say About Jesus?" and October 30, "What's Wrong with Horoscopes, Fortune-Telling, and Ouija Boards?"

APRIL 24

What Is the Holy Spirit's Gift of Distinguishing Between Spirits?

*Do not stop the work of the Holy Spirit. Do not treat prophecy
as if it were not important. But test everything. Keep what
is good. And stay away from everything that is evil.*
—1 THESSALONIANS 5:19—22

To *distinguish* **between spirits means** to be able to supernaturally *discern*, or tell the difference, between good and evil. There are many differences between heaven and earth. Heaven exists mostly outside our time and space. It's where God and the angels live. It is a place of love and goodness. One day, thanks to Jesus, we will live in heaven too.

God allows heaven to break through to accomplish His purposes every day! Sometimes God does this through His faithful angels, who do His bidding. Another way is through believers, filled with His Holy Spirit. Because evil exists, sometimes the gifts of the Holy Spirit must be tested. Believers with the Holy Spirit's gift of discernment are able to answer this question: Is this really true and from God? The Holy Spirit's gift of distinguishing between spirits protects us from evil and helps make sure God's loving will is being done.

> *Thank You, God, for Your Holy Spirit's supernatural gift
> of distinguishing between good and evil spirits!*

? Want to know more? See November 18 and November 19, "Are There Really Angels? (Parts 1 and 2)" and November 22, "Are There Really Demons?"

What Are the Holy Spirit's Gifts of Speaking in and Interpreting Different Kinds of Tongues? (Part 1)

They were all filled with the Holy Spirit, and they
began to speak different languages.
—ACTS 2:4

Another word for the Holy Spirit's gift of speaking in different kinds of tongues is *glossolalia*. It comes from a Greek phrase that means "to speak in, with, or by languages other than one's own." When this happened at Pentecost, it marked the arrival of God's Holy Spirit on earth. About ten days after Jesus ascended into heaven, the disciples gathered in Jerusalem with other Jews to celebrate Pentecost. Suddenly, God's Holy Spirit arrived, and they found themselves miraculously speaking about God's love in languages they did not know! The crowd was amazed because "each one heard them speaking in his own language" (Acts 2:5). Many new people came to believe in Jesus that day. In this first example of God's gift of speaking in tongues, the purpose was to *evangelize*, or spread the good news of God's love through faith in Jesus.

Thank You, Holy Spirit, that language is no barrier for You!

? Want to know more? See April 14, "What Is Pentecost?" and June 30, "Why Are Matthew, Mark, Luke, and John Known as the Four Evangelists?"

What Are the Holy Spirit's Gifts of Speaking in and Interpreting Different Kinds of Tongues? (Part 2)

The one who has the [Holy Spirit's supernatural] gift of speaking in a different language should pray that he can also interpret what he says.
—1 CORINTHIANS 14:13

Sometimes the Holy Spirit's gift of speaking in tongues happens in a language not known on Earth. It's made up of fluid, speech-like syllables that ebb and flow, as the Holy Spirit inspires. The apostle Paul calls this the language of angels (1 Corinthians 13:1). Paul didn't want this to seem odd or confusing. Why? The purpose of all spiritual gifts is *not* to confuse or divide, but to strengthen and unite believers. Paul believed that speaking in tongues in church should be orderly and that believers with the gift of interpreting tongues should also be present. "When you meet together, one person . . . speaks in a different language, and another person interprets that language. The purpose of all these things should be to help the church grow strong" (1 Corinthians 14:26). Speaking in and interpreting different kinds of tongues are powerful examples of God's beautiful gifts.

Thank You, God, for Your Holy Spirit's supernatural gifts of speaking in and interpreting different kinds of tongues!

What Is the Most Important Gift of the Holy Spirit?

*So these three things continue forever: faith, hope
and love. And the greatest of these is love.*
—1 Corinthians 13:13

The purpose of the Holy Spirit is to help you think, speak, and act like Jesus. This can be summed up in one word: *love*. The word *love* means "to deeply care for" and is used in lots of ways. You can love riding your bike, chocolate chip cookies, and your dog. You can love family and friends.

Christian love is caring for another person as much as you care for yourself. Another word for this is *agape* (ah-*gah*-pay) love, or love that has the other person's best interests at heart. The apostle Paul described it: "Love is patient and kind. Love is not jealous, it does not brag, and it is not proud. . . . Love patiently accepts all things. It always trusts, always hopes, and always continues strong. Love never ends" (1 Corinthians 13:4–8). Isn't that beautiful? Paul believed that of all the gifts of the Holy Spirit, the greatest gift is *love*. Christian love is not just a feeling. It's feelings put into action.

> *Thank You, God, for Your gift of love! Help me put Your love
> in to action by helping, praying, and caring for others.*

? **Want to know more?** See January 12, "How Can I Share God's Love?" and April 28, "How Are God's Gifts of the Holy Spirit Different from Natural God-Given Gifts?"

How Are God's Gifts of the Holy Spirit Different from Natural God-Given Gifts?

We all have different gifts. Each gift came because of the grace that God gave us.
—ROMANS 12:6

The gifts of the Holy Spirit are awesome! But just as important in God's eyes are His natural gifts, such as serving, helping, teaching, and encouraging others (Romans 12:6–8). The Gospel of Mark tells a story about a paralyzed man who wanted to be healed. Because he couldn't walk, he couldn't go see Jesus on his own. Thankfully, he had four loving, faithful friends. They carried him to the house where Jesus was staying, but the crowd was so large they couldn't get in. Still, they didn't give up! They climbed on the roof, dug a hole, and lowered their friend down to Jesus. When Jesus saw their faith, He healed the paralyzed man, and everyone was amazed (Mark 2:3–5; 11–12)! Without the help of his friends, the man may never have been healed. This story shows how God's natural gift of helping is *just as important* as His supernatural gift of healing. Simple things such as helping someone shows God's love.

> *Thank You, God, for Your natural, everyday gifts. Help me be Your faithful helper!*

? **Want to know more?** See January 12, "How Can I Share God's Love?"

How Can I Discover My God-Given Gifts and Talents?

Everything you say and everything you do should all be done for Jesus your Lord. And in all you do, give thanks to God the Father through Jesus.
—COLOSSIANS 3:17

How can you know what your God-given gifts and talents are? God has given you a way to discover His special gifts. He has already planted it in your heart. It's God's gift of enthusiasm (en-*thoo*-zee-az-um). *Enthusiasm* means "to be inspired and indwelled by God." That's why when you feel enthusiasm, it is a good idea to pay attention!

Ask yourself: What is it you love to do? What is it that excites and energizes you? Perhaps it is spending time with your grandma and grandpa . . . or playing on a sports team . . . or learning everything you can about a subject such as astronomy, or dinosaurs, or computers . . . or reading . . . or spending time with little ones . . . or singing . . . or caring for animals . . . or painting . . . or making your friends laugh . . . or dancing . . .

Whatever it is, just follow your natural enthusiasm. There is only one you, and God has special plans for you. He loves to reveal to you His unique gifts and purposes for your life!

> Thank You, God, for enthusiasm! Help me discover
> the special gifts and talents You've given me.

What Is the Fruit of the Holy Spirit?

We all show the Lord's glory, and we are being changed to be like him. This . . . comes from the Lord, who is the Spirit.
—2 CORINTHIANS 3:18

When God's Holy Spirit lives in your heart, others can tell. That's because over time, the Holy Spirit *transforms* or changes you. The Holy Spirit produces outward, visible signs that He's living in you and helping you be more like Jesus.

These signs of the Holy Spirit are sometimes called "fruit." They are called fruit because fruit is an outward sign of a healthy, living plant. Fruit is beautiful to look at. Fruit is delicious to eat. Fruit nourishes the body. The fruit that the Holy Spirit produces is an outward sign of a healthy soul.

What is the fruit of the Holy Spirit?

The apostle Paul wrote that the fruit of the Spirit is "love, joy, peace, patience, kindness, goodness, faithfulness, gentleness, self-control" (Galatians 5:22–23). Isn't that wonderful?

> *Thank You, God, for the beautiful fruit of Your Holy Spirit! Help it grow in my life.*

? Want to know more? See October 20, "What Does the Bible Mean When It Says My Body Is the 'Temple of God'?"

125

MAY

What Is the Most Famous Song About God's Holy Spirit?

Be filled with the Spirit. Speak to each other with
psalms, hymns, and spiritual songs.
—EPHESIANS 5:18–19

Over the centuries, countless hymns have been written about God's Holy Spirit. The word *hymn* means "a song of praise." The most famous hymn about the Holy Spirit was written in the ninth century by a Christian named Rabanus Maurus. The hymn's original Latin title is *Veni Creator Spiritus*, which means "Come, Creator Spirit." Although it was written more than a thousand years ago, "Come, Creator Spirit" continues to be joyfully sung by Christians around the world. Many churches sing "Come, Creator Spirit" on Pentecost, the day Christians celebrate the Holy Spirit's arrival on earth and the birth of the church. Here is how it begins: *Come, Holy Ghost, Creator, come from thy bright heav'nly throne; Come, take possession of our souls, and make them all thine own. . . . Thou who art sevenfold in thy grace, finger of God's right hand; His promise teaching little ones to speak and understand.*

> *Veni Creator Spiritus . . . Come, Creator Spirit!*

? **Want to know more?** See April 13, "Who Is the Holy Spirit?";
April 14, "What Is Pentecost?"; April 16, "Is the Holy Ghost
Really a Ghost?"; and September 28, "Why Do We Sing Hymns
in Church?"

What Is the Bible?

All Scripture is inspired by God.
—2 Timothy 3:16

The Bible is the most important book in the world. Why? Because the Bible is the true, living Holy Word of God.

The apostle Paul described the Bible as *inspired* or "God-breathed" (2 Timothy 3:16 NIV). God breathed through the hearts and minds of the people who wrote the Bible. That makes the Bible different from all other books.

When you pick up a Bible, you are actually holding a whole library! That's because the Bible contains sixty-six books, written by forty different people, over a period of approximately two thousand years.

In the Bible you will discover an awesome collection of real, true-life stories about kings and queens, angels and prophets, adventure and love, plus poetry, songs, prayers, and letters—even predictions about the future! Best of all, you will read the real, true-life story of Jesus, God's only Son, sent to earth to save the world. Talk about exciting!

The Bible is not a dry, boring book. It is the living Word of God. The Bible is God's special love letter to you!

Thank You, God, for Your amazing, living Holy Word, the Bible.

How Did We Get the Bible?

"Get a scroll. Write on it all the words I have spoken to you."
—JEREMIAH 36:2

The Bible begins with the oldest stories about how God created the universe. In ancient times, most people didn't know how to read or write, so they passed stories down *orally*, or by mouth. Parents told their children, who told their children, and so on. Over time, people wrote down the stories—first on papyrus scrolls, later on parchment. In the early Christian church, people who loved God had *councils*, or special meetings, to decide which books would be included in the Bible. They prayed for God's Holy Spirit to help them choose. Some books were written in Hebrew and Aramaic, and others in Greek. In the fourth century AD, an Italian Christian named Jerome translated many of the books into Latin. In the fifteenth century, the mechanical printing press was invented by a man named Johann Gutenberg in Germany. In 1457, Gutenberg's Bible was the very first complete book ever printed. It was written in Latin, the language of the church at that time, and it was printed in two huge volumes of 1,282 unnumbered pages! The Bible is the world's best-selling book and has been translated into more than two thousand languages so that people everywhere can learn about God's great love.

> *Help me get to know and love You better, God,*
> *through Your living Holy Word, the Bible.*

? **Want to know more?** See May 4, "How Did the Bible Get Its Name?"

How Did the Bible Get Its Name?

"Workers of Byblos were on board ship with you. . . .
Their sailors came alongside to trade with you."
—EZEKIEL 27:9

In what is now the country of Lebanon, the Phoenician city of Gebal was once a busy Mediterranean seaport. In Bible times, the Greek name for Gebal was *Byblos*. *Byblos* was also the Greek word for *papyrus*, the grassy reed from which the earliest form of paper was made. Maybe this is because trading paper was a big business in Byblos, or maybe it's because that's where papyrus grew. No one knows for sure.

At any rate, the word *byblos*, or papyrus, gives us the Greek word *biblios*, which means "books." Papyrus is the kind of paper the scribes used when writing down the books of the Bible. In ancient times, the only people able to read and write were called *scribes*, which comes from the Latin word that means "to write."

Today the English word *Bible* literally means "The Book."

Here's a fun fact: the word *Bible* is not found in the Bible! This is because the term didn't come into use until long after the all the books of the Bible were completed and chosen.

Thank You, God, for the people of ancient times who worked so
hard to provide the Bible for all Your children—including me!

How Do I Know the Bible Is True?

*God's word is alive and working. . . . God's word judges
the thoughts and feelings in our hearts.*

—HEBREWS 4:12

The Bible is different from every other book in the world. Why? Because it was written by many different people who wrote under the inspiration of God. Through His Holy Spirit, God *breathed His truth into the hearts and minds of the writers*. God inspired the writers so they would know just what to write. God's Holy Spirit is alive today in the pages of every Bible! The Bible speaks God's truth to our hearts. This is why it's often called "God's Word." The Bible has the power to speak God's truth to *you*!

Here is an important and interesting fact: the Bible is the *most documented and reliable book* in the world. Scholars of the Bible have more than *thirteen thousand* ancient copies of portions of the New Testament, which they continue to study and learn from this very day! New discoveries by biblical archaeologists also help to prove that events in the Bible really happened. An *archaeologist* is a scientist who studies human history by digging up artifacts and remains. Isn't that amazing?

Thank You, God, for how Your Holy Word lives and speaks in every Bible—including mine!

? Want to know more? See May 10, "Was There Really a Flood During the Time of Noah?"

What's the Difference Between the Old Testament and the New Testament? (Part 1)

"I will make an agreement between me and you and all your descendants from now on: I will be your God and the God of all your descendants."
—GENESIS 17:7

The books of the Bible are divided into two sections: the Old Testament and the New Testament. The word *testament* means "covenant," which then means "a promise or agreement." In the Bible, the covenant is between God and His children, which includes *you!*

The Old Testament starts before the beginning of time and covers thousands of years. It's more than twice as long as the New Testament. In it, we learn about God's love for the Jews, the people of Israel. God made a covenant with His people (Genesis 13:14–17) and expected them to believe in Him, love Him, and obey His laws (Exodus 20:1–17). This was not always easy!

Most of the Old Testament was written in Hebrew, the language of Israel, or Aramaic, a language similar to Hebrew. The Old and New Testaments are separated in history by approximately four hundred years. If you like, open your Bible and turn to the table of contents to see the thirty-nine books of the Old Testament!

Thank You, God, for the awesome story of Your covenant of love in the Old Testament.

What's the Difference Between the Old Testament and the New Testament? (Part 2)

The Spirit that we have makes us children of God.
—ROMANS 8:15

Yesterday we learned about the Old Testament of the Bible. Today we will learn about the New Testament. The books of the New Testament were originally written in Greek. It begins with the birth of God's Son, Jesus (Matthew 1:18–25). The books of Matthew, Mark, Luke, John, and Acts tell the story of Jesus. Acts also tells about the exciting arrival of God's Holy Spirit, and about the birth and growth of the early church. Many books in the New Testament are letters from people who personally knew Jesus. The last book, Revelation, is the apostle John's vision about the future.

In the New Testament, God makes a new *covenant*, or agreement, with His people. Through believing in His Son, Jesus, God invites everyone to become one of His chosen people—including you (Romans 8:14). Open your Bible and turn to the table of contents to see the twenty-seven books of the New Testament!

Thank You, God, for Your new covenant. I am so happy to be a member of Your great, big, beautiful family!

? **Want to know more?** See June 22, "Does the Old Testament Have Anything to Say About Jesus?"

What Is the Difference Between a Jew and a Gentile?

I am not ashamed of the gospel, because it is the power of God that brings salvation to everyone who believes: first to the Jew, then to the Gentile.
—ROMANS 1:16 NIV

The word *Jew* is the most commonly used name for the people of Israel (Ezra 5:5; Jeremiah 32:12). The word *Jew* is derived from the Hebrew word *Yehudi*, meaning "one who comes from Judea." Judea was the ancient region of southern Palestine—now the southern part of the country Israel and the southwestern part of the country Jordan in the Middle East. Jews are also sometimes called Hebrews or Israelites. *Hebrew* is the official language of the Jews. *Israel* is a nation.

A Gentile is, quite simply, any person who is not Jewish. The word *gentile* comes from a Latin word which means "of a family or nation, or of the same clan."

Today there are many Gentiles and Jews who love God very much!

> *Thank You, God, for how You love all Your children, Jews and Gentiles alike.*

Why Does God's Name Sometimes Appear as "LORD" in the Old Testament?

"You must not use the name of the Lord your God thoughtlessly."
—EXODUS 20:7

God's name was so holy to the Jews that, out of reverence, they didn't write or say it out loud. They wanted to obey the third commandment: "You must not use the name of the Lord your God thoughtlessly" (Exodus 20:7). The ancient Hebrew alphabet had no written vowels (*a*, *e*, *i*, *o*, or *u*). In the original Old Testament manuscripts, the name of God was written as four Hebrew consonants, which translate into English as YHWH or JHVH. Some English versions of the Bible add vowels to create the words Yahweh (*Ya*-way) and Jehovah (Je-*ho*-va). Most Bibles translate YHWH and JHVH as LORD (with big and small capital letters). Even today, some Jewish people substitute God's name with *Adonai* (*Add*-on-eye), which means "my Lord," or *HaShem*, which means "the Name." Some Jewish people write the English word *God* with the middle letter deleted, so it looks like this: G-d. All this is done out of reverence and a desire to obey God's law.

Thank You, God, for all Your beautiful names! Help me to never use Your holy name thoughtlessly.

? Want to know more? See May 29 and May 30, "What Are the Ten Commandments? (Parts 1 and 2)."

Was There Really a Flood During the Time of Noah?

Water flooded the earth for 40 days. As the water rose, it lifted the boat off the ground.
—Genesis 7:17

Yes, there really was a flood during the time of Noah! The name *Noah* means "comfort and rest." Noah was a faithful man who loved God. This was rare in his day, as humans had mostly forgotten God and grown evil. This broke God's heart (Genesis 6:5–6). God warned Noah that a great flood was coming that would destroy all life. He gave Noah instructions for building a huge *ark*, or floatable container, that would save Noah and his family. God told Noah to take into the ark one pair of every living animal on earth! And then—just as God said—the rain fell and the earth flooded. Everything was destroyed except the ark (Genesis 7:23). When the rain finally stopped, the ark came to rest in the mountains of Ararat, in modern-day Turkey. God filled the sky with a beautiful rainbow as a sign of His promise to never again destroy the earth by water (Genesis 9:12–15). Modern-day underwater archaeologists and geologists confirm that there truly *was* a huge flood in Noah's day. Scientific evidence shows it happened around 5000 BC.

> *Thank You, God, for the amazing life and faith of Noah!*

? Want to know more? See December 11, "Can I Believe in Science and Still Believe in God?"

Who Is Abraham, and What Is a Patriarch?

Abram believed the Lord. And the Lord accepted Abram's faith, and that faith made him right with God.
—GENESIS 15:6

Abraham is the first patriarch (*pay*-tree-ark) of the Jewish people. The word *patriarch* means "father." He is one of our spiritual forefathers too! Abraham was born in the ancient city of Ur in what is now Iraq. He was given the name *Abram*, which means "exalted father" (Genesis 11:27–28). Back then, people believed in many *deities*, or false gods. Abram's father, Terah, was, according to tradition, an idol merchant.

Not much is known about Abram's childhood, but over the years he stopped believing in his father's idols. Abram came to believe in the one true Creator, Father God. Back then, this was remarkable, and it made God *very* happy

Because of Abram's great, unshakeable faith, God said to him, "I am changing your name from Abram to Abraham. . . . I am making you a father of many nations" (Genesis 17:5). The name *Abraham* means "father of many." The Bible says Abraham "died at a good old age" (Genesis 25:8 NIV) and was buried with his beloved wife, Sarah. He was 175 years old (Genesis 25:7)! We'll learn more about this amazing man of faith tomorrow.

Thank You, God, for Abraham's great, unshakeable faith!

What Are the Twelve Tests of Abraham?

"I will make you a great nation, and I will bless you."
—GENESIS 12:2

God made Abram an offer. If Abram would take his family and leave his country for the Promised Land, God would make his descendants a great nation. Abram agreed (Genesis 12:1–4). This *covenant*, or agreement, between God and Abram is known as the "Abrahamic covenant." During his lifetime, Abram went through twelve tests of faith to prove his trustworthiness to God. He made mistakes, but because he loved and trusted God with all his heart, he passed all of God's tests! The tests included: (1) leaving his homeland for an unknown future; (2 and 3) parting with and then rescuing his nephew Lot; (4) refusing to give money to an evil king; (5) trusting that he would one day have a son; (6) trusting that his people would one day get to the Promised Land; (7) circumcising the males in his family; (8) praying for the people of Sodom; (9) welcoming angels in disguise; (10) apologizing for lying to a king; (11) peacefully resolving a fight over land; and (12) trusting God so much that he was willing to sacrifice his beloved son, Isaac.

Thank You, God, for Abraham!

? Want to know more? See May 14 and 15, "Who Is Isaac? (Parts 1 and 2)"; June 23, "Who Is King Melchizedek?"; and November 18 and November 19, "Are There Really Angels? (Parts 1 and 2)."

Who Is Sarah?

God said to Abraham, "I will change the name of Sarai, your
wife. Her new name will be Sarah. I will bless her."
—Genesis 17:15–16

Sarah was Abraham's wife. When Sarah and Abraham were married, she was known as *Sarai*, which means "quarrelsome." Before Isaac's birth, God changed her name to *Sarah*, which means "princess" or "noblewoman." Just as God chose Abraham to become the *patriarch*, or father of the Jewish people, He chose Sarah to become the *matriarch*, or mother.

Sarah was beautiful. She was also unable to have children (Genesis 11:30). This made Sarah very sad. It also made God's promise of a son seem impossible. When Sarah was ninety, and Abraham was almost one hundred years old, three strangers came to visit them at their tent. Sent by God, they were actually angels with a very important message: "About this time a year from now . . . Sarah will have a son" (Genesis 18:10). Can you imagine? Sarah laughed because she thought this was impossible. But nothing's impossible with God! She gave birth to a son and named him *Isaac*, which means "laughter."

Sarah died at 127 years of age (Genesis 23:1). She's the only woman in the Bible whose age at her death is given, and she was buried with Abraham in the Promised Land (Genesis 23:19).

Thank You, God, for Sarah!

Who Is Isaac? (Part 1)

God tested Abraham's faith.
—Genesis 22:1

Isaac was the only beloved son of Abraham and his wife, Sarah. His birth was a miracle because his mother was ninety years old when she had him!

Isaac is the second *patriarch*, or father, of the Jewish people. Like his father, Isaac loved God and knew He could be trusted. But he was about to be part of a very hard test. In Isaac's day, when faithful people worshipped God, they often sacrificed an animal. The word *sacrifice* comes from a Latin word that means "holy." The sacrificed animal was usually a goat, ram, lamb, or calf. First it was killed, then it was put on a fire and cooked as a "burnt offering." Meat was valuable, and the animal was considered a gift to God.

One day, when Isaac was still a boy, God commanded Abraham to take his only beloved son and offer him as a sacrifice (Genesis 22:1–2). How could this be?

Although Abraham must have been scared and confused, he did not argue. He loved and trusted God. But can you imagine? How could a loving God make such a request?

Tomorrow we will find out what happened next!

> God, when I don't understand Your ways, help me
> never to lose my faith and to trust in You.

Who Is Isaac? (Part 2)

[Abraham] tied up his son Isaac. And he laid Isaac on the wood on the altar.
—Genesis 22:9

Yesterday we learned how God asked Abraham to sacrifice his son, Isaac, and Abraham did not argue but obeyed. Still, why would God make such a terrible request? Here's what happened next: Abraham went up the mountain with Isaac. On their way up, Isaac asked where the animal to be sacrificed was. Abraham said, "God will give us the lamb." At a certain spot they stopped, and Abraham built an altar. Then he tied Isaac up to sacrifice him! Suddenly, an angel called out, "Stop! Let him go." There in a thicket of bushes, trapped by his horns, was a big old ram. God had provided a perfect sacrifice. Because Abraham was obedient, God blessed him *and* Isaac for generations (Genesis 22)! This is a story of amazing trust. For Christians, it also foreshadows Jesus' sacrificial death on the cross hundreds of years later.

Isaac was approximately thirty-seven years old when his mother, Sarah, died. Isaac loved his mother dearly and grieved her loss. Abraham sent his servant to find heartbroken Isaac a good wife. He returned with beautiful Rebekah. Isaac loved her, and she comforted him in his sorrow. The Bible says that Isaac, like his father Abraham, lived a long life and was 180 years old when he died (Genesis 35:28–29).

Thank You, God, for Isaac!

? **Want to know more?** See May 16, "How Are Isaac and Jesus Similar?"

How Are Isaac and
Jesus Similar?

*Abraham believed that God could raise the dead. And really,
it was as if Abraham got Isaac back from death.*

—HEBREWS 11:19

Throughout the Bible, many people, stories, animals, and even objects *foreshadow* future events. God can do this because He knows *everything*, including the future! Abraham's willingness to sacrifice his beloved son, Isaac, is a foreshadowing of God's sacrifice of His Son. Amazingly, these two events happened hundreds of years apart. Here a few ways Isaac and Jesus are similar: They both were the beloved sons of their fathers (Isaac: Genesis 22:2; Jesus: John 3:16); were named and their births foretold by God (Isaac: Genesis 17:19; Jesus: Matthew 1:21). They were born miraculously (Isaac: Genesis 21:1–3; Jesus: Luke 1:34–35). They obeyed the will of their fathers, even when it was *very* difficult (Isaac: Genesis 22:9–10; Jesus: Philippians 2:8). They were saved from death by God in totally unexpected, surprising ways (Isaac: Genesis 22:10–14; Jesus: Matthew 28:2–5). They fulfilled important promises by God that would change the course of world and human history (Isaac: Genesis 12:3; Jesus: Acts 13:23).

Thank You, God, for how You know everything!

? Want to know more? See January 1, "Who Invented Time?";
January 14, "What Is the Kingdom of God?"; and June 22, "Does
the Old Testament Have Anything to Say About God?"

143

Who Is Jacob? (Part 1)

*When the second baby was born, he was holding on to
Esau's heel. So that baby was named Jacob.*
—GENESIS 25:26

Jacob is the third and final *patriarch*, or father, of the Jewish people. He was the second-born twin son of Isaac and Rebekah. Even in his mother's womb, Jacob struggled with his brother, Esau (Genesis 25:22). The name *Jacob* means "holder of the heel" or "one who overthrows."

Jacob and Esau did not get along. Esau was his father's favorite, and Jacob was Rebekah's favorite. In Bible days, firstborn sons received an *inheritance*, or special gift. Esau didn't understand how valuable his inheritance was. Jacob, however, did. And he plotted to take advantage of Esau.

One day Jacob made a pot of soup. Esau came in hungry from hunting all day and asked for a delicious bowlful. Jacob said sure—as long as Esau would trade him his inheritance. Esau was so hungry he agreed (Genesis 25:29–34)!

That's not all. Years later, Jacob tricked his father into giving him an important firstborn blessing meant for Esau. When Esau found out, he was so angry he wanted to kill Jacob! So Jacob fled (Genesis 27:1–45).

Yes, Jacob was a liar, cheater, and trickster. But his story doesn't end here. More tomorrow!

Thank You, God, that You can use imperfect people do great things.

Who Is Jacob? (Part 2)

"Your name will no longer be Jacob. Your name will now be Israel, because you have wrestled with God and with men. And you have won."
—GENESIS 32:28

Yesterday we learned how Jacob tricked his brother, Esau. Esau was so angry he wanted to kill Jacob! Afraid for his life, Jacob fled to live in a faraway land. Years passed. Jacob had his own family and desperately wanted to return home. His missed his mother and father. He even missed Esau. When God told Jacob in a dream to go home, Jacob was happy to obey. There was only one problem: Esau. How would his angry brother react? Jacob asked for God's protection (Genesis 32:9–12). The night before Jacob's meeting with Esau, a mysterious man unexpectedly showed up and demanded that Jacob wrestle with him. All night long, the two men fought. The man hurt Jacob's hip, but Jacob still wouldn't give up. "I won't let you go until you bless me," Jacob demanded. Before blessing Jacob, the man did something very strange. He gave Jacob a new name, *Israel*, which means "he struggles with God." It turned out the "man" was actually God's angel (Genesis 32:26–28)! When Jacob finally met up with Esau, all was forgiven and the brothers hugged and cried (Genesis 33:4). Jacob lived to be 147 (Genesis 47:28). Before Jacob died, he blessed all his sons, who would go on to become the heads of the "Twelve Tribes of Israel" (Genesis 49:1–28).

Thank You, God, for Jacob!

? **Want to know more?** See May 22, "What Are the Twelve Tribes of Israel?"

145

What Is Jacob's Ladder?

Jacob dreamed that there was a ladder resting on the earth and reaching up into heaven. And he saw angels of God going up and coming down the ladder.
—GENESIS 28:12

God speaks to us in many ways—through the Bible, through His Holy Spirit, and through other people of faith. Sometimes God speaks to us through our dreams. That's what happened to Jacob.

Yesterday we learned how after tricking his brother, Esau, Jacob feared for his life and fled to a faraway land. He was very worried about his future. One night while on the run, Jacob lay down to sleep under the stars, using a stone for a pillow. He dreamed of a huge ladder going up, up, up to heaven, with angels climbing up and down! Then God spoke to Jacob and promised that one day his descendants would be many and blessed. "I am with you," God said, "and I will protect you everywhere you go. And I will bring you back to this land. I will not leave you until I have done what I have promised you" (Genesis 28:15). God encouraged Jacob and also affirmed Jacob's destiny as the third and final *patriarch*, or father, of the Jewish people.

> *Thank You, God, for the ways You speak to Your children—even in dreams!*

? Want to know more? See May 17 and 18, "Who Is Jacob? (Parts 1 and 2)."

Who Is Joseph? (Part 1)

Joseph's brothers saw that their father loved Joseph more than he loved them. So they hated their brother and could not speak to him politely.
—Genesis 37:4

Joseph was the eleventh of Jacob's twelve sons. The name *Joseph* means "God increases." Because Joseph was his father's favorite, his ten older brothers resented him. On top of that, Joseph actually *was* a little stuck-up and bratty! Once Jacob gave Joseph a beautiful, fancy coat. His brothers were furious. They were also jealous that Joseph had the supernatural gift of prophecy and could interpret dreams. When Joseph told them that he dreamed he would one day rule over them, they were so angry they plotted to kill him!

One day, while out working in the fields, the brothers grabbed Joseph, took his coat, and threw him into a deep pit. At the last minute, instead of killing him, they decided to sell him as a slave to Ishmaelite traders. As the traders' caravan pulled away, Joseph's brothers smeared his coat with goat's blood. They showed the bloody coat to their father and lied, saying Joseph had been killed by wild animals. Jacob was devastated. Joseph was seventeen when he was sold into slavery in Egypt. Joseph's story doesn't end here. More tomorrow!

Thank You, God, that You love and watch over me.

? Want to know more? See April 23, "What Is the Holy Spirit's Gift of Prophecy?"

Who Is Joseph? (Part 2)

You intended to harm me, but God intended it for good to accomplish what is now being done, the saving of many lives.
—GENESIS 50:20 NIV

Joseph's brothers sold him as a slave. His new owner was an Egyptian official, Potiphar. Potiphar's wife tried to flirt with Joseph, but when he rejected her, she had him thrown into jail! Still, Joseph never lost his faith in God. In jail, he interpreted dreams for his fellow prisoners (Genesis 40). Word of his gift reached Egypt's *pharaoh* (*fare*-oh), or king, who'd been having upsetting dreams. The pharaoh called Joseph to his palace. Joseph told the pharaoh that his dreams were God's warning that Egypt would have seven years of good harvests but then seven years of famine (Genesis 41:28–32). As a reward, The pharaoh put Joseph in charge of Egypt's grain supply. During the famine, Jacob sent the brothers to Egypt to buy grain (Genesis 42:1–3). When they met with Joseph, they didn't recognize him. In fact, they *bowed down to him*, fulfilling Joseph's prophetic childhood dream! When Joseph finally revealed his identity, his brothers were afraid. But filled with God's love, Joseph forgave them. "You intended to harm me," he said, "but God intended it for good." Joseph understood that God's love can turn even the worst situation into something beautiful and good.

Thank You, God, for Joseph!

? Want to know more? See May 20, "Who Is Joseph (Part 1)" and December 7, "How Can Anything Good Come Out of Pain and Suffering?"

What Are the Twelve Tribes of Israel?

Jacob had 12 sons.
—GENESIS 35:22

Back in Bible days, it was common for men to have more than one wife. Jacob had four wives and was the father of twelve sons! Jacob's sons were Reuben, Simeon, Levi, Judah, Dan, Naphtali, Gad, Asher, Issachar, Zebulun, Joseph, and Benjamin—the ancestors of what became known as the twelve tribes of Israel. There was no tribe named Joseph, but two tribes were named after Joseph's sons, Manasseh and Ephraim. Each tribe had its own land. The tribe of Levi did not stay in one place but served all the tribes as priests.

Like their forefathers, Jacob's sons and grandsons weren't perfect. Throughout their history the twelve tribes struggled with God and with one another. Still, God chose them to be His people.

Eventually the tribes split up into two kingdoms, Judah in the south, and Israel in the north. We know from the Bible that God's Son, Jesus, was a descendant of the tribe of Judah. John the Baptist was from the tribe of Levi. The apostle Paul was from the tribe of Benjamin.

Thank You, God, that even though I am not perfect, You love me and choose me.

? Want to know more? See December 31, "What Does Jesus Mean When He Tells Us to Be Perfect?"

Who Is Moses?

There has never been another prophet like Moses.
The Lord knew Moses face to face.
—DEUTERONOMY 34:10

Moses is the most important prophet and heroic leader of the Jewish people. He is best known for leading the Israelites out of slavery in Egypt and to the Promised Land and for delivering God's Ten Commandments. Moses is so important that he appears in the New Testament, too, when he and the prophet Elijah meet up with God's Son, Jesus, at an event we call the transfiguration (Matthew 17:1–9). Moses was an unlikely and reluctant leader. The Bible says, "Moses was very humble. He was the least proud person on earth" (Numbers 12:3)! When God called him to lead His people, Moses asked Him to send someone else! He was not a skilled speaker, and God eventually gave Moses permission to let his older brother, Aaron, speak for him (Exodus 4:14–16). The important thing about Moses is that he loved and trusted God with all his heart and soul and mind. And God loved him back. Despite his human weaknesses, when Moses was called by God, he obeyed. His faith in God was unshakeable, and God gave him everything he needed to be God's helper.

Thank You, God, that when You call me to be Your helper,
You give me everything I need to get the job done!

? Want to know more? See March 7, "What Is the Transfiguration of Jesus?"

Is It True That Moses Was Adopted?

So the king commanded all his people: "Every time a boy is born to the Hebrews, you must throw him into the Nile River."

—EXODUS 1:22

When Moses was born, the twelve tribes of Israel had become slaves in Egypt. The Egyptian *pharaoh* (*fare*-oh), or king, punished the Israelites by commanding that their male children be drowned in the Nile River!

For three months Moses' mother hid her newborn boy. When she could no longer hide him, she found a sturdy basket and waterproofed it with tar. With a heavy heart, she tucked her son in the basket and sent it floating among the reeds in the Nile. Of all people, guess who found him? The pharaoh's daughter! Upon seeing the sweet baby, she pulled the basket from the river. Best of all, she unknowingly hired Moses' birth mother to nurse and look after the child throughout his early years.

When Moses grew older, he was returned to the pharaoh's daughter, who officially adopted him. She named the boy Moses because she "had pulled him out of the water" (Exodus 2:10). The name *Moses* means "to draw out or deliver."

Moses lived in a palace, but he never forgot who he was and where he came from. He never stopped loving God and His people.

Thank You, God, that You always take care of Your children—including me!

Is It True That God Spoke to Moses in a Burning Bush?

Moses said, "I will go closer to this strange thing. How can
a bush continue burning without burning up?"
—Exodus 3:3

Yes, it is true that God spoke to Moses through a burning bush. When God wants to get our attention, He can do anything! One day Moses witnessed an Egyptian beating a Hebrew slave. Moses, a Hebrew himself, was so angry that he murdered the Egyptian! When the pharaoh found out, he sought to kill Moses. Fearing for his life, Moses fled to a faraway desert (Exodus 2:11–15). Later Moses was tending sheep when noticed a strange sight. A bush was on fire but not burning up. Then, he heard a voice calling him from the flames: "I am the God of your ancestors. I am the God of Abraham, the God of Isaac and the God of Jacob" (Exodus 3:6). God told Moses to lead the Israelites out of slavery in Egypt. "Who should I say sent me?" Moses asked. God replied, "Tell them, 'I AM sent me to you'" (Exodus 3:14). Because Moses loved and trusted God, he obeyed. What happened next is truly amazing. More tomorrow!

Thank You, God, for being the great "I AM"—
our eternal, unchanging Father.

? Want to know more? See May 9, "Why Does God's Name Sometimes Appear as 'LORD' in the Old Testament?" and May 28, "Is It True That Moses Parted the Red Sea?"

MAY 26

What Are the Ten Plagues of Egypt?

This is what the Lord, the God of Israel says: "Let my people go."
—Exodus 5:1

As God commanded, Moses returned to Egypt. There was a new the pharaoh now, and Moses and his brother, Aaron, met with him and asked him to set the Israelite slaves free. But the pharaoh refused. He ordered them to work even harder!

The Egyptians believed in many gods. It was up to Moses to show the reality and power of the Israelites' one true God. *Plague* comes from a Latin word that means "to strike or wound." The ten plagues of Egypt were disasters allowed by God to change the pharaoh's mind. They were (1) the Nile River turned to blood; (2) frogs infested Egypt; (3) gnats swarmed everywhere; (4) flies swarmed everywhere; (5) all the livestock died; (6) everyone suffered sores and boils; (7) a terrible storm destroyed the land; (8) locusts ate their crops; (9) darkness covered the land; and (10) every firstborn son died (Exodus 7:20–12:30). Through all of this, God miraculously protected the Israelites.

Finally, overwhelmed by grief over the death of his firstborn son, the pharaoh agreed to let the Israelites go. At last he was convinced of the reality and power of the Israelites' one true God.

Thank You, God, for never forgetting Your people.

? Want to know more? See May 27, "What Is Passover?"

What Is Passover?

God said, "I will pass over you. . . . You are always to remember this day."
—Exodus 12:13–14

Passover is one of the most important Jewish holidays. It is an eight-day festival that takes place in spring. Passover celebrates how God delivered the Israelites from slavery in Egypt.

Yesterday we learned how God used ten plagues to convince the pharaoh to let His people go. The tenth and worst plague was the death of all firstborns.

God had saved the Israelites from the first nine plagues. But with the tenth plague, God required an act of faith on their part. Through Moses, God commanded each Israelite family to take an *unblemished*, or healthy, male lamb and kill it. The blood of the lamb was to be smeared on the *lintels*, or tops and sides of their doorways, and the lamb was to be roasted and eaten that night.

God warned that, at midnight, death would visit every house. The only protection for the Israelites was the blood of the sacrificed lamb. "The blood will be a sign . . . and when I see the blood, I will pass over you," God said (Exodus 12:13). This is how Passover got its English name. God kept His promise. He always does.

> *Sometimes, God, Your ways are hard for me to understand.*
> *Help me remember that You are both loving and*
> *powerful—and that You always keep Your promises.*

Is It True That Moses Parted the Red Sea?

Then Moses and the Israelites sang this song to the Lord: "I will sing to the Lord. . . . He has thrown the horse and its rider into the sea."

—EXODUS 15:1

Yes, it is true that with God's help, Moses parted the Red Sea. God can do anything!

After the pharaoh let the Israelites go, Moses led them to Egypt's border on the shore of the Red Sea. But the pharaoh changed his mind and ordered his great army to attack the Israelites. Moses and his people were trapped between the advancing soldiers and the Red Sea.

Moses reached out his hand over the sea, and a great wind started blowing back the waters. Dry land appeared in the middle, between two walls of water. The Israelites moved forward, but the Egyptians followed. God slowed the Egyptians by confusing them and causing their chariots to break. As soon as the Israelites had crossed to the other shore, God told Moses to stretch out his hand again and bring the waters back down on the Egyptians. Moses obeyed, and all the soldiers were washed away!

When the Israelites saw this, "they trusted the Lord and his servant Moses" (Exodus 14:31). This was important because the Israelites had a long, hard journey ahead.

Thank You, God, that when You help Your children, nothing is impossible!

What Are the Ten Commandments? (Part 1)

"I am the Lord your God. I brought you out of the land of Egypt where you were slaves."
—Exodus 20:1–2

God chose Moses to be His most important prophet and leader of the Jewish people. Moses loved and obeyed God. For generations, the Israelites had been without a home, held as slaves in Egypt. God chose Moses to lead them out of Egypt to *Canaan*, or "the promised land," which had been promised by God to Abraham's descendants (Genesis 12:7). In 1300 BC, Moses led the Israelites out of slavery in what is called the *exodus*—a word meaning "a mass departure of people." Moses was a good leader, but still the people got into trouble. They needed rules to live by.

God loved His people. He wanted them to enjoy faith-filled, happy, healthy, meaningful lives. He called Moses to the top of Mount Sinai, where He wrote His rules for living on two stone tablets (Deuteronomy 10:1–5). God's rules became known as the Ten Commandments. Even today, the Ten Commandments form the basis for many of our laws and our ideas of right and wrong. They are all based on love—the unchanging love of God for all His children. And that includes *you*!

Thank You, God, for showing us how to live faith-filled, happy lives.

? **Want to know more?** See May 11, "Who Is Abraham, and What Is a Patriarch?"

What Are the Ten Commandments? (Part 2)

"I tell you to obey my commands."
—Exodus 19:5 ERV

God gave Moses and His people the Ten Commandments because He wanted them to enjoy faith-filled, happy, healthy, meaningful lives. They are as important and helpful today as ever.

1) "You must not have any other gods except me"; 2) "You must not worship or serve any idol." An *idol* is any person, place, thing, or idea that's loved more than God; 3) "You must not use the name of the Lord your God thoughtlessly"; 4) "Remember to keep the Sabbath as a holy day." The Sabbath is a day set aside for worship and quiet time with God; 5) "Honor your father and your mother"; 6) "You must not murder anyone"; 7) "You must not be guilty of adultery." *Adultery* means "to be unfaithful to a marriage partner"; 8) "You must not steal"; 9) "You must not tell lies" (Exodus 20:3–16); and 10) "You must not be envious" (Exodus 20:17 TLB). The commandments are based on love and help us know how to love God and others.

Thank You, God, for Your timeless Ten Commandments!

? **Want to know more?** See January 25, "What Are God's Promises for Me When I Am Envious or Jealous?"; October 24, "What Is a Quiet Time?"; and November 12, "Who Is Eric Liddell?"

What Is the Greatest Commandment?

*Hear, O Israel: The LORD our God, the LORD is one. Love the LORD with
all your heart and with all your soul and with all your strength.*
—DEUTERONOMY 6:4–5 NIV

In the New Testament, the Jewish religious leaders asked Jesus,
"Which of the commands is most important?" Jesus replied, "Love
the Lord your God. Love him with all your heart, all your soul, all your
mind, and all your strength" (Mark 12:28–30). The leaders were testing
Jesus. He answered correctly. This famous passage is part of the Shema
prayer, which Jewish children learn from the earliest age. The Hebrew
word *shema* means "Hear, O Israel" (Deuteronomy 6:4–5 NIV). Jesus'
mother, Mary, and her husband, Joseph, would have recited the Shema
with Him twice daily: once in the morning and again as a bedtime
prayer. Mary and Joseph followed the command to teach their children
about God's love and rules for living: "Talk about them when you sit at
home and walk along the road. . . . Write them on your doors and gates"
(Deuteronomy 6:7–9). To this day, faithful Jews attach to their door-
frames a small cylinder-shaped case containing a tiny parchment scroll
with words from Deuteronomy. It's called a *mezuzah* (meh-*zoo*-zah),
which comes from a Hebrew word meaning "doorpost."

Teach me how to love You, God, with all my heart, soul, and strength!

? Want to know more? See May 9, "Why Does God's Name
Sometimes Appear as 'LORD' in the Old Testament?"

JUNE

What Is the Golden Rule?

"Love your neighbor as you love yourself."
—Matthew 22:39

Yesterday we learned how Jesus correctly answered the Jewish religious leaders' question about the greatest commandment. He went on to surprise everyone by adding this brand-new, equally important commandment: "Do to others what you would have them do to you" (Matthew 7:12).

Over the years, this has come to be known as the Golden Rule. Why? Gold is of great value. The Golden Rule is of such great value that Jesus repeats it several times in the Bible (Matthew 7:12; Luke 6:31). When we show God's love to others, we show God that we love Him.

Because we are human, following the Golden Rule is not always easy. What about days when we are down in the dumps? Or days when it's hard to love ourselves, much less others? Not to worry! The Bible promises that God's love has been poured into our hearts through the Holy Spirit (Romans 5:5 NIV). The Bible also promises that we are able to love because God first loved us (1 John 4:19 NIV). When it comes to following the Golden Rule, God has given us all the love we need.

Thank You, God, that because You love me, I am able to love others!

? Want to know more? See January 20, "What Are Some of God's Promises for Me?" and May 31, "What Is the Greatest Commandment?"

What Is Manna from Heaven?

The Israelites called the food manna. It was white like
coriander seed, and it tasted like honey wafers.
—EXODUS 16:31

After they left Egypt, and before reaching the Promised Land of Canaan, Moses and the Israelites spent forty years in the wilderness. Conditions were harsh, and they didn't have enough food.

God loved His children, so He miraculously provided Moses and the Israelites with a mysterious food called manna, which appeared each morning on the ground like a sweet, flaky dew or frost. The word *manna* is Hebrew for "What is it?" which is, of course, the question everyone was asking!

Moses told the Israelites to quickly gather the manna each morning, before it melted in the sun. Each person was allowed a daily amount of one *omer*, or approximately 3.64 liters.

God provided manna for forty years. No one knows for sure what manna was made of, but the Bible says, "It was white like coriander seed, and it tasted like honey wafers." Sounds delicious! Once the Jews reached the Promised Land and began to farm food, the manna stopped appearing (Joshua 5:12).

Manna is a wonderful example of how our loving Father God meets His children's needs.

Thank You, God, for always providing for Your children—including me!

JUNE 3

Is It True That Moses Died Before Entering God's Promised Land?

The LORD said to Moses, "This is the land I promised on oath to Abraham, Isaac, and Jacob when I said, 'I will give it to your descendants.' I have now allowed you to see it with your own eyes, but you will not enter the land."
—DEUTERONOMY 34:4 NLT

Yes, it's true that Moses died before actually crossing over into Canaan, God's Promised Land. God did, however, allow Moses to see Canaan in the distance before he died. How thrilled and moved Moses must have been to see God's promise fulfilled! The Bible describes Canaan as "a good and spacious land . . . flowing with milk and honey" (Exodus 3:8 NIV). *Yum!* Remember, Moses was an ordinary, flawed human being. When God first called him to lead the Israelites, Moses thought God must have chosen the wrong man! Sometimes Moses was stubborn. Sometimes he argued with God and made mistakes. But like his Jewish patriarch ancestors—Abraham, Isaac, and Jacob—he wanted to obey and please God. He never stopped believing in God's promises. He never lost his faith. Moses is an awesome example of how God can take ordinary humans and inspire them to do extraordinary things—and that includes you!

Thank You, God, for Moses!

? Want to know more? See May 23, "Who Is Moses?"

Is There Really a Lost Ark of the Covenant?

"Cover the Ark of the Covenant inside and out with pure gold."
—Exodus 25:11

Yes, there really is a historic lost ark of the covenant! Remember the Ten Commandments? They represented God's *covenant*, or agreement, with Moses and the Israelites. God wrote them for Moses on two stone tablets, and He gave detailed instructions for building an *ark*, or chest, to contain them. We call it the ark of the covenant (Exodus 25:10–22).

The ark was very beautiful and fancy, covered in pure gold. The lid was decorated with two golden *cherubim*, a kind of heavenly creature with wings (Exodus 25:17–22). During the Israelites' forty years in the wilderness, the ark of the covenant was housed in a special *tabernacle*, or tent for worshipping, in the desert. The ark of the covenant contained the holy presence and power of God! The Jewish people carried it everywhere, especially into battles. Eventually it was placed in the first Jewish temple in Jerusalem. After the first temple was destroyed, the ark went missing. Today, the whereabouts of the ark of the covenant is one of history's most fascinating, unsolved mysteries.

Thank You, God, for Your many miracles and mysteries!

? Want to know more? See May 29 and May 30, "What Are the Ten Commandments? (Parts 1 and 2)" and June 6, "What Is the Story of Joshua and the Battle of Jericho?"

Who Is Joshua?

Moses said [to Joshua], "Be strong and brave. Lead these people into the land the Lord promised to give their ancestors. Help the people take it as their own."
—DEUTERONOMY 31:7

Joshua is known as one of the Bible's greatest military leaders and courageous men of faith. He was born a Hebrew slave in Egypt, and he went with Moses on their journey to the Promised Land. During the Israelites' forty years in the wilderness, Joshua was Moses' second-in-command. The Bible says Moses changed Joshua's name from *Hoshea*, which means "salvation," to *Joshua*, which means "God is salvation" (Numbers 13:16). Scholars think Moses did this because of Joshua's extraordinary faith and closeness to God. Before Moses died, God told him to appoint Joshua to lead the Israelites into Canaan, the Promised Land (Numbers 27:18–21).

Entering Canaan would not be easy. There was the Jordan River to cross. There were giant warriors living there in great, fortified cities. Against all the odds, Joshua led the Israelites in many battles against fierce enemies. When God spoke, Joshua listened. It took Joshua seven years of fighting before the Israelites finally controlled Canaan, in fulfillment of God's promise. Tomorrow we will learn about Joshua's most famous, miraculous battle!

Thank You, God, for Joshua!

What Is the Story of Joshua and the Battle of Jericho?

"They will make one long blast on the trumpets. When you hear that sound, have all the people give a loud shout. Then the walls of the city will fall. And the people will go straight into the city."
—JOSHUA 6:5

One of Joshua's most famous battles was against the city of Jericho, which was surrounded by a tall, massive wall made of bricks and stone. God spoke to Joshua and gave him detailed battle plans. Joshua listened and obeyed. But for this battle, God's instructions were *very* strange!

Once a day, for six days, Joshua and the Israelite army marched around Jericho's great wall. Seven priests with rams' horn trumpets marched one time in front of others who were carrying the ark of the covenant.

As God instructed, on the seventh day they marched around the wall seven times. Then they stopped. At Joshua's command, the priests blew their trumpets, the soldiers shouted, and suddenly—just as God promised—the great wall miraculously fell (Joshua 6:1–20)! Against all odds, and in a most memorable way, the Israelite army had won. *Hooray!*

> *Thank You, God, for Your sometimes strange and mysterious ways. With You, nothing is impossible!*

? Want to know more? See June 4, "Is There Really a Lost Ark of the Covenant?"

Who Is Gideon?

The angel of the Lord appeared to Gideon and said,
"The Lord is with you, mighty warrior!"
—JUDGES 6:12

Gideon was a famous warrior, leader, and prophet of the Jewish people. In the years after Joshua's death, God's children forgot about God and His laws. Because of their disobedience, the Israelites faced hard times. When enemies invaded, they cried out for help. Because God still loved his children, He heard their cries and answered. Gideon was an ordinary person, but God saw his potential. God sent an angel to tell Gideon he'd been chosen to lead the Israelites. At first Gideon was not so sure about this. So he asked God to prove Himself by performing miracles! The first miracle took place when God's angel caused fire to shoot out of a rock. Because Gideon's faith was not so strong, he needed more signs. In the most famous story, Gideon told God, "I'm going to lay a piece of wool fleece on the ground. If You really want me to be Your leader, make the wool wet with dew in the morning and the ground dry." God did it! You'd think that would satisfy Gideon. But no! The next night he asked for the opposite—dry fleece, wet ground. Again, God did it. Finally, Gideon stopped asking God for signs and led the Israelites to victory!

Thank You, God, for Gideon!

? Want to know more? See April 13, "Who Is the Holy Spirit?"; May 2, "What Is the Bible?"; and July 11, "What Is a Gideon's Bible?"

Who Is Ruth?

But Ruth said, "Don't ask me to leave you! Don't beg me not to follow you! Every place you go, I will go. Every place you live, I will live. Your people will be my people. Your God will be my God."
—RUTH 1:16

Ruth was from the ancient kingdom of Moab. The name *Ruth* means "friend." As you will see, this name describes Ruth perfectly!

The Moabites did not worship the God of Israel, but Ruth married an Israelite who did. Over time, Ruth came to know and love God. Sadly, Ruth's beloved husband, brother-in-law, *and* father-in-law died. Ruth, her mother-in-law, and her sister-in-law were widows. Back then, widows had very hard lives—especially if they didn't have a family to provide for them.

The three widows were heartbroken. They had to decide what to do to survive. Ruth's sister-in-law decided to stay in Moab, where she had family. But her mother-in-law, Naomi, was moving back to her hometown of Bethlehem. Naomi tried to convince Ruth to stay in Moab, but Ruth could not bear it! She vowed to stay with Naomi always.

Today's verse, Ruth's faithful vow of loyalty and love, is so famous that it's often read aloud at weddings. Ruth went to Bethlehem with Naomi, and God blessed them both in surprising ways. To learn more about this loving friend, you can read Ruth's book in the Old Testament!

Thank You, God, for Ruth!

Who Is the Prophet Samuel?

The Lord called Samuel. Samuel answered, "I am here!"
—1 SAMUEL 3:4

Samuel was one of God's greatest prophets. The name *Samuel* means "God hears." Samuel's birth was God's miraculous answer to the prayers of his mother, Hannah. She sent the boy to live with an old Jewish priest named Eli, who would be Samuel's teacher (1 Samuel 1). With all his heart and mind, Samuel wanted to hear God's voice. Then one night, something amazing happened.

As Samuel was lying down to sleep, suddenly God called Samuel's name. But Samuel thought it was Eli calling! The boy ran to his teacher's bedside and said, "I am here. You called me." But Eli said no, he hadn't. Confused, Samuel went back to bed. Two more times this happened! Finally, Eli realized the Lord was calling the boy. So he said, "If He calls you again, say, 'Speak, Lord. I am your servant, and I am listening'" (1 Samuel 3:2–10).

From then on, Samuel was filled with God's Holy Spirit and spoke freely with God. God told Samuel to *anoint*, or choose for service, the first and second Jewish kings—Saul and David.

Thank You, God, for Samuel!

JUNE 10

Did David Really Kill a Giant with a Slingshot?

The stone hit the Philistine on his forehead and sank
into it. Goliath fell facedown on the ground.
—1 SAMUEL 17:49

Yes, David really did kill a giant with a slingshot! Although David would grow up to be one of Israel's most famous kings, he started out as a humble shepherd boy during the reign of King Saul. For years, King Saul had problems with the neighboring Philistines, people who hated God and loved war. Their scariest soldier was a giant named Goliath who stood more than nine feet tall! He wore bronze armor and carried a big sword. In all of King Saul's army, there was no one brave enough to fight him. Day after day Goliath taunted the Israelite soldiers, insulting and mocking God. This made young David, who loved God with all his heart, furious! Filled with God's Holy Spirit, David chose five smooth stones from a stream, took out his slingshot, and boldly approached the giant. "You come to me using a sword," David said, "But I come to you in the name of the Lord of heaven's armies" (1 Samuel 17:45)! He sent a stone flying, and it hit the giant in the forehead, knocking him out. Then David took the giant's sword and killed him. Everyone was amazed.

Thank You, God, for David!

? Want to know more? See June 13, "What Is the Shepherd's Psalm?" and July 18, "What Are Some of the Bible's Most Amazing Fun Facts? (Part 1)."

169

What Are the Psalms?

I will praise the Lord all my life. I will sing praises to my God as long as I live.
—PSALM 146:2

The psalms are 150 beautiful poems and songs for worship. They were written over many centuries by different authors, including King David, King Solomon, and Moses. The Hebrew name for the book of Psalms was the book of Praises. That's because so many of the psalms are songs of praise to God.

Many psalms were written by King David. God loved David, and King David loved God back. We know from the Bible that David loved to sing and dance. Many of his psalms are joyful. But because David was human, sometimes he made mistakes. Sometimes he was ashamed, brokenhearted, or afraid. So David also wrote psalms to tell God about his feelings.

The word *psalm* comes from the Greek word *psalmos*, which means "to pluck or play the harp." Isn't it easy to imagine beautiful voices singing the psalms? We, like King David, can use psalms to sing to God about everything.

The book of Psalms is easy to find. It's right in the middle of your Bible!

Thank You, God, for Your beautiful psalms!

Why Does the Word *Selah* Appear in the Margins of Psalms?

Praise him with trumpet blasts. Praise him with harps and lyres. Praise him with tambourines and dancing. Praise him with stringed instruments and flutes. Praise him with loud cymbals. Praise him with crashing cymbals. Let everything that breathes praise the Lord.
—PSALM 150:3–6

Many of the psalms were written as songs of praise to God. The word *selah* is a musical sign that might mean "to lift up." It was written in the margins as a direction to the singers to "lift up loud" their voices. It was also a direction to the members of the orchestra to "lift up loud" their instruments. The word *selah* appears more than seventy times in the book of Psalms. It also appears three times in Habakkuk. Musical instruments in the days of the Bible included harps, lyres, lutes, horns, trumpets, cornets, flutes, bagpipes, dulcimers, bells, drums, triangles, castanets, cymbals, timbrels, and tambourines. Imagine the sound!

*Thank You, God, for Your beautiful gift of music.
Show me how to sing Your praises!*

? **Want to know more?** See April 4, "Why Do We Say 'Alleluia!' at Easter?" and September 28, "Why Do We Sing Hymns in Church?"

What Is the Shepherd's Psalm?

"I am the good shepherd. I know my sheep, and my sheep know me. . . . I give my life for the sheep."
—JOHN 10:14–15

The Twenty-third Psalm is the most famous of all the psalms. It is a beautiful song about God, written by King David of Israel. King David loved and trusted God with all his heart, just as a sheep trusts his shepherd. Because David actually worked as a shepherd when he was a boy, he knew what he was talking about. David recognized God's voice in his heart, just as a sheep recognizes his shepherd's voice. He depended on God to provide for his needs, just as a sheep depends on his shepherd to lead him to food, water, and safe shelter.

When you are worried or sad, the Twenty-third Psalm is a very comforting psalm to read. It also helps us understand what Jesus meant when He said, "I am the good shepherd" (John 10:11). It starts like this: "The Lord is my shepherd. I have everything I need. He gives me rest in green pastures. He leads me to calm water. He gives me new strength" (vv. 1–3). Isn't that beautiful?

> *Thank You, God, for being my Good Shepherd!*

? Want to know more? See February 25, "Who Did Jesus Say He Was?"

What Is the Surprise Message Hiding in Psalm 118:8?

It is better to trust the Lord than to trust people.
—Psalm 118:8

Psalm 118:8 is famous for its surprising location in the Bible, and for its special message from our Father God. Consider these fun facts about this truly amazing verse:

The middle chapter of the Bible is Psalm 118.

The shortest chapter of the Bible is Psalm 117.

The longest chapter of the Bible is Psalm 119.

There are 594 chapters before *and* after Psalm 118.

And what's the verse located in the exact center of the Bible? It's Psalm 118:8, which says: "It is better to trust the Lord than to trust people." In other words, in the exact center of the Bible, we discover the heart of our loving Father God! In Psalm 118:8, God tells us to trust and "get centered" on Him. God reassures us that no matter what storms life may bring, we can find refuge in Him. The word *refuge* means "safe shelter." This is very good news!

Thank You, God, for Your Holy Word.

* Psalm 118:8 is located in the center of most, but not all, Bibles. This is because there are different translations of the Bible, and some translations have slightly different chapter, verse, and word counts.

Who Is the Prophet Elijah?

[Elijah] prayed, "Lord, you are the God of Abraham,
Isaac and Israel. I ask you now to prove that you are the
God of Israel. And prove that I am your servant."
—1 KINGS 18:36

Elijah is among the most important of all God's prophets. The name *Elijah* means "my God is the Lord." Like Moses, Elijah was an ordinary, flawed human being who loved God. When Elijah's faith was strong, God used him to do amazing things. When Elijah's faith was weak, he lost confidence and got scared and depressed. Still, he never lost his faith nor stopped listening to God. Elijah's prophecies always came true—the sign of a true prophet. Filled with God's Holy Spirit, he also performed many miracles, including bringing a widow's dead son back to life (1 Kings 17:17–24)! Elijah is also famous for how he did not experience earthly death, but was miraculously swept up to heaven by God in a "whirlwind," riding a "chariot and horses of fire" (2 Kings 2:11)! God promises that one day Elijah will return to earth to announce the coming of the Messiah (Malachi 4:5). Elijah is so important, he appears in the New Testament, too, when he and Moses meet with Jesus in a supernatural event called the transfiguration (Matthew 17:1–3).

> *Thank You, God, for Elijah!*

? Want to know more? See March 7, "What Is the Transfiguration of Jesus?" and April 23, "What Is the Holy Spirit's Gift of Prophecy?"

What Is a Proverb?

These are the wise words of Solomon son of David. . . . They teach wisdom and self-control. They give understanding.
—Proverbs 1:1–2

The book of Proverbs in the Old Testament was written mostly by Israel's good King Solomon, who was known for his great wisdom. Other contributors include a man named Agur, King Lemuel, and *anonymous*, or unnamed, scribes. A proverb is a pithy saying—easy to understand and remember—that offers practical advice for living a good life that pleases God. *Pithy* means "short, forceful, and to the point." The word *proverb* comes from the Latin *proverbium*, which means "to put forth a word." Proverbs are not promises. Rather, they are solid bits of hard-earned wisdom, based on common-sense truths.

To gain important wisdom, all you have to do is open your Bible to the book of Proverbs! Here are few famous ones to get you started:

- "The beginning of wisdom is this: Get wisdom." (Proverbs 4:7 NIV)
- "Trust the Lord with all your heart. Don't depend on your own understanding." (Proverbs 3:5)
- "A gentle answer will calm a person's anger. But an unkind answer will cause more anger." (Proverbs 15:1)
- "A happy heart is like good medicine." (Proverbs 17:22)

Thank You, God, for the wisdom of Your proverbs!

Who Is the Prophet Isaiah?

Then I heard the Lord's voice. He said, "Whom
can I send? Who will go for us?"
So I said, "Here I am. Send me!"
—Isaiah 6:8

Isaiah (I-*zay*-ya) is one of the most famous and important of God's prophets. The name *Isaiah* means "God is salvation." In the New Testament, Isaiah is the most quoted book of the Old Testament, with 419 references! Isaiah served as a prophet for more than fifty years, from 740 to 687 BC. He is famous for his amazingly detailed prophecies about God's promised *Messiah*, or anointed Savior of the world, which were fulfilled in Jesus (Isaiah 7:14). Isaiah's eager, willing, and obedient response to God's call is the inspiration for Christians everywhere. When God called for someone to do His work, Isaiah said, "Here I am. Send me!"

Today God continues to ask His children to be His helpers. When God calls your name, you—like Isaiah—can say, "Here I am! Send me!" Isn't that exciting?

Thank You, God, for Isaiah!

? Want to know more? See June 22, "Does the Old Testament Have Anything to Say About Jesus?"

Who Is the Prophet Jeremiah?

"I know what I have planned for you," says the Lord. "I have good plans for you. I don't plan to hurt you. I plan to give you hope and a good future."
—JEREMIAH 29:11

Jeremiah is a major prophet called by God when he was very young, approximately seventeen years old. The name *Jeremiah* means "God has lifted up." When God called Jeremiah, he said, "I don't know how to speak. I am only a boy." But God said, "Don't say, 'I am only a boy.' . . . Don't be afraid of anyone, because I am with you." True to His word, God stayed with Jeremiah and told him exactly what to say (Jeremiah 1:6–8).

Jeremiah lived during the dark, difficult days leading up to the downfall of Jerusalem. Sadly, the Jewish people didn't want to hear Jeremiah's dire prophecies. In fact, they turned their backs on him! This broke Jeremiah's heart, and he often wept for his fallen nation and people. That's why he's known as "the weeping prophet" (Jeremiah 13:17).

Almost everyone abandoned Jeremiah—with one happy exception: a friend named Baruch, who helped Jeremiah write his book of prophecies, which you can read in your Bible today. How loving God is to provide good friends and helpers in times of need!

Thank You, God, for Jeremiah!

Was Daniel Really Thrown into a Den of Lions?

King Darius gave the order. They brought Daniel
and threw him into the lions' den.
—DANIEL 6:16

Yes, Daniel really was thrown into a den of lions! Daniel was a prophet who loved God. The name *Daniel* means "God is my judge." The Babylonian people conquered the Jews and sent many of them away to the great walled and wicked city, Babylon. The people of Babylon worshipped many false gods. But Daniel stayed close to his one true God in prayer. He was hardworking and honest. The Babylonian King Darius was so impressed he considered giving Daniel the top job in all the land! This made a group of men so jealous that they tricked King Darius into making a law against praying. Anyone who prayed—except to the king—would be thrown into a den of lions!

But Daniel kept on praying. When the jealous men reported this to King Darius, he was heartbroken. He didn't want to punish Daniel. But he had to follow his own law, so he threw Daniel into the lions' den. In his heart, he hoped that Daniel's God would protect him. That night, King Darius didn't sleep a wink. When morning came, he hurried to the den, where Daniel was alive! Daniel told the king how God had sent an angel to shut the mouths of the lions. Then the two men rejoiced and thanked God together (Daniel 6).

Thank You, God, for Daniel!

Did Jonah Really Get Swallowed by a Huge Fish?

The Lord caused a very big fish to swallow Jonah.
—JONAH 1:17

Yes, the prophet Jonah was swallowed by a big marine animal! The Bible's Hebrew word for "huge fish" can also mean "sea monster." Bible scholars believe that Jonah was most likely swallowed by a sperm whale, which scientists today classify as a mammal.

Jonah was a prophet of God who lived in Israel. The name *Jonah* means "dove." God told Jonah go to the evil city of Nineveh and tell the people to stop being so wicked. But Jonah didn't want to. Instead, he hopped on a ship going the opposite direction. Talk about being disobedient! God was *not* pleased. A great storm arose, and Jonah was tossed overboard and swallowed by a huge fish. For three days and nights, Jonah was trapped in the big fish's belly. Still, Jonah never stopped talking to God. He apologized for his disobedience. With that, God commanded the fish to vomit Jonah up onto a beach. *Yuck!*

God gave Jonah got a second chance to preach to the people of Nineveh—and guess what? They changed their ways and followed God!

Thank You, God, for Jonah!

? Want to know more? See December 11, "Can I Believe in Science and Still Believe in God?"

What Does It Mean When God Changes a Person's Name?

"I am changing your name from Abram to Abraham."
—Genesis 17:5

In the Bible, a person's name captures a person's *essence*, or most important quality in God's eyes. So when God changes a person's name, He's giving the person a new name that reflects the person's special purpose. God only did this four times in the Bible:

Abram became Abraham (Genesis 17:5). *Abram* means "exalted father." *Abraham* means "father of many."

Abraham's wife, Sarai, became Sarah (Genesis 17:15). *Sarai* means "quarrelsome." *Sarah* means "princess."

Jacob became Israel (Genesis 32:28). *Jacob* means "one who overthrows." *Israel* means "he struggles with God."

Simon became Peter (Mark 3:16; John 1:42). *Simon* means "he (God) has heard." *Peter* means "stone" or "rock."

In the New Testament, the apostle John suggests that God will give His children new names in heaven (Revelation 2:17)!

> *Thank You, God, for knowing my name.*

? Want to know more? See March 3, "Who Are the Apostles: Simon Peter, Andrew, James, and John?"; May 11, "Who Is Abraham, and What Is a Patriarch?"; May 13, "Who Is Sarah?"; and May 17 and 18, "Who Is Jacob? (Parts 1 and 2)."

Does the Old Testament Have Anything to Say About Jesus?

For to us a child is born, to us a son is given. . . . And he will be called Wonderful Counselor, Mighty God, Everlasting Father, Prince of Peace.
—ISAIAH 9:6 NIV

God gave lots of exciting clues in the Old Testament about His Son, Jesus, coming to earth. These clues are called *prophecies*. God gave these clues because He wanted His children to recognize Jesus when He arrived. God sent Jesus to save His children—and that includes *you!* Finding prophecies about Jesus in the Old Testament is fun. It is like being a detective. Here are some of the Old Testament prophecies about Jesus that are fulfilled in the New Testament:

- Jesus would be born of a virgin. (Isaiah 7:14; fulfilled in Matthew 1:23–25)
- Jesus would be born in Bethlehem. (Micah 5:2; fulfilled in Luke 2:4–7)
- Jesus would heal many. (Isaiah 53:4; fulfilled in Matthew 8:16)
- Jesus is our "good shepherd." (Isaiah 40:11; fulfilled in John 10:11–14)
- Jesus would die with sinners. (Isaiah 53:12; fulfilled in Matthew 27:38)

Thank you, God, for Your prophecies about Jesus in the Old Testament, revealing that Jesus truly is Your beloved Son.

? Want to know more? See January 1, "Who Invented Time?"; April 23, "What Is the Holy Spirit's Gift of Prophecy?"; and June 17, "Who Is the Prophet Isaiah?"

Who Is King Melchizedek?

Melchizedek king of Salem also went to meet
Abram. Melchizedek was a priest for God Most High.
—GENESIS 14:18

King Melchizedek (mel-*ki*-ze-dek) is one of the Bible's most mysterious and fascinating characters. Melchizedek was both a king and a priest. He was the King of Salem, or *Jerusalem*. He was a priest of *El Elyon*, or "God most high." King Melchizedek is first mentioned in the Bible when, out of the blue, he shows up to bestow a blessing on Abram (before God changed his name to Abraham). What makes King Melchizedek so mysterious? Many Bible scholars believe he foreshadows Jesus and His earthly ministry. Some think he may be an actual earthly appearance of Jesus!

In the book of Psalms, King David describes God's promised Messiah as "a priest forever, in the order of Melchizedek" (Psalm 110:4 NIV). The New Testament book of Hebrews says, "Without father or mother, without genealogy, without beginning of days or end of life, resembling the Son of God, he remains a priest forever" (Hebrews 7:3 NIV). Does King Melchizedek foreshadow Jesus? Is it possible that King Melchizedek and Jesus are one and the same? What do you think?

> *Thank You, God, for good King Melchizedek!*
> *Oh, how I love Your mysterious ways!*

? Want to know more? See May 11, "Who Is Abraham, and What Is a Patriarch?"

What Are the Four Gospels?

*Jesus went about all Galilee, teaching in their synagogues, preaching
the gospel of the kingdom, and healing all kinds of sickness.*
—MATTHEW 4:23 NKJV

The word *gospel* means "good news." The first four books of the New
Testament are known as the four Gospels because they tell the good
news about Jesus! The four Gospels are Matthew, Mark, Luke, and John.
They were written by men who actually walked and talked with Jesus, or
knew people who did.

Matthew, Mark, and Luke focus on the life and teachings of Jesus.
Because they share many similar stories, they are called the Synoptic
(sin-*op*-tik) Gospels. The word *synoptic* means they "look alike." The
Gospel of John is written in a very different style and looks back in time
at Matthew, Mark, and Luke, revealing their deep spiritual meaning.

The four Gospels are doors that we open to discover Jesus. This is
because they not only tell us *about* Jesus, but they also invite us to have a
personal encounter *with* Jesus. Because the Bible is God's living Word,
when you read Jesus' words in the Gospels, He can actually speak to you!
Over the next four days, we will learn more about these exciting four
books!

*Thank You, God, for the four Gospels and how
they help me know Your Son, Jesus!*

Who Is the Gospel Writer Matthew?

This is the family history of Jesus Christ. He came from the family of David. David came from the family of Abraham.
—MATTHEW 1:1

Matthew was a tax collector. The name *Matthew* means "gift of God." Because Matthew was a tax collector for the Romans, he was considered a traitor by his fellow Jews and had few friends. When Matthew met Jesus, he stopped being a tax collector. Jesus taught him how to love God and people more than money, and soon Matthew had many friends. Matthew wrote his Gospel around AD 60–70, or approximately thirty years after Jesus' ascension to heaven. Paying special attention to Jesus' teachings and sermons, Matthew wrote for a mostly Jewish audience. He wanted to prove to the Jews that Jesus was the long-awaited Messiah, or God's *anointed* ruler, descended from King David and Abraham. This is why Matthew opens his Gospel with a long, detailed *genealogy*, or family history, of Jesus (Matthew 1:1–17). For us, this long list of names may not be so interesting, but for the Jewish people it was very important. It proved that Jesus was the long-prophesied "Son of David," King of the Jews.

> *Thank You, God, for Matthew's Gospel!*

? Want to know more? See May 11, "Who Is Abraham and What Is a Patriarch?"; and June 22, "Does the Old Testament Have Anything to Say About Jesus?"

Who Is the Gospel Writer Mark?

"The Son of Man came to give his life to save many people."
—MARK 10:45

Mark's full name was John Mark. *John* means "God is gracious," and *Mark* means "war-like." Mark was a teenager when Jesus and His followers met in Mark's mother's house in Jerusalem. Scholars think Mark watched and listened to Jesus as He taught. He may have been present when Jesus died on the cross.

Mark wrote his Gospel around AD 55–65. It is the earliest written and shortest Gospel. It's full of action—Mark uses the word "immediately" at least forty times!

Mark wrote his Gospel for a largely *Gentile*, or non-Jewish, audience. He pointed out that Jesus described Himself as "the Son of Man" (Mark 8:31), who must suffer and die. The disciples didn't understand or like it when Jesus talked about Himself this way. But later they saw that Jesus was fulfilling the Old Testament prophecies about the Messiah dying for our sins (Isaiah 52:13–15; 53). Jesus suffered and gave up His life for us in order that our sins can be forgiven and we can live forever with God in heaven.

> *Thank You, God, for Mark's Gospel!*

? Want to know more? See May 8, "What Is the Difference Between a Jew and a Gentile?" and June 22, "Does the Old Testament Have Anything to Say About Jesus?"

Who Is the Gospel Writer Luke?

I write these things so that you can know that
what you have been taught is true.
—LUKE 1:4

Luke was a Greek-speaking doctor and dear friend of many in the early church. The name *Luke* means "light giving." Luke is the only *Gentile*, or non-Jewish, author of the New Testament. Luke didn't know Jesus personally, but he carefully researched His life by speaking to many people who did. He was an excellent reporter.

Luke wrote his Gospel around AD 60–70. Luke also wrote the book of Acts in the New Testament, which tells the story of the arrival of God's Holy Spirit on earth and the story of the early Christian church. The Gospel of Luke includes many details not found in the other Gospels, paying special attention to Jesus' parables.

The Gospel of Luke includes famous hymns, including the *Song of Mary* (Luke 1:46–55) and the *Gloria in Excelsis* sung by all the angels when Jesus was born. *Gloria in Excelsis* means "Glory to God in the highest!" The angels went on to sing, "And on earth peace, goodwill toward men" (Luke 2:14 NKJV).

Thank You, God, for Luke's Gospel!

? **Want to know more?** See February 11, "What Is the *Song of Mary*?"; July 7, "What Is a Parable?"; and December 18, "What Does *Gloria in Excelsis Deo* Mean?"

Who Is the Gospel Writer John?

Before the world began, there was the Word. The Word was with
God, and the Word was God. He was with God in the beginning.
—JOHN 1:1—2

John was one of Jesus' original twelve apostles. The name *John* means
"God is gracious." Like his older brother, James, John was a fisherman
from the Sea of Galilee. Jesus' affectionate nickname for John and James
was "Sons of Thunder" (Mark 3:17). This is because John and James had
very big voices and bold personalities!

Over time, John became especially close to Jesus. Many scholars
believe that John was Jesus' best friend. John wrote his Gospel around
AD 70—90. He also wrote three letters in the New Testament and the
book of Revelation.

The Gospel of John is different from the other three Gospels. John
looks back in time at Matthew, Mark, and Luke, revealing their deep
spiritual meaning. John does not begin his Gospel with Jesus' birth.
Instead, he goes back to *before* the creation of the world (John 1:1—14)! He
does this to show how God and Jesus have always existed. He also shows
us how God and Jesus relate to one another—and to each one of us—in an
endless, eternal circle of life and love.

Thank You, God, for John's Gospel!

? **Want to know more?** See July 23, "Why Do Some Christians
Carry Signs That Say 'John 3:16' at Sporting Events?"

If the Four Gospels Are All About Jesus, Why Are They Different?

There are many other things that Jesus did. If every one of them were written down, I think the whole world would not be big enough for all the books that would be written.

—JOHN 21:25

Each of the four Gospels tells a slightly different story of Jesus because they come from four different people—Matthew, Mark, Luke, and John.

This makes lots of sense. Imagine that four of your friends wrote a story about you. Parts would be the same. But because each friend knows you differently and you do different things together, parts would be different. All four stories together would give the best, most complete picture of you.

Together, all four Gospels give the best, most complete picture of Jesus. Remember, the Bible is meant to be read and understood in its entirety. The Old Testament looks forward to Jesus' arrival in human history. The New Testament, starting with the Gospels, introduces us to Jesus and explains how and why God sent Him. You could sum up the entire Bible in one simple sentence: *God redeems helpless humanity.* The word *redeem* means "to save."

Thank You, God, for how the four Gospels show us the best picture of Jesus!

Why Are Matthew, Mark, Luke, and John Known As the Four Evangelists?

How beautiful is the person who comes to bring good news.
—ROMANS 10:15

The word *evangelist* (ee-*van*-jel-ist) means "one who brings good news." Matthew, Mark, Luke, and John are known as the four Evangelists because their four Gospels in the New Testament bring the good news of Jesus. Over the years, through Christian art and architecture, believers have given Matthew, Mark, Luke, and John certain symbols that stand for different qualities of Jesus. The next time you're in a church with stained glass windows or visiting an art museum, see if you can spot these ancient symbols of the four Evangelists:

- Matthew's is the winged man, representing Jesus' humanity (Matthew 16:13; 17:9, 22; 20:28).
- Mark's is the winged lion, representing Jesus' kingship (Mark 15:2, 9, 12, 18, 26).
- Luke's is the winged ox, representing Jesus' priesthood (Luke 24:50–52).
- John's is the eagle, representing Jesus' *divine*, or godly, nature (John 20:31).

Thank You, God, for Your faithful evangelists, Matthew, Mark, Luke, and John. Help me be Your faithful evangelist too!

? Want to know more? See June 24, "What Are the Four Gospels?"

JULY

?

What Are the Epistles?

I am Paul, and I end this letter now in my own handwriting.
All my letters have this to show they are from me. . . . May
our Lord Jesus Christ show all of you his grace.
—2 THESSALONIANS 3:17–18

The *epistles* are a collection of letters in the New Testament. The word *epistle* (ee-*pis*-ell) means "to send a message." Another word for epistles is *letters*.

The New Testament letters were written by different men who lived at the same time as Jesus. Some of them actually walked and talked with Jesus! One of the most famous epistle writers was the apostle Paul, about whom we will learn more tomorrow.

The letters were written to teach and encourage early Christians in different communities in the ancient world. Some letters are named after the writer (James; Peter; John; Jude). Others are named after the people the letter was for (Timothy; Titus; Philemon; Hebrews). Still other letters are named after the places the letter was sent (Romans; Corinthians; Galatians; Ephesians; Philippians; Colossians; Thessalonians).

Today the *epistles*, or letters, of the New Testament still teach and encourage Christians around the world—including *you*!

> *Thank You, God, for Your New Testament letter*
> *writers and for their beautiful words.*

Who Is the Apostle Paul?

Saul said, "Who are you, Lord?"
The voice answered, "I am Jesus. I am the One you are trying to hurt."
—ACTS 9:5–6

The apostle Paul's original name was *Saul*, which means "asked or prayed for." Saul was a brilliant, learned Jew who loved God but didn't understand how Jesus could be God's Son. In fact, he hated Christians so much that he persecuted them! The word *persecute* means "to chase in order to hurt someone." When Saul heard about Christians in a town called Damascus, he could hardly wait to hunt them down and throw them in jail! On his way to Damascus, suddenly a bright light from heaven flashed around him. Saul heard a voice say, "Saul, Saul! Why are you doing things against me?" It was Jesus! Saul was so terrified, he fell to the ground. Jesus told Saul to get up and carry on his journey and that He would tell him what to do next (Acts 9:3–6), which He did. Saul was shocked by Jesus' total forgiveness and love for him. His heart was filled with God's Holy Spirit, and his life was totally turned around. He stopped persecuting Christians and shared the good news of Jesus' love with everyone he met. Because he was like a new man, Saul changed his name to the Greek name *Paul*, which means "small or humble." This also helped him more easily share the good news of Jesus with Gentiles, or people who aren't Jewish.

Thank You, God, for Paul!

What Is the Thorn in Paul's Flesh?

In order to keep me from becoming conceited, I was given a thorn in my flesh.
—2 CORINTHIANS 12:7 NIV

Paul was a very smart and gifted man of faith. Still, he was human, and he struggled mightily with something he called "a thorn in [his] flesh." This was a common saying back then. It didn't mean an actual thorn, but a "thorny" or difficult and painful problem (Numbers 33:55).

No one knows for sure what Paul's "thorn in the flesh" was. But we do know it hurt him all the time. It could have been pain in his body, constant temptation, a bad habit, or a troubled relationship. It was so bad he asked God to remove it three times! Paul believed that God didn't put it there, but that God allowed it to remain. Why? Paul believed it was to keep him from being too conceited! To be *conceited* is to think you're better than others. That's *not* loving. The thorn in Paul's flesh kept him humble and compassionate. As God said to him, "My grace is sufficient for you, for my power is made perfect in weakness" (2 Corinthians 12:9 NIV). God can take anything—even suffering—and turn it into something beautiful and good.

> Thank You, God, that when I am weak, You are strong and help me.

? Want to know more? See October 23, "How Is It Possible to Be Weak and Strong at the Same Time?" and December 7, "How Can Anything Good Come Out of Pain and Suffering?"

Was George Washington Truly a Man of Faith?

The Lord is the Spirit. And where the Spirit of the Lord is, there is freedom.
—2 CORINTHIANS 3:17

George Washington, America's Founding Father, was truly a man of faith. George Washington was commander-in-chief of the Continental Army and America's first president. It's a historical fact that George Washington also loved Jesus. Washington wasn't ashamed to write and speak about the truth of the Bible and the life-transforming power of Christian faith.

Here, in his own words, is a prayer from Washington's handwritten prayer journal. The language is old-fashioned, but if you read the words slowly and carefully, you can tell they are from the president's heart: "Increase my faith in the sweet promises of the gospel; give me repentance from dead works; pardon my wanderings, and direct my thoughts unto thyself, the God of my salvation; teach me how to live in thy fear, labor in thy service, and ever to run in the ways of thy commandments."

Today is Independence Day in America. The word *independence* means "freedom." George Washington understood that true freedom is found in knowing and loving God, and seeking His guidance in prayer.

Thank You, God, for George Washington and for the freedom that comes from knowing and loving You!

? Want to know more? See August 31, "What Is a Prayer Journal?"

What's the Difference Between the Dead Sea and the Sea of Galilee?

"If a person believes in me, rivers of living water will flow out from his heart."
—John 7:38

The Dead Sea is mentioned many times in the Bible. Located between modern-day Israel and Jordan, the Dead Sea is actually a large salt lake. At 1,407 feet below sea level, it's the lowest spot on Earth! Hardly anything lives in the Dead Sea because it contains so much salt and other toxic minerals. In fact, its waters are so deadly that birds will not fly over them! In contrast, just eighty miles north is the Sea of Galilee, a large lake that teems with plant and animal life.

Both bodies of water receive water from the River Jordan, so what makes the two so different? The Sea of Galilee thrives because as it receives water from the Jordan River, it also *passes the water on* through outlets. The Dead Sea has no outlets, which causes its water to stay and stagnate, building up life-killing levels of salt and minerals.

Guess what? If we think of the life-giving waters of the Jordan River as God's life-giving love, our hearts are the same way. To live full lives, we need to pass love on, not just receive it. Jesus put it this way: "Freely you have received; freely give" (Matthew 10:8 NIV).

Thank You, God, for the gift of Your life-giving love—and help me pass it on to others!

What Are the Beatitudes and the Sermon on the Mount?

Now when Jesus saw the crowds, he went up on a mountainside and sat down. His disciples came to him, and he began to teach them.
—MATTHEW 5:1–2 NIV

The word *beatitude* **comes from** a Latin word that means "happy." One day after healing many people, Jesus climbed up a steep hill and began to teach. We call this the Sermon on the Mount (Matthew 5:1–2; Luke 6:20–23). Jesus taught about what makes people truly happy.

Over the years, these nine famous teachings became known as the Beatitudes. I have a friend who calls them the "Be Attitudes," because they teach us how God wants us to be! You can find the Beatitudes in your Bible in Matthew 5:1–12. Remember when you read them that the word *blessed* means "happy." Here are the first five to get you started:

"Blessed are the poor in spirit, for theirs is the kingdom of heaven. Blessed are those who mourn, for they will be comforted. Blessed are the meek, for they will inherit the earth. Blessed are those who hunger and thirst for righteousness, for they will be filled. Blessed are the merciful, for they will be shown mercy" (Matthew 5:3–7 NIV). Aren't they beautiful?

Thank You, God, for Your Beatitudes.

What Is a Parable?

*Jesus spoke all these things to the crowd in parables; he did
not say anything to them without using a parable.*
—MATTHEW 13:34 NIV

A *parable* is a simple story that teaches a big idea. The word *parable*
comes from a Latin word that means "comparison." When Jesus walked
and talked on the earth, He shared lots of important truths about God
and His kingdom. Sometimes He did this by telling parables.

Jesus taught an all-new message of God's love; parables were an all-
new way to share it. For example, in the parable of the lost sheep, Jesus
teaches how much God loves His children (Matthew 18:10–14). If one of
His children wanders away like a lost sheep, God will leave the entire
flock and search and search until He finds that child. For the common,
everyday shepherd listening to Jesus, this would be a very impractical
and extravagant thing to do! But that's how God's love is—surprising in
every way. Remember that this parable is about how much God loves
you—His very special child!

> *Thank You, God, for sending Jesus to teach us about Your love,
> and thank You for His surprising and wonderful parables!*

Who Is the Good Samaritan?

He said to Jesus, "And who is my neighbor?"
—LUKE 10:29

The parable of the good Samaritan is one of Jesus' best-known teachings. *Samaritans* were part-Jewish, but the Jews back then didn't accept them. In fact, the Samaritans and Jews hated one another so much that they wouldn't go near or speak to one another (Luke 9:52–53). Jewish religious leaders were shocked when Jesus used a Samaritan to answer the question, "Who is my neighbor?"

In the story, a Jewish man was walking on the road when robbers attacked and beat him up, leaving him badly hurt on the roadside. A Jewish priest walked by and didn't stop to help the man. Another very religious Jew walked by and didn't help either. Finally, a Samaritan stopped and, even though the injured man was Jewish, took pity. He bandaged him up, took him to an inn, and told the innkeeper to look after him—the Samaritan paid for everything. *He* was a good neighbor (Luke 10:25–37).

The parable of the good Samaritan teaches how God wants us to have hearts full of love for everyone. God wants us to welcome and care for strangers. He wants us to show mercy. Your neighbor is everyone you encounter along life's way. Whom will you meet today?

Thank You, God, for the amazing story of the good Samaritan!

What Are Some Famous Sayings from the Bible?

"Arise, shine, for your light has come, and the glory of the LORD rises upon you."
—ISAIAH 60:1 NIV

Did you know there are more sayings in our modern-day language that come from the Bible than from any other book in human history? This is amazing, since the Bible is thousands of years old. But even though times may change, our human hearts do not. We still laugh and cry, struggle and dream, live and die. The good news is that our Father God knows and loves us. He sent His Holy Word, the Bible, to guide us! Here are just a few famous sayings that come from the Bible.

"Rise and shine!" (Isaiah 60:1)

"Can a leopard change his spots?" (Jeremiah 13:23)

"Eat, drink, and be merry!" (Ecclesiastes 8:15)

"Woe is me!" (Isaiah 6:5)

"A drop in the bucket" (Isaiah 40:15)

"A wolf in sheep's clothing" (Matthew 7:15)

"The blind leading the blind" (Matthew 15:14)

"The apple of my eye" (Deuteronomy 32:10)

"A little birdie told me." (Ecclesiastes 10:20)

"Nothing but skin and bones" (Job 19:20)

Thank You, God, for how Your Holy Word, the Bible, lives forever!

Is It True That the Saying "God Helps Those Who Help Themselves" Isn't in the Bible?

Don't add to these commands. And don't leave anything out. But obey the commands of the Lord your God that I give you.
—DEUTERONOMY 4:2

Yes, it is true that the saying "God helps those who helps themselves" is not in the Bible. In fact, our loving Father sent His Son, Jesus, not only to help but to save those who *cannot* help themselves, which includes everyone (Romans 3:23)! Here are a few more popular sayings that you will not find in the Bible:

"Cleanliness is next to godliness."   "This too shall pass."

"Hate the sin, love the sinner."   "Money is the root of all evil."

Some of these may sound like they're from the Bible, and they may even include parts of Scripture. For example, "Money is the root of all evil" is very close to 1 Timothy 6:10: "For the love of money is a root of all kinds of evil" (NIV). Money in itself is neither good nor bad. But to *love* money above all else—or to be *greedy*—can cause all kinds of evil. Now you know!

Thank You, God, for the unchanging truth of the Bible!

? Want to know more? See July 27, "What Is Sin?" and August 2, "What Are the Seven Deadly Sins?"

What Is a Gideon's Bible?

*"We pray that the Lord Jesus Christ himself and
God our Father will comfort you."*
—2 Thessalonians 2:16

Did you ever stay in a hotel and find a Bible in the nightstand? If so, it was likely placed there by a Christian organization called Gideons International, which for more than a hundred years has distributed more than two billion free Bibles and New Testaments, in more than ninety languages around the world.

The Gideons organization was founded by two traveling salesmen. In 1898, John H. Nicholson arrived exhausted at a hotel in Wisconsin. But the hotel was so crowded, he had to share a room with another salesman, Samuel E. Hill. It didn't take long for the two strangers to realize they both loved Jesus! They got down on their knees and prayed together for themselves and for the other traveling salesmen far away from home.

Nicholson and Hill became best of friends. They dreamed of reaching out and comforting lonely travelers with God's Word. So they joined with other Christians to form the Gideons, which they named after the great biblical hero Gideon. Their mission: to put a Bible in every hotel room in America!

*Thank You, God, that wherever I go, the Bible gives
me Your loving words of comfort and hope.*

? Want to know more? See June 7, "Who Is Gideon?"

Why Do Some Bibles Have Red Letters?

When Jesus talked to us on the road, it felt like a fire burning in us. It was exciting when he explained the true meaning of the Scriptures.
—LUKE 24:32

Some Bibles use red letters for Jesus' spoken words. The red letters show the importance of Jesus' words and make them easier to find. Why red? Over time, red became the symbolic color of the Holy Spirit. When the Holy Spirit arrived on earth, the Bible says "something that looked like flames of fire" came to rest above the heads of the apostles (Acts 2:1–4). Red is the color of fire. And Jesus' words are aflame with God's Holy Spirit!

Because red is a symbol of God's Holy Spirit, many churches have red-painted doors. The red doors say, "Holy Spirit, You are welcome here!" Some churches that celebrate Pentecost have a red cloth on the altar and red-colored robes for the minister. I know a pastor who wears red shoes so that wherever his feet take him, he remembers that the Holy Spirit lives in his heart and helps him share the good news of Jesus. He especially loves it when people ask, "Why are you wearing red shoes?"

> *Thank You, God, for Jesus' words! Remind me of Your Holy Spirit when I see the color red.*

? **Want to know more?** See February 5, "Who Is Jesus?" and April 14, "What Is Pentecost?"

Which Bible Is Right for Me?

"It is written in the Scriptures, 'A person does not live only by eating bread. But a person lives by everything the Lord says.'"
—MATTHEW 4:4

Some Bibles have colorful pictures and maps. Others have study guides and notes. Some Bibles use literal translations from the original Hebrew and Greek manuscripts. Others use modern language. Some Bibles are bound in leather and trimmed with gold. Others are paperback. Some Bibles can be read as e-books on your computer or phone!

The best way to discover which Bible is right for you is to visit your church library or local bookstore and look at different Bibles. Hold the Bible in your hands. Open it up. Flip through the pages. Read a few passages. You need a Bible you can understand. God wants you to understand how much He loves you!

If you can't afford to buy a Bible, talk to your pastor, youth minister, or other trusted grown-up who loves Jesus. Tell him or her that you would very much like to have your own Bible. God wants all His children to have a Bible. And that includes *you*!

> *Thank You, God, for the Bible. Lead me to the Bible that's just right for me.*

What Are Some Helpful Hints for Reading My Bible?

We pray that you will also have great wisdom and
understanding in spiritual things.
—COLOSSIANS 1:9

The Bible is not just any book. It's the true, inspired Holy Word of God! Because the Bible is the living Word of God, when you read your Bible, God can actually speak to you. The next time you open your Bible, try these helpful hints.

- Before you start reading, take a moment to pray. Ask God to open your mind to understand His Word and to hear His voice.
- Ask yourself, "What kind of book is this?" Remember, the Bible is actually a library of different kinds of books!
- Read a short section of the Bible carefully. Think deeply about what the words mean.
- Ask yourself, "What is God trying to say to me right now?"
- Decide how you can act on what you've learned. For example, if the Bible passage you read is about showing love to others, ask God if there is someone special He wants you to love with a kind word or action.

> *God, help me hear Your voice when I read my*
> *Bible. I want to get to know You better!*

? Want to know more? See May 2, "What Is the Bible?"

Is It Okay to Write in My Bible?

"I will put my teachings in their minds. And I will write them on their hearts."
—JEREMIAH 31:33

We know from the Bible that God wants you to remember His words (Deuteronomy 11:18). Some people find it helpful to underline or highlight certain verses of the Bible. Others make notes in the margins of their Bibles. When you remember God's words, you can use them in your day-to-day life.

If your mom and dad say it is all right, then, yes, it's okay to write in your Bible. Maybe you're using an e-book or online version of the Bible. That's okay too. But some people prefer a paper version. That's because with a traditional book, you can really see where you are in the Bible. When you go back and forth from the pages of the Old Testament to the New Testament, it's a little like going back and forth in time too! And although you can make notes in some electronic versions, there's still something special about underlining, highlighting, and writing notes with your own hand.

> *Thank You, God, for showing me the best way to understand and remember Your living Holy Word, the Bible.*

? Want to know more? See July 16, "What's the Point of Memorizing Bible Verses?" and July 17, "What Are Some Helpful Hints for Memorizing Bible Verses?"

What's the Point of Memorizing Bible Verses?

Your word is like a lamp for my feet and a light for my way.
—PSALM 119:105

When you memorize a Bible verse, you are carrying the Word of God in your mind and in your heart. This is a very helpful thing. Why? Because if, for example, you're facing a task that seems impossible, you can remember that "all things are possible for him who believes" (Mark 9:23).

Because we're human, life is full of ups and downs. The Bible says that God's Word is like a light that shines in the dark to show you the way (Psalm 119:105). The more you know about God's Word, the easier it is for you to hear His loving voice (Isaiah 30:21).

But what if you're not good at memorizing? Don't worry! Memorizing Bible verses is fun and easy. Everyone learns in different ways. Some of us can look at a short Bible verse and remember it right away. Others have to work a bit harder. With a little practice, I promise you will find the way that works best for you.

> *Thank You, God, for how I can carry Your living Word in my mind and heart wherever I go!*

? Want to know more? See January 20, "What Are Some of God's Promises for Me?"

What Are Some Helpful Hints for Memorizing Bible Verses?

Get wisdom and understanding. Don't forget or ignore my words.
—PROVERBS 4:5

Memorizing Bible verses is easier than you may think. Because everyone learns differently, there are no "right" or "wrong" ways to memorize Bible verses. Here are a few helpful hints!

- *Listen* as someone else reads a Bible verse to you, or record yourself reading the verse and listen to it several times. Keep listening to it until you have the verse memorized.
- *Read* the Bible verse to yourself over and over, out loud or silently, until you can say it out loud by memory.
- *Write* the Bible verse ten times. When you think you have the verse memorized, say it out loud.
- *Sing!* If the verse is short, make up a little tune to go with the words. Sing it over and over, until you remember it.
- *Imagine* a story or pictures in your mind that will help you remember the verse.
- *Memorize with a friend or family member.* Encourage each other as you see which methods work best for each of you.

> *Thank You, God, for how there is no "right" or "wrong" way to memorize Bible verses. I am so eager to remember Your words!*

? Want to know more? See June 16, "What Is a Proverb?"

What Are Some of the Bible's Most Amazing, Fun Facts? (Part 1)

So Methuselah lived a total of 969 years. Then he died.
—GENESIS 5:27

The Bible is filled with amazing, fun facts. You might want to look up some of these facts for yourself. Who knows? You may discover new ones!

The tallest man in the Bible is Goliath, who stood more than nine feet tall (1 Samuel 17:4)! The longest name in the Bible is *Maher-Shalal-Hash-Baz*, which means "Hurry to the spoils!" (Isaiah 8:3). The shortest book in the Old Testament is Obadiah. The shortest book in the New Testament is 3 John, which contains only 294 words in its 14 verses. The longest book in the Old Testament is the book of Psalms, which contains 150 psalms. The longest verse in the Bible is Esther 8:98, which has 90 words! The shortest verse in the Bible is John 11:35: "Jesus wept."

Thank You, God, for the amazing facts found in the Bible!

? **Want to know more?** See June 10, "Did David Really Kill a Giant with a Slingshot?"

What Are Some of the Bible's Most Amazing, Fun Facts? (Part 2)

When Jezebel heard about it, she put on eye makeup,
arranged her hair and looked out of a window.
—2 KINGS 9:30 NIV

Even in the Bible, women wore eye makeup and fussed with their hair! Here are some more amazing, fun facts from the Bible:

In the New Testament, the most quoted Old Testament book is Isaiah, with 419 references. Sheep are the most popular animal in the Bible, mentioned more than 400 times!

Dogs are mentioned 14 times in the Bible, and lions are mentioned 55 times, but cats are not mentioned at all. Also, there is a donkey in the Bible that talks (Numbers 22:28)!

The fruit eaten by Adam and Eve in the Garden of Eden was probably not an apple, but an apricot (Song of Songs 2:3).

The last word in the Bible is *"Amen"* (Revelation 22:21), which means "so be it."

Thank You, God, for Your awesome, fun, fact-filled, living Bible!

? Want to know more? See July 28 and 29, "Who Are Adam and Eve, and How Did Sin Enter the World? (Parts 1 and 2)."

What Is Religion?

*[God] has made everything beautiful in its time. He
has also set eternity in the human heart.*
—Ecclesiastes 3:11 NIV

Religion comes from the desire God has put in every human heart
to get closer to Him. Religion is commonly defined as a "set of beliefs"
about being human.

The word *religion* is rooted in the Latin word *ligare*, which means
"bound together." When you add the letters *re* in front of *ligare*, you get
re-ligare, or religion. So it means "to *re*-bind or *re*-connect together"
something that has come undone. Hiding in this little word is the very
big idea that God wants us to *reconnect* with Him!

The Bible teaches that God created us to be in a loving, personal,
two-way relationship with Him. Because God loves us, He wants us to
know Him and love Him back.

Of all the religions in the world, Christianity is the only one that
offers believers a completely and perfectly restored relationship with
God, through faith in His Son, Jesus (John 3:16). Tomorrow we will learn
more about what makes Christianity so special and true.

Thank You, God, for sending Your Son, Jesus, to reconnect us with You.

JULY 21

What Is Christianity?

In Antioch the followers were called Christians for the first time.
—ACTS 11:26

Christianity is a religion based on the life and teachings of Jesus Christ. Christianity began with a few disciples more than two thousand years ago. People who believe in and follow Jesus Christ are called Christians. The early believers were originally called followers of "the Way," because they followed the way of Jesus (Acts 9:2 NIV). They were first called "Christians" in Antioch, which is located in modern-day Turkey (Acts 11:26).

The Bible records that the early Christians "devoted themselves to the apostles' teaching and . . . to prayer. . . . And the Lord added to their number daily those who were being saved" (Acts 2:42, 47 NIV). From Jerusalem, Christianity quickly spread to other places.

Today Christians live in every nation of the world. More than two billion people, or approximately one-third of the people on Earth, call themselves Christians. It's estimated that more than 700 million Christians are 15 years old or younger. That's a lot of Christian kids!

Tomorrow we will discover what makes Christianity different from all other religions.

> *Thank You, God, for Christianity! Please watch over all of Jesus' followers, especially the kids!*

? Want to know more? See February 9, "Is 'Christ' Jesus' Last Name?"

What's the Difference Between Christianity and Other Religions?

"I am in my Father. You will know that you are in me and I am in you."
—John 14:20

Christianity is not just another religion that teaches *about* God. It's about having a *personal relationship with* God through faith in His Son, Jesus. God is alive and has a special plan for each person. Christians do not worship teachings and rules, but a living, loving God! Christianity is different because the Bible says that God knows and loves His children even before they are born (Psalm 139:13–16)! God's deepest desire is for His children to know and love Him too (1 John 3:1). Christianity is also different from many other religions because Christians believe our human bodies are very important. The Bible teaches that all of God's creation, including our bodies, is beautiful and good, and God uses our bodies to accomplish His will on earth (1 Corinthians 6:19-20). Christianity is not just a set of "pie in the sky" beliefs. It's a practical faith, rooted in love, that God uses to offer hope in a broken world.

Thank You, God, for living in my heart!

? **Want to know more?** See January 17, "Does God Care What My Body Looks Like?" and October 20, "What Does the Bible Mean When It Says My Body Is the 'Temple of God'?"

Why Do Some Christians Carry Signs That Say "John 3:16" at Sporting Events?

*"For God so loved the world that he gave his one and only Son, that
whoever believes in him shall not perish but have eternal life."*
—JOHN 3:16 NIV

John 3:16, which appears in the Gospel of John, is one of the most famous verses in the Bible.

It is famous because in just a few words, Jesus sums up the good news of Christianity. Because it is so short, it is a good Bible verse to put on a banner or sign. When you see someone holding up a banner or sign that says "John 3:16" at a sporting event, he is sharing the message of God's love for all to see!

Because John 3:16 is so short, it is also a good Bible verse to memorize!

Thank You, God, for Jesus' words in John 3:16 in the Bible.
How beautifully and perfectly they sum up Your great love
for the world and all Your children—including me!

? Want to know more? See July 17, "What Are Some Helpful Hints for Memorizing Bible Verses?"

What Is the Apostles' Creed?

*Believe in the Lord Jesus and you will be saved—
you and all the people in your house.*
—ACTS 16:31

The word *creed* **means** "a statement of belief." The Apostles' Creed helps Christians around the world remember what they know and believe about God, Jesus, and the Holy Spirit. It goes like this:

I believe in God, the Father Almighty, creator of heaven and earth. I believe in Jesus Christ, his only Son, our Lord. He was conceived by the power of the Holy Spirit and born of the Virgin Mary. He suffered under Pontius Pilate, was crucified, died, and was buried. He descended to the dead.* On the third day he rose again. He ascended into heaven, and is seated at the right hand of the Father. He will come again to judge the living and the dead. I believe in the Holy Spirit, the holy catholic** church, the communion of saints, the forgiveness of sins, the resurrection of the body, and the life everlasting. Amen.

*Some churches do not include this line. **See definition on July 25.

Thank You, God, for the Apostles' Creed!

What Does the Word *Catholic* Mean in the Apostles' Creed?

*As the Scripture says: "Their message went out through
all the world. It goes everywhere on earth."*
—ROMANS 10:18

The word *catholic* means "universal." As is appears in the Apostles' Creed, the "holy catholic church" refers to the universal or worldwide Christian church. The holy catholic church includes all the believers in Jesus who have ever lived!

When the word *Catholic* is capitalized, it refers to the Roman Catholic Church, which makes up part of the worldwide Christian church and has its headquarters in Vatican City, near Rome, Italy.

Since its beginning more than two thousand years ago, the Christian church around the world continues to thrive and grow. Every day, in towns and cities far and wide, more than two billion people who know and love Jesus are busy helping God's kingdom grow with loving prayers and acts of kindness.

Thank You, God, for Your worldwide Christian church and for the billions of believers busy at work, spreading the good news of Jesus!

? Want to know more? See July 24, "What Is the Apostles' Creed?" and October 12–15, "How Did the Christian Church Grow Over the Ages? (Parts 1–4)."

What Is Faith?

*"Truly I tell you, if you have faith as small as a mustard
seed…nothing will be impossible for you."*
—MATTHEW 17:20 NIV

The Bible teaches, "Faith means being sure of the things we hope
for. And faith means knowing that something is real even if we do not
see it" (Hebrews 11:1). The word *faith* means "to trust and believe with
confidence."

Faith is a gift from God, your Creator and heavenly Father. When
you are born as God's child, you come hard-wired with faith. Faith is
not something that you have to scrunch up your eyes and nose and try
to muster up. It's as natural as breathing. It is already planted in your
heart. In today's verse, Jesus says that all it takes is faith no bigger than
a teeny-tiny mustard seed to do great and beautiful things for God!

Would you like your faith in God to grow? Then here's good news:
All you have to do is ask God to grow your faith, and He promises that
He will! Why does God want to help your faith grow? Because God loves
you (1 John 3:1).

> *Thank You, God, for growing my faith, which
> You have planted as a gift in my heart.*

? **Want to know more?** See January 29, "What Are God's Promises
for Me When I Need More Faith?" and December 27, "What Is
the Difference Between an Atheist and an Agnostic?"

What Is Sin?

All people have sinned and are not good enough for God's glory.
—Romans 3:23

God is perfect. Human beings are not.

Sin is the imperfect condition of the human body, mind, and soul. The word *sin* comes from an Old English word that means "guilty." Sin is part of our human nature. It's the way we are born. Human beings make mistakes. We forget how to love. Sometimes we're selfish or unkind. Sometimes we do bad things on purpose. Sin is what separates us from God. It's why we need Jesus to be our Savior.

Sins are unloving thoughts, words, and behaviors. When a person thinks, *Oh, she is so stupid,* or *He's such a jerk,* those are sinful thoughts. When a person cheats on a test, or gossips about a friend, or tells a lie, or steals a candy bar, those are sinful behaviors.

Everyone is born with a sinful human nature (Romans 3:23). It's all part of being human. There was only one person ever born without a sinful nature. That person is Jesus (Hebrews 4:15).

Thank You, God, for sending Your Son, Jesus, to save me from my sins!

? **Want to know more?** See February 13, "Did Jesus Ever Do Anything Wrong?" and February 15, "What Is the Temptation of Christ?"

Who Are Adam and Eve, and How Did Sin Enter the World? (Part 1)

Sin came into the world because of what one man [Adam] did.
—ROMANS 5:12

The Bible says God created the first man, Adam, from the earth. But God recognized that Adam was lonely, so He created the first woman, Eve (Genesis 2:18; 3:20). They lived happily in a beautiful garden called Eden. God loved them dearly, and they loved and trusted God. God gave Adam and Eve everything they needed for a healthy, happy life. He had only one rule: don't go near the tree of the "knowledge of good and evil" (Genesis 2:17), because if they ate its fruit, they would die! For a while, Adam and Eve obeyed. But one day Eve came across a tricky serpent, or snake. "Why do you listen to God?" the serpent hissed. "He doesn't really care about you. Eat the fruit and you'll be fine," he lied. At that moment, Eve forgot all about loving and trusting God. She believed the serpent and ate the fruit. Then she shared it with Adam. At once, just as God had warned, sin and death entered God's beautiful world. Thankfully, this is not the end of the story.

> *God, when I am tempted, help me remember everything
> I know about You that is good and true.*

? Want to know more? See January 30, "What Are God's Promises for Me When I Am Tempted?"

219

Who Are Adam and Eve, and How Did Sin Enter the World? (Part 2)

The man and his wife hid from the Lord God among the trees in the garden.
But the Lord God called to the man. The Lord said, "Where are you?"
—GENESIS 3:8–9

Adam and Eve made a big mistake when they ate the forbidden fruit! Knowing they had disobeyed, God came looking for His children in the cool breeze of the early evening. "Where are you?" He called. But Adam and Eve were nowhere to be found. They were hiding. For the first time, they felt the sickening pain of shame. Guilt. Anger. Betrayal. Hopelessness. Fear. For the first time, they felt the pain of separation from each other and—worst of all—from their beloved Father. Oh, what a dark day for the world! Over the years, people have called the story of how sin came into the world "the Fall of Man" or "the fall." But here is good news: Even though Adam and Eve sinned, God never stopped loving them. Likewise, even when we sin, God never stops loving us. He loves us so much that He sent His only Son, Jesus, to overcome sin and death!

Thank You, God, for saving me from sin and death through Jesus!

? Want to know more? See January 31, "What Are God's Promises for Me When I Feel Guilty?"; February 5, "Who Is Jesus?"; and February 18, "Why Did Jesus Come to Earth?"

Does God Stop Loving Me When I Sin?

Christ died for us while we were still sinners. In this way God shows his great love for us.
—ROMANS 5:8

The Bible teaches that sin is what breaks our relationship with God. This is because God is holy. The word *holy* means "set apart by God," who is perfect.

Human beings are not holy. But because God created and loves us, He made a way for our sins to be forgiven. The word *forgive* means "to excuse or pardon." And when God forgives our sins, He also forgets them (Jeremiah 31:34)!

God loves us so much He sent Jesus to die for our sins (Romans 5:8). Because our sins are forgiven when we believe in Jesus, we can be friends with God. When you sin, you make God very sad—but God never stops loving you. His love for you is bigger than any sin. There is nothing you can think or say or do that will make God love you any more or any less! But when we do sin, God wants us to talk to Him about it. He wants us to admit what we did wrong, say we're sorry, and ask for His forgiveness.

Thank You, God, for Your unconditional love!

? **Want to know more?** See November 9 and 10, "Who Is Fred Rogers? (Parts 1 and 2)."

Why Do I Still Sin, Even When I Don't Want To?

*I do not understand the things I do. I do not do the good things
I want to do. And I do the bad things I hate to do.*
—ROMANS 7:15

Everyone makes mistakes. It is part of being human. Even the apostle
Paul struggled with sin! He was human, just like you and me. And when
Paul sinned, he absolutely hated it!

When you give in to sin, you feel guilty. The word *guilty* means to
feel responsible (and probably a little ashamed) for having thought,
said, or done something you know is wrong. Guilt is a very unpleasant
and painful feeling. But that's okay. Sometimes painful feelings are
God's way of protecting you! Like physical pain warns you of danger to
your body, emotional pain warns you of danger to your soul.

So when you sin and feel a pang of guilt, what can you do? Talk to
God. *Confess*, or admit, your sin. Tell God you are truly sorry and you
want to do better. Ask God to help you. Because Jesus died for your sins,
God promises that He will forgive you. No matter what.

> *Thank You, God, that Your love for me is bigger than any sin.*

? Want to know more? See January 30, "What Are God's Promises
for Me When I Am Tempted?"; January 31, "What Are God's
Promises for Me When I Feel Guilty?"; and February 13, "Did
Jesus Ever Do Anything Wrong?"

AUGUST

Are There Special Words I Need to Say When I Confess My Sins to God?

If we confess our sins, he will forgive our sins. We can trust God.
—1 John 1:9

There are no special words that you need to say when you confess your sins to God. That's because *confessing*, or admitting, to God that you are sorry for having sinned has more to do with what's inside your heart than with your words.

When we confess our sins, the Bible says that God wants us to come to Him with "a humble and contrite heart" (Isaiah 66:2 NLT). A *humble* heart is a heart that is not proud or puffed up. A *contrite* heart is a heart that is truly sorry.

Still, many beautiful prayers have been written by Christians with humble and contrite hearts. Here is one of my favorites, adapted from *The Book of Common Prayer*:

"Dear God, I confess that I have sinned against You in thought, word, and deed; by things I have done, and by things I have left undone. I have not loved you with my whole heart, and I have not loved my neighbors as myself. I am truly sorry and I humbly repent. For the sake of Your Son, Jesus, have mercy on me and forgive me, that I may delight in Your will and walk in Your ways, to the glory of Your Name. Amen."

Thank You, God, for forgiving me when I confess my sins.

What Are the Seven Deadly Sins?

Happy are they whose sins are forgiven, whose wrongs are pardoned.
—ROMANS 4:7–8

The "seven deadly sins" don't appear as an actual list in the Bible, but they agree with biblical teachings. Despite being called "deadly," they are no more dangerous than any other sins. In fact, they are common! Everyone sins (Romans 3:23). The good news is God forgives us. The seven deadly sins are:

> *Pride*, which means to have such a high opinion of yourself that you think you don't need God (Proverbs 16:18); *Wrath*, which means out-of-control, destructive anger (Proverbs 15:1); *Envy*, which means desire for something that belongs to someone else (1 Peter 2:1); *Greed*, which means an extreme love of money and a desire for more things (Luke 12:15); *Laziness*, which means an extreme unwillingness to work (Proverbs 10:4); *Lust*, which means out-of-control desire (1 John 2:16); *Gluttony*, which means out-of-control eating and drinking (Proverbs 23:21).

Thank You, God, for forgiving my sins.

? Want to know more? See July 27, "What Is Sin?"; July 30, "Does God Stop Loving Me When I Sin?"; and January 25, "What Are God's Promises for Me When I Am Envious or Jealous?"

What Is Christian Hope?

*This hope will never disappoint us, because God
has poured out his love to fill our hearts.*
—Romans 5:5

Christian hope, like faith, is a gift from God. The word *hope* comes from
an old Dutch word, *hopen*, which means "to anticipate or expect." *Hope* is
a word that can be used in a lot of ways. You can hope it doesn't rain. You
can hope you get a good grade on a test. You can hope your team wins.

But Christian hope is something different—and much more powerful. The apostle Peter describes Christian hope this way: God "gave
us a *living hope* because Jesus Christ rose from death. Now we hope for
the blessings God has for his children" (1 Peter 1:3–4).

Christian hope is *alive*. Christian hope has a name: *Jesus*. This is
why Christian hope "will never disappoint us"!

Would you like to grow the hope of Jesus living in your heart? All you
need to do is ask God, who promises that He will do it (1 Thessalonians
5:24).

Why does God want to grow your hope? Because God loves you!

> *Thank You, God, that the hope of Jesus does not disappoint.*

? **Want to know more?** See January 14, "What Is the Kingdom of
God?" and February 2, "What Are God's Promises for Me When
I Need Hope?"

Why Did Christians Invent Orphanages and Hospitals?

*Religion that God the Father accepts is this: caring
for orphans or widows who need help.*

—JAMES 1:27

Jesus came to show us what God is like. Jesus taught that God loves *everyone*. He put His love into action. When Jesus saw hungry people, He fed them. He healed sick people, and He encouraged people who were lonely. He welcomed people who had no friends. To explain why people should help one another, Jesus said, "I tell you the truth. Anything you did for any of my people here, you also did for me" (Matthew 25:40). In other words, through Jesus, we are all connected. Christians in the early church took Jesus' teachings to heart. They made a special effort to take care of orphans, widows, and older people. They visited people in prison. Over time, Christians developed hospitals to take care of sick people and orphanages to take care of children without parents. Christians also developed many organizations to help hungry, struggling, and hurting people around the world. When we help other people, we are actually helping Jesus!

*Thank You, God, for sending Jesus to teach
us how to love and help others.*

? Want to know more? See November 4, "Who Is Mother Teresa of Calcutta?"

AUGUST 5

What Can I Do to Help People in Need?

She welcomes the poor. She helps the needy.
—Proverbs 31:20

Our life on earth is a gift from God. God wants us to care about people in need. Jesus said, "Everyone who has been given much will be responsible for much. Much more will be expected from the one who has been given more" (Luke 12:48). Once we care about others, God asks us to do something more. He asks us to use our lives to reach out and help. This is called putting our Christian faith into action. Here are a few ideas for how you can help people in need:

- You can pray for someone.
- You can visit an older person who is lonely.
- You can listen to your friend who is in trouble or sad.
- You can write an encouraging letter to a soldier far away from home.

Talk to your mom and dad, or your pastor or youth minister at church. They will have lots of good ideas too!

> *Open and grow room in my heart, God, for truly caring more about others.*

? Want to know more? See January 12, "How Can I Share God's Love?"; August 11, "What Is Prayer?"; and September 2, "What Is Intercessory Prayer?"

What Is the "I Give You My Hands" Prayer?

Again Jesus put his hands on the man's eyes. Then the man opened his eyes wide. His eyes were healed, and he was able to see everything clearly.
—MARK 8:25

Yesterday we talked about putting our Christian faith into action. When we do that, Jesus works through us! We help God's kingdom grow when we share the good news of His love for all His children. Here is a great prayer about putting our Christian faith into action:

I Give You My Hands

Lord Jesus, I give You my hands to do Your work. I give You my feet to go Your way. I give You my eyes to see as You do. I give You my tongue to speak Your words. I give You my mind that You may think in me. Above all, I give You my heart that You may love, in me, Your Father and all humankind. I give You my whole self that You may grow in me, so that it is You, Lord Jesus, who lives and works and prays in me.
—LANCELOT ANDREWES, BISHOP OF WINCHESTER, ENGLAND, 1555–1626

> *Lord Jesus, I give You my hands to do Your will.*

Why Is Taking Care of Our Planet Important to Christians?

The Lord God put the man in the garden of Eden to care for it and work it.
—GENESIS 2:15

God created our planet Earth and everything in it. God loves the world (John 3:16). God loves His children (1 John 3:1). God made everything in the world for His children. He gives us water to drink. He gives us delicious fruits and vegetables, chicken and fish, and other foods to eat. He gives us trees and stone to build houses. He gives us coal, oil, gas, water, sunshine, and wind for power. What a generous Father God we have! God instructed humans to take care of His creation (Genesis 1:26; 2:15). Taking care of the Earth is called *stewardship*, which means "to care for another's property."

Our beautiful planet doesn't belong to us. We didn't make it. It belongs to God. Our job is to take good care of it. Christians believe it's important to keep our air and water clean and be careful with our natural resources such as trees and oil. It's important not to litter. Why take good care of our planet? It's one way of saying "Thank You!" to God.

> *Teach me, God, to be a good steward of our planet Earth.*

? **Want to know more?** See December 30, "Is It Really Possible for Mountains and Trees to Sing?"

Why Do Some Christians Put Fish-Shaped Symbols on Their Cars?

Jesus said to them, "Come and follow me. I will make you fishermen for men."
—MARK 1:17

In the early days of the church, Christians were persecuted by the government. They had to meet in secret. Because of the danger they faced, the early Christians developed secret signs to identify one another. One secret sign was the fish. One Christian would draw a simple curve-shaped line of half a fish on the wall or in the dirt. Most people passing by wouldn't notice. But another Christian knew what to do and completed the sign by drawing the other half of the fish! The sign helped Christians feel not so alone and reminded them of what they believed. Why a fish? Jesus' first disciples, Peter and his brother Andrew, were fishermen. When Jesus saw them casting their nets, He called out, "Come and follow me. I will make you fishermen for men" (Luke 5:10). Two thousand years later, the symbol of the fish is still being used by Christians around the world.

Thank You, God, for the Christian symbol of the fish. Make me a fisher of people too!

? Want to know more? See March 3, "Who Are the Apostles: Simon Peter, Andrew, James, and John?" and August 9, "What Is the Secret Message Hiding in the Greek Word for Fish?"

231

What Is the Secret Message Hiding in the Greek Word for Fish?

Grace and peace to you from God the Father and Christ Jesus our Savior.
—TITUS 1:4

Here is the best part about the Christian symbol of the fish. In the days of the early Christians, many people wrote and spoke Greek. In fact, all the books of the New Testament were first written in Greek. The Greek word for "fish" is *ichthus*. The letters of the word *ichthus* contained a secret, encouraging message for the early Christians. Here's the secret message:

- Iesous is Greek for *Jesus*
- CHristos is Greek for *Christ*
- Theous is Greek for *God's*
- HUios is Greek for *Son*
- Soter is Greek for *Savior*

So, the letters of *ichthus*, the Greek word for fish, stand for "Jesus Christ, God's Son, Savior." For early Christians, *ichthus* offered a clever way to remember what they believed about Jesus.

> *Thank You, God, for how I can discover You in the most surprising ways!*

Is There a Way to Tell Christians Apart from Other People?

"People will know that you are my followers if you love each other."
—John 13:35

Loving other people is not always easy. Jesus said, "I give you a new command: Love each other. You must love each other as I have loved you" (John 13:34). Because we are human, sometimes it can seem impossible to love others or even love ourselves! But Jesus would not ask us to do something impossible. When you're having a hard time loving others (or yourself!), remember:

- We are able to love because God first loved us. (1 John 4:19)
- God loves His children (and that includes you!) so much that He sent His Son, Jesus, so we can live with Him in heaven. (John 3:16)
- God has poured His love into our hearts with His Holy Spirit. (Romans 5:5)
- The Bible says that nothing can separate us from God's love. (Romans 8:38–39)
- With God, *all things* are possible! (Matthew 19:26)

Thank You, God, for helping me love myself and others.

? Want to know more? See January 12, "How Can I Share God's Love?"

AUGUST 11

What Is Prayer?

I call to you, God, and you answer me. Listen to me now. Hear what I say.
—PSALM 17:6

Prayer is a conversation with God. One part of a conversation is talking. The other part is listening. God created you to enjoy a personal relationship with Him. The more time you spend with God, the better you get to know Him and the more you grow to love Him.

God wants to listen to you (Psalm 34:15). God is interested in all your thoughts and feelings. He's interested in all your friendships, hopes, and dreams. He's interested in everything about you (Psalm 139:1).

God wants to talk to you (Isaiah 30:21). God wants to comfort you when you are feeling sad, lonely, worried, or afraid. He wants to laugh with you when you are happy. He wants to help you when you have a difficult decision to make.

Why is God so interested in listening and talking to you? Because He loves you (1 John 3:1).

> *How wonderful, God, that You want to listen and talk to me, because I want to listen and talk to You too!*

? Want to know more? See January 20, "What Are Some of God's Promises for Me?" and October 24, "What Is a Quiet Time?"

Do I Need to Use Special Words When I Pray?

[Jesus] prayed, "Abba, Father! You can do all things."
—MARK 14:36

You don't need to use special words when you pray. You don't need to use fancy language. You don't need to memorize prayers. You don't need to recite prayers written by other people. You don't need to write down your thoughts before you pray. You don't even need to speak out loud. It's perfectly fine to have a conversation with God silently. This is because God hears your thoughts (Matthew 6:8).

When you pray, just be yourself. Talk to God as if He is your best friend in the whole world. It is all right to cry when you pray. It is all right to laugh too.

Jesus was so close to God that when He prayed, He called God *"Abba,"* which in his native Aramaic language means "Daddy" or "Papa."

What should you pray about? Everything!

Dearest "Abba," Daddy, please bring me closer to You through prayer.

? **Want to know more?** See February 17, "What Makes Jesus So Important?"

Do I Have to Kneel When I Pray?

*Pray about everything. Tell God what you need,
and thank him for all he has done.*
—PHILIPPIANS 4:6 NLT

You don't have to kneel when you pray. You don't have to close your eyes. You don't have to bow your head. You can pray standing, walking, sitting, or riding the bus to school. You can pray while you are walking the dog. You can pray while you are lying in your bed at night. If you like, you can pray while you are standing on your head!

Many Christians pray standing up, with their hands held apart, palms open and facing up toward God. Open palms can mean being open to hearing God's voice. Other Christians kneel when they pray. Kneeling can symbolize that you are approaching God with a humble heart. The word *humble* means "not proud" and comes from a Latin word that literally means "lowly or close to the ground."

Bowing your head and closing your eyes can help you concentrate, but God doesn't care what position you are in when you pray. God just cares that you pray (Romans 12:12).

> *Thank You, God, that I can pray to You about
> anything, anywhere, in any way I want!*

Why Do We Say "Amen" at the End of Prayers?

Praise the Lord, the God of Israel, forever and forever. All the people said, "Amen" and "Praise the Lord."
—1 CHRONICLES 16:36

The word *amen* comes from the Hebrew language and means "Yes, it is certain" or "So be it."

We say amen at the end of a prayer to show that what we have said to God is true. We say it to show that we believe that God has heard our prayer. We say it to show that we believe God will answer our prayer. He is real and loves us, and He always hears us when we pray.

> God, with each passing day, help my love for You to grow. So be it. Amen!

? Want to know more? See August 24, "Can I Know for Sure That God Hears My Prayers?" and August 25, "Can I Know for Sure That God Will Answer My Prayers?"

What Is the Lord's Prayer? (Part 1)

One time Jesus was praying in a place. When he finished, one of his followers said to him, . . . "Lord, please teach us how to pray, too."
—LUKE 11:1

When Jesus walked and talked, the disciples noticed He had a different way of praying. Jesus didn't use fancy language or call attention to Himself when He talked to God. When Jesus prayed, it was like He was talking to His best friend. Jesus' disciples wanted to pray like He did. So they asked Him to teach them how. Jesus' answer became known as the Lord's Prayer. It's the most famous prayer in the world:

Our Father who art in heaven, hallowed be thy name. Thy kingdom come. Thy will be done, on earth, as it is in heaven. Give us this day our daily bread; and forgive us our debts, as we also have forgiven our debtors. And lead us not into temptation, but deliver us from evil. *For thine is the kingdom, and the power, and the glory, for ever and ever.** Amen. (Matthew 6:9–13 KJV)

*This last line appears in the King James Version of the Bible (Matthew 6:13 KJV). Because it does not appear in all translations, some Christian churches don't include it.

Thank You, God, for sending Jesus to teach me how to pray!

What Is the Lord's Prayer? (Part 2)

"Our Father who art in heaven . . ."
—MATTHEW 6:9 RSV

The Lord's Prayer opens with: "Our Father who art in heaven." This line might be so familiar that we don't think much about it. But there is a lot hidden in these six carefully chosen words. (In case you are wondering, *art* is simply an old-fashioned word for *is*.)

First, notice that Jesus didn't say "My Father." Jesus used the word *our* to remind us that we belong to the larger, worldwide family of God, which includes all Christians everywhere! Did you ever want to be part of a great, big, loving, caring family? Now, thanks to Jesus, you are! The word *our* also reminds us that we are not alone. It reminds us of how God wants us to pray with and help one another through loving acts of kindness. Worshipping and working together is a wonderful way for Christians to be God's helpers on earth.

Finally, "Our Father" reminds us of the awesome fact that we *share the same Father* in heaven as Jesus! Who knew there was so much waiting to be discovered in the first line of the Lord's Prayer? Tomorrow we'll learn more!

Thank You, God, for being our heavenly Father!

? Want to know more? See September 17, "What Is the Church?" and September 20, "Why Does God Want Me to Be Involved in a Church?"

What Is the Lord's Prayer? (Part 3)

"Hallowed be thy name. Thy kingdom come. Thy will be done, on earth as it is in heaven. Give us this day our daily bread."

—MATTHEW 6:9–11 RSV

In the Lord's Prayer, Jesus described our Father God's name as "hallowed." The word *hallow* means "holy or set apart." Because God is holy, the Bible says that we are to honor, respect, and be in total awe of Him. Our holy God loves His earthly children perfectly (1 John 3:1). This is very good news! Jesus went on: "Thy kingdom come. Thy will be done, on earth as it is in heaven." (In case you are wondering, *thy* is simply an old-fashioned word for *your*.) Jesus was talking about the kingdom of God, or heaven. Each time we share God's love with others, we help His kingdom "come," or break through on earth! Then Jesus said: "Give us this day our daily bread." God loves us and wants us to be well-nourished in our bodies! We also need to feed our spirits. We can do this by praying, reading the Bible, and learning about God. In fact, you're feeding your spirit right now! *Yum!*

> *Thank You, holy God, for Your kingdom and for nourishing my spirit!*

? Want to know more? See January 4, "If God Is My Creator, How Is He Different from My Parents?"; January 14, "What Is the Kingdom of God?"; and September 25 and 26, "What Is Communion? (Parts 1 and 2)."

What Is the Lord's Prayer? (Part 4)

"Forgive us our debts, as we also have forgiven our debtors."
—MATTHEW 6:12 RSV

In the Lord's Prayer, Jesus said, "Forgive us our debts, as we also have forgiven our debtors." The word *debt* means "something owed." A *debtor* is a person who owes a debt. A debt can be money, but it can also be something else, such as a favor returned. Some Christian churches use the words, "Forgive us our *trespasses* as we forgive those who *trespass* against us." Here, the word *trespass* means sin. Jesus said, "If you forgive men their trespasses, your heavenly Father also will forgive you" (Matthew 6:14 RSV).

The key word here is *forgive*, which means "to excuse or pardon." Jesus reminds us not only to ask for forgiveness but to forgive others too. This is because refusing to forgive causes deep anger, sadness, and spiritual sickness. There is an old saying that "Being unforgiving is like drinking poison and expecting the other person to die." *Yikes!*

It is not always easy to forgive. But if we ask God to give us forgiving hearts, He will. Because God forgives us, we are able to forgive others.

> *Thank You, God, for forgiving my sins and teaching me to forgive others.*

What Is the Lord's Prayer? (Part 5)

"And lead us not into temptation, but deliver us from evil."
—MATTHEW 6:13 KJV

At the end of the Lord's Prayer, Jesus prayed, "And lead us not into temptation." This is another way of saying, "God, lead me *away* from temptation!" We're all tempted to do things we shouldn't, but the good news is that God is always by our side, ready to grab our hand and pull us away from danger. Finally, He prayed, "Deliver us from evil." Evil, sin, and death entered the world when Adam and Eve gave in to temptation and disobeyed God. Now the world and all human beings are fallen and broken. This is not what God intended! The word *deliver* here means "to save or rescue." God loves us so much, He sent Jesus to rescue us from sin and death, so we can live forever with God and Jesus in heaven (John 3:16). But for now, we live in a world where evil, sin, and death still exist. This is why it's not easy being human! Our heavenly Father understands how filled with danger life can be. Because He loves us, He wants to protect us and keep us safe.

> *Thank You, God, for leading me away from temptation and rescuing me from sin and evil.*

? **Want to know more?** See January 30, "What Are God's Promises for Me When I Am Tempted?" and July 28 and 29, "Who Are Adam and Eve, and How Did Sin Enter the World? (Parts 1 and 2)."

What Is the Lord's Prayer? (Part 6)

"For thine is the kingdom, and the power, and the glory, for ever. Amen."
—MATTHEW 6:13 KJV

Today's verse is the traditional ending to the Lord's Prayer! This ending comes from the King James Version of the Bible, which was published in 1611. (The word *thine* is simply an old-fashioned way of saying *yours*.)

This beautiful conclusion to the world's most famous prayer is a way of saying, "Everything belongs to You, our Creator and Father God! Your heavenly kingdom, and our planet Earth, the sun and the moon and the stars . . . everything! How awesome You are! You alone are worthy of our praise and love. To You alone belong all the power and glory in heaven and on earth, forever and ever!" (Psalm 148, paraphrased; 1 Peter 4:11).

The final one-word line of the Lord's Prayer, *Amen*, means "yes, it is certain" or "so be it."

How loving Jesus was to teach this beautiful and powerful prayer to His disciples and all believers—including *you*!

> *The kingdom, and power, and glory are Yours, dear Father—now and forever! Amen!*

What's the Difference Between "Saying Grace" and "Saying a Blessing" Before Meals?

Jesus took the five loaves of bread and two fish. He looked up to heaven and thanked God for the food.
—LUKE 9:16

Grace is a beautiful word. It is used in many ways and comes from a Latin word that means "thankful or pleasing." In the Bible, *grace* describes unearned, unconditional love, freely given by God to His children. To "say grace" is to offer a prayer of thanksgiving before a meal. Some Christians describe the mealtime prayer as "saying a blessing." This means asking God to bless the food we're about to eat. The word *bless* comes from an old English word that means "to consecrate, or set apart as holy." In today's verse, Jesus took time to pray over bread before giving it to the disciples to serve more than five thousand hungry people.

Some Christians make up a new prayer each time they eat. Others say a short memorized prayer. Sometimes we are so hungry, it is easy to forget to thank God for our food. But even if you're in a hurry, saying grace doesn't have to take a long time. You can just say, "Thank You, Father, for this food! Amen."

Even when I'm in a hurry, help me remember to thank You, God, for my food—and for Your unconditional love!

Is It Okay to Say Grace in a Restaurant?

"When you come before God, don't turn that into a theatrical production either. All these people making a regular show out of their prayers, hoping for stardom! Do you think God sits in a box seat?"
—MATTHEW 6:5 MSG

Yes, it is okay to say grace in a restaurant. God is happy to hear from you anytime, anywhere!

At the same time, when you say grace in a restaurant, remember to be considerate of other people dining around you. The purpose of saying grace is not to draw attention to yourself. The purpose is simply to thank God.

Here are three short blessings many Christians say before eating:

- God is great. God is good. Let us thank Him for our food. Amen.
- Thank You for the world so sweet. Thank You for the food we eat. Thank You for the birds that sing. Thank You, God, for everything! Amen.
- Bless us, O Lord, and these Your gifts, which we are about to receive from Your bounty. Through Christ our Lord, amen.

*Fill my heart to overflowing with thankfulness, God—
not only at mealtimes, but all day long!*

What Is a Good Bedtime Prayer?

He has put his angels in charge of you. They will
watch over you wherever you go.
—PSALM 91:11

Bedtime is a great time to talk to God. You can thank Him for the day you just had. You can talk to Him about tomorrow. You can even ask God to send His angels to watch over you while you sleep (Psalm 91:11). You can use the quiet moments before you fall asleep as a time to listen for God's still, small voice.

Here's a popular bedtime prayer for children. The word *Thee* is an old-fashioned way of saying *You*. The word *Thy* is an old-fashioned way of saying *Your*.

Nighty-night, and sweet dreams!

Now I lay me down to sleep. I pray Thee, Lord, my soul to keep. Let Thy love guide me through the night. And wake me with Thy morning light. God bless . . . (Here you can have fun listing everyone in the whole world you love and care about!) I pray all these things in Jesus' name. Amen.

Thank You, God, for being with me when I
am awake and when I am sleeping.

Can I Know for Sure That God Hears My Prayers?

The Lord sees the good people. He listens to their prayers.
—PSALM 34:15

Yes, you can know for sure that God hears you when you pray. You can also know that God sees you when you pray. How can you know this for sure? Because this is what today's Bible verse promises!

God's Word also promises "how gracious [God] will be when you cry for help! As soon as he hears he will answer you" (Isaiah 30:19 NIV). In the book of Psalms, King David wrote, "The Lord has heard my cry for help. The Lord will answer my prayer" (Psalm 6:9). And Jesus' closest friend, the apostle John, wrote, "We can come to God with no doubts. This means that when we ask God for things (and those things agree with what God wants for us), then God cares about what we say" (1 John 5:14).

God promises that He hears and sees you when you pray. You can trust God about this because He always keeps His promises (Deuteronomy 7:9).

> *Thank You, God, for hearing and seeing me when I pray!*

? Want to know more? See January 20, "What Are Some of God's Promises for Me?"

Can I Know for Sure That God Will Answer My Prayers?

God listens to us every time we ask him. So we know that
he gives us the things that we ask from him.
—1 JOHN 5:15

Yes, you can know for sure that God will answer your prayers.

Jesus promised, "I tell you to ask for things in prayer. And if you believe that you have received those things, then they will be yours" (Mark 11:24). Jesus also promised, "Continue to ask, and God will give to you. Continue to search, and you will find. Continue to knock, and the door will open for you" (Matthew 7:7).

God promises that He will answer your prayers. Sometimes God's answers are not what we want to hear. Sometimes His answer is, "No." Sometimes His answer is, "Wait." God may not always give you want you want. But you can trust that God will always give you what you need. That's because God loves you and knows what is best for you.

You can trust that God always gives you the perfect answer to your prayer.

Thank You, God, for Your perfect love and for how You know what is best for me. Help me be patient and trusting as I wait for Your answer.

Can God Actually Talk to Me?

If you go the wrong way—to the right or to the left—you will hear a voice behind you. It will say, "This is the right way. You should go this way."
—ISAIAH 30:21

Yes, God can actually talk to you! The secret is to learn how to hear His voice. Sometimes that means taking time to be quiet and listen. This is not always easy to do. It is easy to be distracted by the TV. Or the sound of cars going by. Or the smell of chocolate chip cookies. Sometimes it is easy to be distracted by the noise of your own thoughts!

God's voice is different from our thoughts. God often says things you might never think of yourself. Sometimes God speaks to you through a Bible verse or the words in a book or sermon. Many times God speaks through people we love.

Sometimes God speaks a tender word of comfort or a stern word of wisdom. He could give you a new spiritual idea or instruction. God always knows exactly what you need to hear (Isaiah 30:21). It's good to take time to listen to God.

Teach me, God, to hear and recognize Your voice.

? Want to know more? See October 24, "What Is a Quiet Time?" and October 25, "How Can I Make the Most of My Quiet Times with God?"

Is It Okay to Pray for Help on a Test?

Give your worries to the Lord. He will take care of
you. He will never let good people down.
—Psalm 55:22

Yes, it is okay to pray for help on a test. But prayer is not an excuse for not being prepared! Prayer is not a magic wand. God expects you to do your homework and study for tests. That's your responsibility.

On the day of the test, you might pray, "God, You know how hard I've studied for this test. Please help me not to be nervous. Help me remember everything I can and do my best. Thank You for caring so much. I love You! In Jesus' name I pray. Amen."

If you have not done your homework or studied as you should, ask God to forgive you and help you be better prepared next time! If you are really struggling with your schoolwork, be sure to tell your mom and dad and teacher. They will want to work with you to help you do better.

God wants to help you do well in school too because He wants the best for you in all things (Jeremiah 29:11)!

Thank You, God, that I can talk to You about
everything, including school!

What Does It Mean to Pray "In Jesus' Name"?

*"You have never asked for anything in my name. Ask and
you will receive. And your joy will be the fullest joy."*
—JOHN 16:24

Many Christians close their prayers with the words, "in Jesus' name, amen." That's because Jesus said to the disciples, "If you ask for anything in my name, I will do it for you" (John 14:13). Saying the words "in Jesus' name" at the end of a prayer is not a magic formula. It doesn't guarantee that God will answer your prayer exactly the way you want. But it is a way of saying you know and love Jesus. You're saying, "Whatever You think is best for me, God."

You don't have to end every prayer with the words, "in Jesus' name." This is because God doesn't care about the exact words you use when you pray. God does care that you mean what you say. When you pray, God wants you to speak to Him sincerely, from the bottom of your heart. Why is this? Because God loves you (1 John 3:1)!

> *God, when I talk to You, help me speak from the
> bottom of my heart. In Jesus' name I pray. Amen!*

? Want to know more? See August 26, "Can God Actually Talk to Me?"

Is It Okay to Pray Out Loud with Another Person?

"If two or three people come together in my name, I am there with them."
—MATTHEW 18:20

Yes, it is okay to pray out loud with another person. In fact, you can pray with as many people as you like! This is because there is special power when you pray with other people.

Jesus said to the disciples, "If two or three people come together in my name, I am there with them." Isn't that amazing? When two or three—or more—gather to pray in Jesus' name, it's a regular prayer party!

In case you are wondering, it's also okay to pray with a friend over the phone or on your computer. God hears your prayers, no matter where you say them. God hears your unspoken prayers too. He is such a good listener that He knows what you need even before you ask Him (Matthew 6:8)!

The next time you are talking to a friend in person, or over the phone or computer, you might want to try praying together. Tomorrow we will consider some helpful tips on how to pray out loud with others!

> *Thank You, God, for Your powerful gift of Jesus'*
> *presence when I pray with others!*

What Are Some Tips for Praying with Others?

"I tell you that if two of you on earth agree about something, then you can pray for it. And the thing you ask for will be done for you by my Father in heaven."
—MATTHEW 18:19

Yesterday we learned how God gives us the special gift of Jesus' presence when we pray with others. Here are some tips:

- You might sit or stand in a circle—whatever is comfortable.
- You might hold hands and close your eyes.
- Invite God's Holy Spirit to be with you to help guide and inspire your thoughts and prayers.
- Expect times of silence. Use the silence to listen for God's Holy Spirit, who might give you surprising ideas about what to pray!
- When you feel that everyone has had his or her turn speaking, listen to the silence one last time.
- You might close by saying the Lord's Prayer together.

Thank You, God, for Your amazing promise that when we pray out loud with others, Jesus is with us in an extra-special way!

? Want to know more? See September 5, "Is It True That God's Holy Spirit Can Help Me When I Pray?"; August 15, "What Is the Lord's Prayer?"; and September 1, "What Should I Do When I Can't Think of What to Pray?"

What Is a Prayer Journal?

Remember the wonderful things he has done.
Remember his miracles and his decisions.
—PSALM 105:5

A prayer journal is like a diary between you and God. It's a written record of your prayers.

If you decide to keep a prayer journal, it doesn't need to be fancy. It can be as simple as a spiral notebook. Some people write in a prayer journal every day. Others write in it once or twice a week. Whatever works for you is fine. God is always happy to hear from you!

When you write in your prayer journal, put the date at the top of the page. That way, as days and weeks go by, you can go back and see how God has worked in your life. When you're feeling low, reading through your prayer journal can help you remember how God has helped you in the past. That can be an excellent spirit-lifter!

Should you choose to keep a prayer journal, you will be amazed to see how God answers your prayers.

Thank You, God, for how You are always happy to hear from me! Help me look back and remember all the times You have worked in my life.

? **Want to know more?** See July 4, "Was George Washington Truly a Man of Faith?"

SEPTEMBER

What Should I Do When I Can't Think of What to Pray?

They all joined together constantly in prayer.
—ACTS 1:14 NIV

In the Bible, the book of Acts tells the story of the early church. Like Christians today, the first Christians prayed a lot! There is no certain way you *have* to pray, but when you need some guidance, think of the letters in the word *ACTS*.

A: *Adoration*, which means "to deeply love." Begin your prayer time by praising God. Tell God how wonderful He is, how much you love Him, and how much you appreciate His love too!

C: *Confession*, which means "to admit or acknowledge." Confess all the ways you've stumbled. Tell God you're sorry. Ask for His forgiveness.

T: *Thanksgiving*, which means "to thank" God for all the good things in your life. No matter what, there's always much to be thankful for.

S: *Supplication* is a big word that means "to humbly, earnestly ask." Tell God what's going on in your life. Share your prayer requests. Don't hold back. No request is too small or too big for God.

> *Thank You, God, that I can always tell You about everything.*

? Want to know more? See August 1, "Are There Special Words I Need to Say When I Confess My Sins to God?"

What Is Intercessory Prayer?

Confess your sins to each other and pray for each other. Do this so that God can heal you. When a good man prays, great things happen.
—JAMES 5:16

Intercessory **is a big word** that means "asking on another's behalf." Intercessory prayer is praying for another person.

You might have a friend who is very sick—so sick that he can't pray for himself. When you pray for that friend, you're asking God for healing on his behalf. Or you might have a friend whose grandmother has died and she is very sad. When you pray for that friend, you are asking God for comfort on her behalf. To pray for another person is a very loving thing to do. It is also good for you.

The apostle Paul wrote: "Do not worry about anything. But pray and ask God for everything you need" (Philippians 4:6).

When someone you love is in trouble, God doesn't want you to worry. God wants you to pray (1 Peter 5:7)!

Thank You, God, for the power of intercessory prayer. If there's anyone You want me to pray for today, speak to my heart and let me know!

? Want to know more? See September 4, "Is It True That Jesus Is Praying for Me Now in Heaven?"

Is It True That When Jesus Was on Earth, He Prayed for Me?

"Holy Father, keep them safe . . . by the power of your name (the name you gave me), so that they will be one, the same as you and I are one."

—JOHN 17:11

Yes, it's true that when Jesus was on Earth, He prayed for you.

Before Jesus died, He had a big conversation with His Father God. First, He prayed for Himself. Then, He prayed for His disciples. Then, He prayed for all the believers in the world—including believers who hadn't been born yet! He prayed for *you*. Isn't that amazing?

After Jesus prayed for His disciples, He said, "I am also praying for all people who will believe in me because of the teaching of these men. . . . I will be in them and you will be in me. So they will be completely one. Then the world will know that you sent me" (John 17:20, 23).

Jesus prayed that you will know and love God. Jesus also prayed that others will love and believe in Him because of you. Jesus prayed that you will love and enjoy being with other Christians. Why? Because He loves you (John 15:9, 13).

Thank You, God, that Jesus actually prayed for me!

Is It True That Jesus Is Praying for Me Now in Heaven?

Christ Jesus died, but that is not all. He was also raised from death.
And now he is on God's right side and is begging God for us.
—ROMANS 8:34

Yes, it's true that Jesus is praying for you—right this very moment—in heaven!

After Jesus' resurrection, He ascended into heaven, where He is "at the right hand" of His Father (Romans 8:34 NIV), or at His right side. To be at God's right side means to be God's closest aide and helper.

One of the most important, loving things Jesus does as God's right-hand helper is *intercede*, or beg, for all God's children in prayer. To *intercede* means "to earnestly ask on another's behalf." Because Jesus loves you, He's constantly speaking up for you. He's constantly reminding God of your choice to believe in Him, and in God too. Right now, even as you read these words, Jesus is singing your praises to God our Father. In fact, all of heaven is rejoicing that you believe in Jesus (Luke 15:10).

How loving Jesus is to intercede for all God's children—and that includes *you!*

> *Thank You, God, for Your Son, Jesus, who right now is praying for me in heaven.*

? **Want to know more?** See September 2, "What Is Intercessory Prayer?"

SEPTEMBER 5

Is It True That God's Holy Spirit Can Help Me When I Pray?

[God] knows what is in the mind of the Spirit, because the Spirit speaks to God for his people in the way that God wants.
—ROMANS 8:27

Yes, it's true that God's Holy Spirit can help you when you pray.

Because we are human, we sometimes don't know what or how to pray. Maybe our problem is too complicated, or we don't really know all the facts. When this happens, we can trust God's Holy Spirit to do the praying! God's Holy Spirit is alive in our hearts, eager to help us. When you feel confused about praying, start by inviting the Holy Spirit to help you. The apostle Paul put it this way: "The Spirit helps us in our weakness. We do not know what we ought to pray for, but the Spirit himself intercedes for us through wordless groans" (Romans 8:26 NIV). *Intercede* means "to earnestly ask on someone else's behalf." How wonderful that when we don't know what to pray, God's Holy Spirit powerfully intercedes for us, with words we could never think of ourselves. God thinks of everything!

Thank You, God, for how Your Holy Spirit helps me when I pray.

? Want to know more? See April 13, "Who Is the Holy Spirit?";
September 2, "What Is Intercessory Prayer?"; and September
4, "Is It True That Jesus Is Praying for Me Now in Heaven?"

260

Do Miraculous Answers to Prayer Still Happen Today?

"The Father will give you anything you ask for in my name."
—John 15:16

Yes, miracles still happen today, including miraculous answers to prayers!

Miracles are God's way of showing us how much He loves us. Sometimes miracles can help people believe in God. They can also help increase a believer's faith. The word *miracle* comes from the Latin word *miraculum*, which means "object of wonder" or "wonderful." Miracles are not magic tricks. They are things God does that are not bound by the laws of nature. Miracles are very real. The same power God gave to Jesus to help and heal people is available to Christians today. Jesus was very clear about this when He said, "He who believes in me will do the same things that I do. He will do even greater things than these" (John 14:12).

Sometimes, when a prayer is answered with a miracle, it's easy to say, "Oh, that was just a coincidence" or "I was just lucky." But with God, there is no such thing as luck. And as a friend of mine likes to say, "With God there are no coincidences; there are only *God*-incidences!"

Thank You, God, for Your miraculous answers to prayer!

? Want to know more? See February 26, "Why Did Jesus Do Miracles?" and April 22, "What Is the Holy Spirit's Gift of Miraculous Powers?"

Is It Okay to Pray for My Pet?

God made the wild animals, the tame animals and all the small crawling animals to produce more of their own kind. God saw that this was good.
—GENESIS 1:25

Yes, it is okay to pray for your pet! It is okay to pray for all of God's amazing animals.

Our pets are very special creatures. Our pets don't really belong to us; they are given to us on loan from God to love and care for. Loving and taking good care of our pets can help us understand how deeply God loves and wants to care for us.

Let me tell you about our little pug, Max. When we first got Max, he was just ten weeks old, a brand-new, fluffy, snuggly puppy. One day I was taking him for a walk when I bumped into my friend Gail, who was a pastor at our church. "*Oooh!*" she exclaimed. "What a cute little puppy!" She scooped up Max and held him close to her cheek—a warm, wriggly ball of snuffly pug kisses.

"Would it be all right if I prayed for him?" she asked.

"Okay," I agreed, although I had never heard of praying for a dog, or any kind of animal. But my friend's prayer changed our life with Max forever. More about that tomorrow!

Thank You, God, for pets, and for all Your amazing animals!

? **Want to know more?** See August 29, "Is It Okay to Pray Out Loud with Another Person?"

What Is a Good Prayer for My New Pet?

I led them with cords of human kindness, with ties of love. I lifted the yoke from their neck. I bent down and fed them.
—HOSEA 11:4

If you're the owner of a new pet, congratulations! What a very happy event! Yesterday I told you about our little pug, Max, and how my friend Gail offered to pray for him. Here's what happened next:

Gail scooped up Max into her arms and prayed, "Thank You, God, for bringing this precious, little puppy into my friend Kitty's life. Help her provide Max with a safe, happy home. May he be a dog that only knows human kindness. In Jesus' name I pray. Amen."

May he only know human kindness, I thought. *What a beautiful prayer!* You can pray it, too, for your pet—or for any of God's amazing animals!

As years passed, I often remembered Gail's words—especially during challenges that came later in Max's life. Human beings and animals are connected in a deep way, because we share the same Creator God. Pets especially trust and depend on their humans to care for them. Taking care of our pets is not always easy or convenient. It is a big responsibility! Even so, God trusts us to love and care for them.

Thank You, God, that I can offer human kindness to all Your amazing animals.

What Is a Good Prayer for When My Pet Is Sick?

"I have heard your prayer. And I have seen your tears."
—2 KINGS 20:5

I am so sorry if your pet is sick. When our little pug, Max, got sick, it was a very hard time for our whole family. Max's hind legs stopped working because of a nerve problem that would only get worse. Max was still a happy dog, but we were very sad and worried.

A pastor invited Max and me to her church for a "Blessing of the Animals." There the pastor shared the story of Saint Francis, a Christian who lived in thirteenth-century Assisi, Italy. Saint Francis loved Jesus, and he loved all God's creatures. He wrote a prayer for sick animals that we prayed for Max. You can pray it for any sick or injured animal. It is helpful to remember how much God loves all His creatures!

Heavenly Father, you created all things for Your glory and made us stewards of this creature. If it is Your will, restore [Name of Pet] to health and strength. Blessed are You, Lord God, and holy is Your name for ever and ever. Amen.

> *Thank You, God, for Your great love for me, and for all Your animals—including my pet.*

? Want to know more? See December 17, "What Is a Christmas Crèche?"

What Is a Good Prayer for When My Pet Is Close to Death?

Even if I walk through a very dark valley, I will
not be afraid because you are with me.
—Psalm 23:4

There's nothing sadder than losing someone we love—including a pet. Our pets are gifts from God, on loan to us to love—but only for a season. When our vet told us that Max's time had come to die, we cried and cried. Below is the prayer we said aloud to God as our beloved Max peacefully passed away in our arms. I hope it comforts you too:

"Dearest, loving Creator and Father God, our beloved pet and companion [Name of Pet] is on [his/her] final journey. We love [Name] so much and will miss [him/her] dearly! Thank You, God, for the joy and affection that [Name] has given us over the years. Thank You for the honor it has been to be [his/her] people, and for trying to show [Name] human kindness. Thank You for the incredible gift and blessing that [Name] has been to us and to our family. Now, please bless [Name] and grant [him/her] peace. May Your love for [Name] never die. In Jesus' name we pray, amen."

Thank You, God, for the true gift it is to love and care for any of Your precious creatures.

? Want to know more? See December 12, "Will I See My Pet in Heaven?"

What Is the Jesus Prayer?

"The tax collector stood at a distance. . . . He was so sad.
He said, 'God, have mercy on me. I am a sinner!'"
—LUKE 18:13

The Jesus Prayer goes like this: "Lord Jesus Christ, Son of God, have mercy on me, a sinner."

This simple prayer comes from Jesus' parable of the Pharisee and the tax collector. As the story goes, two Jewish men went to the temple to pray. The Pharisee was a Jewish religious leader and very proud of his rule-following. He thought he was far above the Jewish tax collector, whom everyone hated for working for the Roman government.

The tax collector knew he was a sinner. He was so humble, and all he could do was lower his head and pray, "God have mercy on me, a sinner" (Luke 18:13). Because his prayer was so heartfelt, honest, and true, Jesus said, "I tell you, when this man went home, he was right with God," but the Pharisee wasn't (Luke 18:14).

The Jesus Prayer is simple and easy to remember. You can say it aloud or silently, or when you don't know what or how to pray.

> *Lord Jesus Christ, Son of God, have mercy on me, a sinner.*

? Want to know more? See March 11, "What Is the Difference Between the Pharisees and the Sadducees?" and July 7, "What Is a Parable?"

What Is the Serenity Prayer?

"I leave you peace. My peace I give you."
—JOHN 14:27

In 1934, the Christian theologian Reinhold Niebuhr (1892–1971) wrote a prayer for one of his sermons. A *theologian* is a person who studies the nature of God. It went: "O God and heavenly Father, grant to us the serenity of mind to accept that which cannot be changed; courage to change that which can be changed, and wisdom to know the one from the other, through Jesus Christ our Lord, Amen."

Over the years, these powerful words became known as the "Serenity Prayer." The word *serenity* means "the state of feeling calm, peaceful, and untroubled." The prayer quickly appeared in many newspapers, magazines, and books and was widely quoted on the radio. In the early 1950s it became the prayer used by participants in Alcoholics Anonymous, an organization that helps people struggling with addiction to alcohol. To this day it is also used by many other recovery groups and people everywhere.

Several versions of the Serenity Prayer exist. If you like, try reading the prayer again, slowly and thoughtfully. See if you feel a little bit more calm, peaceful, and untroubled.

Thank You, God, for the supernatural gift of Your serenity.

? Want to know more? See January 23, "What Are God's Promises for Me When I Am Worried?"

What Is the Prayer of Saint Francis?

The Lord said . . . "This man is my chosen instrument to proclaim my name."
—ACTS 9:15 NIV

The Prayer of Saint Francis is one of Christianity's most beautiful and beloved prayers. The funny thing is, no one knows for sure that Saint Francis wrote it! We do know that in 1920 a French Franciscan priest printed the words on the back of a picture of the peace-loving Saint Francis, and the title stuck. Here's how it goes:

> Lord, make me an instrument of thy peace. Where there is hatred, let me sow love; Where there is injury, pardon; Where there is doubt, faith; Where there is despair, hope; Where there is darkness, light; Where there is sadness, joy. O divine Master, grant that I may not so much seek to be consoled as to console,
>
> To be understood as to understand, to be loved as to love; For it is in giving that we receive; It is in pardoning that we are pardoned; And it is in dying that we are born to eternal life. Amen.

God, please make me an instrument of Your peace!

What Is Saint Patrick's Breastplate Prayer?

Lord . . . You are all around me—in front and in back.
—PSALM 139:1, 5

In the fifth century, Saint Patrick became famous for converting the people of Ireland to Christianity. He wrote a prayer about how he felt the love of Jesus all around him. The term *breastplate* refers to a piece of armor worn in battle. This is Saint Patrick's famous prayer:

> *I bind unto myself today the strong name of the Trinity,*
> *By invocation* of the same the Three-in-One and One-in-Three. . . .*
> *Christ be with me, Christ within me, Christ behind me, Christ*
> > *before me,*
> *Christ beside me, Christ to win me, Christ to comfort and restore me.*
> *Christ beneath me, Christ above me, Christ in quiet, Christ in danger,*
> *Christ in hearts of all that love me, Christ in mouth of friend and*
> > *stranger.*

—FROM THE *SAINT PATRICK'S BREASTPLATE* TRANSLATION BY CECIL F. ALEXANDER, 1889

*The word *invocation* comes from the word *invoke*, which means "to summon" or "to call upon."

Thank You, God, that Jesus is all around me, everywhere!

? **Want to know more?** See January 8, "Who Is the Trinity?"; March 17, "Was There Really a Saint Patrick?"; and October 21, "What Does It Mean to 'Put On the Armor of God'?"

What Is a Good Everyday Prayer?

We have been cleansed and made free from feelings of guilt.
And our bodies have been washed with pure water.

—HEBREWS 10:22

One of my favorite prayers is the "Collect for Purity" from *The Book of Common Prayer*. *Collect* (coll-ect) is an old-fashioned word for a short prayer. Some churches say it before communion. But like all prayers, it can be said anytime or anywhere! It goes like this: Almighty God, to You all hearts are open, all desires known, and from You no secrets are hid. Cleanse the thoughts of my heart by the inspiration of Your Holy Spirit, that I may perfectly love You, and worthily magnify Your holy Name. Through Christ Jesus our Lord, I pray. Amen.

The beautiful "Collect for Purity" is a wonderful, short, everyday prayer. I like to say it when I water my garden! The sight and sound of the sparkling water raining down on the flowers reminds me of my Christian baptism and the power of faith in Jesus to wash away my sins. It reminds me of how God lovingly nurtures and grows my faith.

Thank You, God, for making me clean and pure!

? Want to know more? See September 23 and 24, "What Is Baptism? (Parts 1 and 2)."

What Is the Most Important Prayer in the World?

*"Here I am! I stand at the door and knock. If anyone hears
my voice and opens the door, I will come in."*
—REVELATION 3:20

Maybe you know a lot about Jesus, but you're still not sure He is living in your heart. Not to worry! We all feel like that sometimes. Read today's verse again. Do you hear Jesus knocking on the door of your heart? If you do, maybe it's time to open the door. It's easy. Just say:

Thank You, Jesus, for being real and loving me so much that You died on the cross for me and my sins. Thank You, Jesus, for forgiving me when I sin and loving me no matter what. Please come into my heart now, live in me, and be my friend forever. Day by day, show me how to live. In Your name I pray, amen.

Guess what? You just prayed the most important prayer in the world! You may not *feel* any different, but you *are*. Jesus is living in your heart, which means you're about to go on a big adventure! Tell someone who loves Jesus and celebrate!

> *Thank You, Jesus, for living in my heart!*

? Want to know more? See April 11, "Can Anyone Believe in Jesus?" and April 12, "How Do I Get to Know Jesus?"

What Is the Church?

The church is Christ's body. The church is filled with
Christ, and Christ fills everything in every way.
—EPHESIANS 1:23

The worldwide church is made up of all the Christians on Earth. The early church was made up of people who lived mostly in the Middle East, northern Africa, and southern Europe. Today Christians live in every nation of the world!

The word *church* comes from an Old English word that means "Lord's house." That word suggests a building. The original New Testament Greek word for *church* is *ecclesia*, which means "assembly" or "congregation." This makes sense because the church is more about people than buildings. The Bible describes the church as the living body of Jesus at work in the world! The church is a living example of God's love for the world and all the people in it. Because Christians have God's Holy Spirit living in their hearts, they can be God's helpers. As the living body of Jesus, Christians help God's kingdom break through and touch others with His love (Luke 4:43; 10:9).

Thank You, God, for Your Christian church.

? Want to know more? See April 13, "Who Is the Holy Spirit?";
July 21, "What Is Christianity?"; September 19, "Does a Church
Have to Have a Building?"; and October 12–15, "How Did the
Christian Church Grow Over the Ages? (Parts 1–4)."

Why Is the Church Called the "Body of Christ"?

All of you together are the body of Christ. Each one of you is a part of that body.

—1 CORINTHIANS 12:27

Take the fingers of one hand and press them gently against the inside of your wrist. Feel your pulse. Every heartbeat is a reminder that Jesus actually lives within us and uses our bodies to show the world God's love! Isn't that amazing?

In today's Bible verse, the apostle Paul explains to members of the early church that they're all part of the body of Christ, with Jesus at "the head" leading the way (Ephesians 1:22–23). Jesus uses the hearts, minds, and bodies of Christians to get God's work done on earth. He uses our minds to think of ways to put God's love into action. He uses our feet to carry us to people who are lonely, sick, or sad. He uses our arms to wrap around people who need a hug. He uses our mouths to speak kind and encouraging words and to tell others about God. Why does Jesus live in the hearts of Christians this way? To show the world God's love (John 3:16).

Thank You, God, that I am part of Your body!

? Want to know more? See January 12, "How Can I Share God's Love?"; August 5, "What Can I Do to Help People in Need?"; and August 6, "What Is the 'I Give You My Hands' Prayer?"

Does a Church Have to Have a Building?

Give my greetings to Priscilla and Aquila. . . . Also, greet
for me the church that meets at their house.
—ROMANS 16:3, 5

Over the years, the word *church* has come to mean a building where Christians meet. But a church doesn't need a building. A church can be any group of Christians who meet together regularly to pray, study the Bible, and worship God.

A church is a community of people who believe in and love Jesus (Acts 9:31). Some churches are very small and meet in people's homes (Philemon v. 2). Other churches are large and meet in huge auditoriums. Some churches have their own buildings. Other churches rent space in schools and gymnasiums. Some churches are old and historic, with beautiful stained glass windows and bell towers. Other churches are brand new and modern, with all the latest audio and video technology.

In God's eyes, the building is the least important part of any church. That's because God doesn't love buildings. God loves people. God loves *you*!

> *Thank You, God, for all the different kinds of churches in the world.*

? **Want to know more?** See September 21, "Why Are There So Many Different Kinds of Churches?"

Why Does God Want Me to Be Involved in a Church?

When we have the opportunity to help anyone, we should do it. But we should give special attention to those who are in the family of believers.
—GALATIANS 6:10

There's an old saying that there are no "Lone Ranger" Christians. *The Lone Ranger* is a TV and movie character who wears a mask and fights outlaws in the Old West. Although he does have one good friend, Tonto, he mostly is alone. God didn't create His children to be alone. The church is God's great big family, and He wants you to be a part of it (1 Timothy 3:15)! God wants you to share His love with others (John 13:35). God wants your faith to grow (2 Thessalonians 1:3). Being involved in a church is a great way to do these things. When you are involved in a church you can: 1) Learn more about God; 2) Pray with other Christians; 3) Worship God with other Christians; 4) Reach out and help other people in need; and 5) Have fun with friends.

Thank You, God, for my local church. Show me how I can be more involved!

? Want to know more? See August 16, "What Is the Lord's Prayer? (Part 2)."

Why Are There So Many Different Kinds of Churches?

*Yes, there are many parts to a body, but all those parts
make only one body. Christ is like that too.*
—1 CORINTHIANS 12:12

No two churches are exactly alike, because no two people are exactly alike. There are many kinds of churches because there are many different kinds of Christians. Some churches have services only on Sunday. Others have services every day. Some churches celebrate Communion one Sunday a month. Others do it every day. Some baptize babies by sprinkling them with water. Others baptize kids and grown-ups in waist-deep pools of water. Some churches have organs and choirs and sing traditional hymns. Other churches have worship teams with electric guitars and sing modern praise songs. Some church leaders wear blue jeans, while others wear special robes.

What do all these churches have in common? They are all made up of people who love Jesus (Acts 2:42, 46–47).

Thank You, God, for all the different kinds of people who love Jesus!

? Want to know more? See September 19, "Does a Church Have to Have a Building?"; September 23–24, "What Is Baptism? (Parts 1 and 2)"; September 25–26, "What Is Communion? (Parts 1 and 2)"; October 12–15, "How Did the Christian Church Grow Over the Ages? (Parts 1–4)"; and October 16, "What Does *Denomination* Mean?"

Is It Okay for Me to Invite a Friend to Visit My Church?

*Faith comes from hearing the Good News. And people hear
the Good News when someone tells them about Christ.*

—ROMANS 10:17

To invite a friend to church is a very loving and generous thing to do. When you invite a friend to church, you are sharing your love for Jesus. This makes God very happy!

God's church is like a beautiful lamp shining in the darkness. Jesus said, "No one lights a lamp and then covers it with a bowl or hides it under a bed. Instead, he puts the lamp on a lampstand so that those who come in will have enough light to see" (Luke 8:16). When we invite others to church, we are sharing the light of God's love. At church, we share the good news of God's love through Jesus (John 3:16). At church, we worship God. It's where Christians pray, learn about the Bible, make new friends, and put God's love into action. For all these reasons, church is a wonderful place for a friend to visit. Before you invite a friend to church, be sure to ask your mom and dad.

> *Thank You, God, for the good news of Jesus.
> Please show me how to share it.*

? Want to know more? See November 15, "How Do I Tell a Friend About Jesus?"

What Is Baptism? (Part 1)

Change your hearts and lives and be baptized, each one of you,
in the name of Jesus Christ for the forgiveness of your sins.
—ACTS 2:38

In Jesus' day, people who wanted to turn away from their sins and toward God were baptized. They waded into a river where a prophet named John the Baptist dipped them in the water and said a prayer. The word *baptize* means "to dip." Water symbolizes the "washing away" and forgiveness of sins. Baptism was very important to Jesus. Jesus was baptized when He was thirty years old, right when he started His ministry. He had no sins that needed to be "washed away," but He was baptized out of loving obedience to His Father God and to set an example for us. Later, before ascending to heaven, Jesus told His disciples, "Go and make followers of all people in the world. Baptize them in the name of the Father and the Son and the Holy Spirit" (Matthew 28:19). The disciples loved Jesus and obeyed.

Thank You, God, for Your gift of holy baptism
as a way to wash away our sins.

? Want to know more? See February 13, "Did Jesus Ever Do Anything Wrong?"; February 15, "What Is the Temptation of Christ?"; February 23, "Who Is John the Baptist?"; February 24, "Who Is the Most Important Person Baptized by John the Baptist?"; and September 15, "What Is a Good Everyday Prayer?"

What Is Baptism? (Part 2)

*Then those people who accepted what Peter said were baptized. About
3,000 people were added to the number of believers that day.*

—ACTS 2:41

From the very earliest days of the church, believers in Jesus were
baptized. Over the ages, Christian churches around the world have
developed different ways of doing baptisms. Some baptize babies and
young children. Other churches require that children be old enough to
make their own decision to be baptized. Sometimes adults are baptized.
You are never too old to be baptized! Some churches sprinkle or pour
water over the head of the one being baptized. Other churches have special indoor pools deep enough for a grown-up to go totally underwater.
Christians around the world are also baptized in rivers, ponds, oceans,
and swimming pools.

Sometimes baptism is called "holy baptism." The word *holy* means
"set apart by and for God." A baptism is a time of great rejoicing and
celebration and is often followed by a special meal or party for family
and friends! Why is baptism so important to Christians around the
world? Because Jesus asks us to do it (Matthew 28:19).

Thank You, God, for Your gift of holy baptism!

? **Want to know more?** See September 21, "Why Are There So
Many Different Kinds of Churches?" and December 29, "What
Is a Godparent?"

What Is Communion? (Part 1)

"Take this bread and eat it. This bread is my body."
—MATTHEW 26:26

On the night before His death, Jesus shared a special Passover meal with His disciples. This meal is now known as the Last Supper. The apostle Paul wrote:

> The Lord Jesus, on the night he was betrayed, took bread, and when he had given thanks, he broke it and said, "This is my body, which is for you; do this in remembrance of me." In the same way, after supper he took the cup, saying: "This cup is the new covenant in my blood; do this, whenever you drink it, in remembrance of me." (1 Corinthians 11:23–25 NIV)

From the very earliest days of the church, believers gathered to break bread and pray together (Acts 2:42; 20:7). To "break bread" means to eat and drink, to share a meal with others, or to enjoy one another's company. When the early Christians did this, they remembered Jesus and felt His presence and love in a powerful way.

This gathering together to share the "body and blood" of Jesus became known as Communion. The word *communion* means "to participate together."

Thank You, God, for how Communion helps me remember Jesus and feel His presence and love in a powerful way.

? Want to know more? See March 30, "What Is the Last Supper?" and October 18, "What Is Christian Fellowship?"

What Is Communion? (Part 2)

*"This is my blood which begins the new agreement
that God makes with his people."*
—MATTHEW 26:28

Churches *celebrate* or offer Communion in many different ways. Some churches celebrate Communion at every service. Others do it once a month or twice a year. Some churches use wine. Others use grape juice. Some churches use bread. Some churches use flat crackers or thin wafers. Different churches have different names for Communion. Some call it holy Communion, the Great Thanksgiving, or holy Eucharist. The word *Eucharist* comes from a Greek word that means "thanksgiving." Other churches call it the Lord's Supper, the mass, the divine liturgy, or the breaking of bread.

When Christians celebrate Communion, the wine or grape juice represents Jesus' blood, which He shed for our sins when He suffered on the cross. The bread represents Jesus' body, which He gave up for our sins when He died on the cross. That's why some churches call the Communion bread the *host*, which means "the sacrificed one." Communion helps us experience the presence and love of Jesus in a powerful way.

Why is Communion so important to Christians? Because Jesus asks us to do it (Luke 22:18–20).

Thank You, God, for Your gift of holy Communion!

? Want to know more? See September 21, "Why Are There So Many Different Kinds of Churches?"

Is It True That an Astronaut Celebrated Communion on the Moon?

When I consider thy heavens, the work of thy fingers, the moon and the stars . . . what is man, that thou art mindful of him?
—PSALM 8:3–4 KJV

July 20, 1969, was an amazing day for Earth, when two astronauts, Neil Armstrong and Edwin "Buzz" Aldrin, became the first humans to land and walk on the moon. But did you know it was also the first time Communion was celebrated far, far away from our planet?

Buzz Aldrin was an astronaut who loved Jesus. A few weeks before his mission, Aldrin asked his pastor to give him a piece of blessed Communion bread and a tiny silver cup containing a sip of Communion wine. Aldrin also carried with him a notecard, with two Bible verses: Psalm 8:3–4 and John 15:5. When the Apollo 11 Lunar Module safely landed on the moon, Aldrin held the notecard and blessed bread and wine. Prayerfully he read the Bible verses and then took Communion. "It was interesting," he later wrote, "to think that the very first liquid ever poured on the moon, and the first food eaten there, were Communion elements." Communion on the moon . . . how truly amazing!

Thank You, God, that Your love travels everywhere—even to the moon!

? Want to know more? See December 11, "Can I Believe in Science and Still Believe in God?"

Why Do We Sing Hymns in Church?

Sing psalms, hymns, and spiritual songs with
thankfulness in your hearts to God.
—COLOSSIANS 3:16

Singing is a way to praise God. There is an old saying, "He who sings prays twice!" That's because when we sing, we praise God with words and song. The word *hymn* means "song of praise." Singing is an important part of worship in almost all Christian churches. Thousands of years ago King David and others wrote and sang songs of praise to God, which can be found in the book of Psalms in your Bible. Jesus and the disciples sang hymns together too (Matthew 26:30). Singing makes your heart glad. God often speaks to His children through music and the words of hymns. What's your favorite spiritual song? "Jesus Loves Me" is one of the world's best-loved hymns for kids. Maybe you know the tune. If so, feel free to sing the words!

Jesus loves me! This I know, for the Bible tells me so;
Little ones to Him belong, they are weak, but He is strong.
Yes, Jesus loves me! Yes, Jesus loves me!
Yes, Jesus loves me! The Bible tells me so.

Thank You, God, that I can sing praises to You!

? **Want to know more?** See June 11, "What Are the Psalms?"

SEPTEMBER 29

What Is the Amazing Story Behind "Amazing Grace"? (Part 1)

You have been saved by grace because you believe. You did not save yourselves. It was a gift from God.
—EPHESIANS 2:8

"Amazing Grace" is one of the most beloved hymns of all time. It was written by an English clergyman named John Newton. John Newton did not always love and know Jesus. When he was eleven years old, he went to sea with his father as a sailor, and he grew up to be a hard-drinking, cruel captain of slave ships. He gambled and swore and saw nothing wrong with the horrible business of slavery.

In 1738, Newton's ship ran into a bad storm and sprang a leak. Newton thought for sure he would die, but God made the ship's cargo shift in a way that plugged the hole! It was a miracle. Amazed, Newton started reading his Bible and asked Jesus into his heart. His hard heart softened, and he eventually realized that slavery was pure evil. In 1754, he quit his job at sea and became a Christian minister. He worked hard to make trading slaves illegal in England. His hymn "Amazing Grace" tells the story of how God lovingly touched his heart and changed him forever.

Thank You, God, that You can transform any heart.

? Want to know more? See November 2, "Who Is William Wilberforce?"

SEPTEMBER 30

What Is the Amazing Story Behind "Amazing Grace"? (Part 2)

One thing I do know. I was blind but now I see!
—JOHN 9:25 NIV

Yesterday we learned the story behind John Newton's "Amazing Grace." Newton included two famous Bible verses in his song. The first verse is from Jesus' parable of the prodigal son. The word *prodigal* means "recklessly wasteful." Jesus told about a young man who, after years of sin-filled living, decided to return home. He was desperate and sad, and he thought his father would be angry. Instead, the father was overjoyed to see him! He threw a party, saying, "My son was dead, but now he is alive again! He was lost, but now he is found!" (Luke 15:24). The second Bible verse describes a time Jesus healed a man who was born blind. No one had ever done such a thing before, and everyone was amazed. The man didn't know how it had happened, but he said, "One thing I do know. I was blind but now I see!" (John 9:25 NIV). There are more Bible verses hiding in "Amazing Grace." Look up the words to this hymn, and see if you can find them!

Thank You, God, for Your amazing grace!

? **Want to know more?** See July 7, "What Is a Parable?" and August 21, "What's the Difference Between 'Saying Grace' and 'Saying a Blessing' Before Meals?"

OCTOBER

What Is a Doxology?

Praise be to the God and Father of our Lord Jesus Christ. In Christ, God has given us every spiritual blessing in heaven.
—EPHESIANS 1:3

A doxology is an expression of praise to God, typically sung as a short hymn in a church service. The word *doxology* comes from a Greek word that means "a saying of glory." Although the word *doxology* doesn't appear in the Bible, people of faith have been saying and singing God's praises for thousands of years. God is so wonderful, there are countless reasons to praise Him—including His love, His blessings, and His total awesomeness! In 1674, an English pastor named Thomas Ken wrote a beautiful doxology that touches on all three of these qualities of God. The doxology called "Praise God from Whom All Blessings Flow" is sung in many churches today. If you know the tune, why not sing it out loud? God loves it when His children sing His praises!

> *Praise God from whom all blessings flow;*
> *Praise Him, all creatures here below;*
> *Praise Him above, ye heavenly host;*
> *Praise Father, Son, and Holy Ghost! Amen.*

Praise You, my great and glorious God, from whom all blessings flow!

? Want to know more? See January 3, "Who Is God?" and November 18 and 19, "Are There Really Angels? (Parts 1 and 2)."

What Does It Mean to Sing the "Gloria Patri"?

"Father, I want these people that you have given me to be with me in every place I am. I want them to see my glory."
—JOHN 17:24

The "Gloria Patri" is a popular and beloved ancient *doxology*, or short hymn of praise, sung in many Christian churches around the world. The original Latin title *Gloria Patri* means "Glory Be to the Father." We sing it to offer praise and glory to our loving Father God, to His beloved Son, Jesus, and to God's Holy Spirit. To sing the "Gloria Patri" is to remember that God is the same yesterday, today, and tomorrow. Because God doesn't change, we can always count on His love for all His children—and that includes you! If you know the tune to the "Gloria Patri" below, you can sing it out loud. God loves it when His children sing His praises!

Glory be to the Father and to the Son and to the Holy Ghost!
As it was in the beginning, is now and ever shall be,
world without end! Amen.

All glory be to You, dear God!

? Want to know more? See January 8, "Who Is the Trinity?" and April 16, "Is the Holy Ghost Really a Ghost?"

What's the Difference Between a Pastor, Priest, and Minister?

An elder [in the church] must be . . . one who loves what is good.
—Titus 1:6, 8 NIV

Leaders of different churches are called by different names. But their jobs are very similar. Pastors, priests, and ministers are responsible for the spiritual well-being of their congregations (Ephesians 4:11–13). They work very hard! They teach about the Bible. They deliver inspired, helpful sermons. They counsel people who are in trouble and suffering. They organize the activities of the church. They celebrate baptisms and Communion. They marry people and bury people. They pray for all their church members and for the world.

The word *pastor* comes from a word that means "shepherd." A pastor, like a shepherd, watches over his or her "flock," or the people in the church. The word *priest* comes from a word that means "superintendent or person in charge." The word *minister* comes from a word that means "servant." What do Christian pastors, priests, and ministers have in common? They love Jesus.

Thank You, God, for all Your pastors, priests, and ministers!

? Want to know more? See September 17, "What Is the Church?" and September 21, "Why Are There So Many Different Kinds of Churches?"

What's the Difference Between a Clergy Person and a Lay Person?

Why is it that he gives us these special abilities to do certain things best? It is that God's people will be equipped to do better work for him, building up the Church, the body of Christ.
—EPHESIANS 4:12 TLB

A clergy person is someone whose official full-time job is to serve God. The word *clergy* (*klur*-jee) comes from a word that means "clerk" or "secretary." Today many clergy people go to college to learn more about Christianity before leading a church. Some clergy choose to teach, work as missionaries, or become Bible scholars. A lay person is anyone in the church who is not a clergy person. The word *lay* or *laity*, means "of the people." They are just as important as clergy! Lay people teach Sunday school, lead Bible studies, sing in choirs, lead worship teams, read aloud from the Bible, and help with Communion. They pray for other members of the church and organize projects to help people. Some even write and deliver sermons!

> *Thank You, God, for the many ways You call Your children to serve You, including me!*

? Want to know more? See April 29, "How Can I Discover My God-Given Gifts and Talents?" and August 5, "What Can I Do to Help People in Need?"

Is It True to Be a Missionary You Have to Travel Far from Home?

Before someone can go and tell them [about God's love], he must be sent.
—Romans 10:15

Jesus said, "Go everywhere in the world. Tell the Good News to everyone" (Mark 16:15). Over the years, this powerful command has become known as the Great Commission. *Commission* means "authority that is given to someone." Jesus gave the disciples authority to tell the whole world about God's love. A Christian missionary is a person who shares the love of Jesus with others. The word *missionary* means "one who is sent off." Some missionaries travel to far parts of the world to share the love of Jesus. Others work close to home. Some help people plant crops and dig wells for fresh water. Other missionaries build schools, houses, orphanages, and hospitals. Some work with adults, and others with teenagers and children. Everyone who loves Jesus is a missionary. This is because wherever you are, you can share the love of Jesus with others. Whether you're at home with your family, or with relatives near and far, you can share the love of Jesus.

Thank You, God, for the honor of being Your missionary.

? Want to know more? See March 6, "What's the Difference Between a Disciple and an Apostle?" and October 29, "Can I Have Friends Who Aren't Christians?"

What Does It Mean to Be Born Again?

"I tell you the truth. Unless you are born again,
you cannot be in God's kingdom."
—John 3:3

To be *born again* is another way of saying "to be converted from unbelief to belief in Jesus." The phrase comes from a famous conversation Jesus had with a Jewish religious leader named Nicodemus. One night Nicodemus came to Jesus and said, "We know that you are a teacher sent from God. No one can do the miracles you do, unless God is with him."

Jesus replied, "I tell you the truth, unless you are born again, you cannot see God's kingdom."

"But if a man is already old, how can he be born again?" Nicodemus asked. "He cannot enter his mother's body again."

Jesus answered, "I tell you the truth. Unless you are born from water and the Spirit, you cannot enter God's kingdom" (John 3:2–6).

When you convert from unbelief to belief in Jesus, you receive a brand-new life. This is because you are spiritually born again.

> *God, how happy I am to be born again!*

? Want to know more? See January 14, "What Is the Kingdom of God?"; April 13, "Who Is the Holy Spirit?"; and September 23 and 24, "What Is Baptism? (Parts 1 and 2)."

Why Do Some Clergy Persons Wear White Collars?

This is what people should think about us: We are servants of Christ.
—1 CORINTHIANS 4:1

Some Christian clergy wear what is called a clerical collar. Others don't. A clerical collar is a narrow band that fastens at the back of the neck. It is almost always white, which symbolizes purity. It was originally made of cotton or linen but is now often made of plastic. Some clergy wear collars only during church, and others wear them with their everyday clothing.

While it may seem old-fashioned, the clerical collar is fairly modern. It was invented in 1827 by a Presbyterian minister in Scotland! Today is it worn by both male and female clergy from a wide variety of Christian churches around the world, including Baptist, Methodist, Lutheran, Anglican, Eastern Orthodox, Roman Catholic, and many others. The clerical collar is a sign to others that the person wearing it is a professional clergy person who works to spread God's love. It is, most importantly, a sign that the person loves Jesus.

Thank You, God, for all Your devoted clergy around the world.

? Want to know more? See September 21, "Why Are There So Many Different Kind of Churches?" and October 4, "What's the Difference Between a Clergy Person and a Lay Person?"

Why Do Some Christians Make the Sign of the Cross?

The cross of our Lord Jesus Christ is my only reason for bragging.
—GALATIANS 6:14

Making the sign of the cross is an ancient Christian custom that goes back to the days of the early church. It's a four-step motion, usually made with the right hand gently touching one's (1) forehead, (2) heart, (3) left shoulder, and (4) right shoulder. Touching our head reminds us to think of Jesus. Touching our heart reminds us to love Jesus. Touching our shoulders reminds us to carry His message of love to all the world. While making the sign of the cross, some Christians pray: "In the name of the Father, the Son, and the Holy Spirit, amen."

There is no right or wrong time or reason to make the sign of the cross. Many Christians make the sign of the cross as a way to begin and end a time of prayer. Some make the sign of the cross as a silent prayer during a time of trouble. Others make it when they simply want to feel close to Jesus. Making the sign of the cross can be a helpful reminder of God's great love for the world and all the people in it—including *you!*

Help me, God, to love and serve You with all my mind, heart, and body!

? Want to know more? See January 8, "Who Is the Trinity?"; September 21, "Why Are There So Many Different Kinds of Churches?"; and October 20, "What Does the Bible Mean When It Says My Body Is the 'Temple of God'?"

Help! What Should I Do When I Think a Church Service Is Boring?

Continue to think about the things that are good and worthy of praise.
—PHILIPPIANS 4:8

Everyone gets a little sleepy or bored during church sometimes. It's not always easy to sit still indoors when outside the sun is shining or to stay awake when you're sleepy. It's not always easy to pay attention if the preacher is talking about something hard to understand. Not to worry! Jesus was human, so He experienced times of restlessness, sleepiness, and boredom too. In other words, God understands. Here are a few ideas to help you the next time you find yourself a little bit sleepy or bored during church:

- Tell God how you feel, and ask Him to help you.
- Make a list of all the things you're thankful for.
- Make a list of nice things you might do for other people.
- Pray for all the people you love.

God, when my thoughts wander, remind me to ask for Your help.

? Want to know more? See August 26, "Can God Actually Talk to Me?"; September 1, "What Should I Do When I Can't Think of What to Pray?"; and November 28, "What Does It Mean to Count My Blessings?"

Why Do Some Crosses Have Jesus on Them and Others Don't?

We saw all the things that Jesus did. . . . But they
killed him by nailing him to a cross.
—ACTS 10:39

The cross has become a symbol for Christianity. That's because through Jesus' obedient, sacrificial death on a cross, God offered salvation to the world and all the people in it! In Jesus' day, death on a cross was a shameful and painful death for criminals. Now it stands for Jesus' love! In many Christian churches, the cross is displayed for all to see. Some crosses are simple and plain. They may be made of carved wood or metal. Crosses that are empty symbolize the *risen* Jesus, who is now in heaven sitting at the right hand of His Father. Other crosses include an image of Jesus during His time of loving sacrifice and suffering. A cross with the figure of Jesus is known as a crucifix. The word *crucifix* comes from a Latin word that means "fixed to a cross." No longer is the cross a symbol of shame. It's a beautiful symbol of God's great love for the world and for all His children.

Thank You, God, for Your Son Jesus' great sacrifice on the cross.

? Want to know more? See March 14, "Why Did Jesus Have to Die?" and September 21, "Why Are There So Many Different Kinds of Churches?"

What Is an Altar Call?

[The disciples] called the blind man. They said, "Cheer up!
Get to your feet. Jesus is calling you." The blind man stood
up quickly. He left his coat there and went to Jesus.
—MARK 10:49–50

Some Christian church services end with an "altar call." The word *altar* refers to the front of the church. At the altar call, the pastor invites people who sense God calling them to give their lives to Jesus to walk to the front of the church. There they are greeted by the pastor and lay people who welcome and pray with them. Some churches sing hymns during altar calls, such as "Softly and Tenderly Jesus Is Calling," part of which appears below. You don't have to be in church to commit your life to Jesus. You can respond to Jesus right now!

> *Softly and tenderly Jesus is calling, Calling for you and for me;*
> *See, on the portals* He's waiting and watching, Watching for*
>   *you and for me.*
> *Come home, come home, You who are weary, come home;*
> *Earnestly, tenderly, Jesus is calling, Calling, "O sinner, come home!"*

*Just in case you are wondering, the word *portal* means "a gateway
or entrance" and refers here to the gates of God's kingdom.

Thank You, God, for calling me!

? **Want to know more?** See September 21, "Why Are There So
Many Different Kinds of Churches?"

How Did the Christian Church Grow Over the Ages? (Part 1)

*They praised God, and all the people liked them. More
and more people were being saved every day; the Lord
was adding those people to the group of believers.*
—ACTS 2:47

The Christian church started approximately two thousand years ago in Jerusalem, Israel. Many early church leaders knew Jesus personally during His time on earth. Early Christians met in one another's homes. The Bible says, "They spent their time learning the apostles' teaching. And they continued to share, to break bread, and to pray together" (Acts 2:42). From Jerusalem, Christianity spread quickly. Over time, Christians became more organized, built churches, and met regularly for worship, prayer, baptisms, Communion, marriages, and burials. The local Christian church became the center of community life. For more than one thousand years, there were two major churches, located in two huge cities: Rome, Italy, and Constantinople (now Istanbul), Turkey. These two big churches influenced many smaller churches around them. Over the years the two developed slightly different teachings and practices.

Thank You, God, for how You watch over, guide, and grow Your church!

? **Want to know more?** See July 21, "What Is Christianity?";
September 17, "What Is the Church?"; and September 21, "Why
Are There So Many Different Kinds of Churches?"

How Did the Christian Church Grow Over the Ages? (Part 2)

We are many, but in Christ we are all one body.
—ROMANS 12:5

Remember: God is perfect. Human beings are not. Because God's church on Earth is made up of imperfect people, sometimes there are disagreements and misunderstandings. Still, God's love is perfect, and He is always watching over, guiding, and protecting His church. Yesterday we learned about the two major branches of the early church in Rome, Italy, and Constantinople (now Istanbul), Turkey. As centuries passed, they developed slightly different teachings and practices. In 1054 the church leaders prayerfully decided to split into the Catholic Church in Rome and the Orthodox Church in Constantinople. Both churches are still large, active, and growing, with millions of faithful believers doing God's work in the world. While Christian churches may be different in some ways, they are alike in the most important way: their people love Jesus and want to share God's love with others.

> *Thank You, God, that even when Your children don't understand Your ways, You still find a way to grow and work wonders.*

? Want to know more? See January 3, "Who Is God?"; January 4, "If God Is My Creator, How Is He Different from My Parents?"; and September 21, "Why Are There So Many Different Kinds of Churches?"

OCTOBER 14

How Did the Christian Church Grow Over the Ages? (Part 3)

You were born again through God's living message that continues forever.
—1 PETER 1:23

Yesterday we learned how the early church spread and grew until it split to form the first two major branches of the Christian church: the Catholic Church, with its headquarters near Rome, and the Orthodox Church, with its headquarters in Constantinople. The third major branch grew from the Protestant Reformation in the sixteenth century. These Christians were called *Protestants* because they *protested*, or disagreed, about certain teachings and practices in the Catholic Church. The Protestants wanted to *reform*, or change, the church by focusing more on studying God's Holy Word, the Bible. In 1457, Johann Gutenberg invented the mechanical printing press in Germany, which made it easier for people to get Bibles to read for themselves. Bible teaching and preaching became very important in Protestant churches, which continue to grow and thrive, spreading the message of God's love and doing good works in the name of Jesus around the world.

Thank You, God, for the invention of the printing press, and for Your living Holy Word, the Bible!

? **Want to know more?** See May 3, "How Did We Get the Bible?" and September 21, "Why Are There So Many Different Kinds of Churches?"

How Did the Christian Church Grow Over the Ages? (Part 4)

*[Jesus said,] "He who believes in me will do the same things
that I do. He will do even greater things than these."*
—JOHN 14:12

The fourth major branch of the Christian church is made up of the Charismatic (kare-iz-*ma*-tik) churches. The modern Charismatic movement started in 1906, at a small church in California. To their great surprise, the church members started speaking and understanding languages that were not their own. They experienced many supernatural gifts of the Holy Spirit, including prophecies and miraculous healings. The word *charismatic* comes from the Greek word *kharism*, which means "favor or grace, freely given." Another name for churches that focus on the gifts of the Holy Spirit is *Pentecostal*. So the four major branches of the Christian church are Catholic, Orthodox, Protestant, and Charismatic. Because the Christian church is the living body of Jesus, many churches are exciting *mixtures* of these four branches! Remember: While Christian churches may be different in some ways, they are alike in the most important way: their people love Jesus and want to share the good news of His love with others.

Thank You, God, for Your great big, beautiful body of Christ!

? Want to know more? See April 14, "What Is Pentecost?"; April 17, "What Are the Gifts of the Holy Spirit?"; and September 21, "Why Are There So Many Different Kinds of Churches?"

What Does *Denomination* Mean?

*You are joined together with peace through the
Spirit. . . . Let peace hold you together.*
—EPHESIANS 4:3

The word *denomination* comes from a Latin word meaning "to give a name to." Today there are many different kinds of churches that make up the great big Christian family of believers working together, each in their own way, to share God's love around the world. If we think of the worldwide Christian church as God's living tree, the many denominations are like the leaves of the tree. The major branches of the tree remain strong, but some leaves last only for a season.

It's a good idea for Christians not to spend too much time on our differences. Instead, God wants us to love and pray for one another. He wants us to focus on and rejoice in the important things we share. When believers in the early church disagreed about this or that, here is what the apostle Paul wrote: "There is one Lord, one faith, and one baptism. There is one God and Father of everything" (Ephesians 4:5–6). In other words, when it comes to loving and serving Jesus, we're all on the same team!

Thank You, God, for all your many beautiful churches. Go, Team Jesus!

? Want to know more? See September 21, "Why Are There So Many Different Kinds of Churches?"

OCTOBER 17

When Does My Eternal Life Begin?

All the days planned for me were written in your book before I was one day old.
—PSALM 139:16

Many people think that eternal life doesn't begin until we die. But that's not so. You're living your eternal life right this very moment! How can this be?

God has no beginning and no end. This is because God, our Creator, is *eternal*—infinite or endless. God also planted eternity in your heart (Ecclesiastes 3:11). He knew and loved you *before* you were born (Psalm 139)! Because God, your Creator, is eternal, you are eternal too. Another word for your eternal identity is *soul*. An old saying goes, "We're not human beings having a spiritual experience, but we are spiritual beings having a human experience." The truth is, we are both! We are fully human, and we are fully spiritual. The Bible says that when we die, our souls continue to live. Like Jesus, we will one day get new bodies designed to live forever in heaven. Isn't that amazing?

> *Thank You, God, for planting eternity in my heart and for knowing and loving me even before I was born!*

? Want to know more? See March 25, "How Is Jesus' Resurrection Body Different from My Body?" and July 22, "What's the Difference Between Christianity and Other Religions?"

What Is Christian Fellowship?

Now we tell you what we have seen and heard because we want you to have fellowship with us. The fellowship we share together is with God the Father and his Son, Jesus Christ.

—1 JOHN 1:3

Christian fellowship is spending time with friends who believe in, know, and love Jesus. Friends who believe in Jesus can share with one another what they know and love about Him. They can study the Bible together. Friends who believe in Jesus can pray with and for one another. Many Christian churches have fellowship halls, dinners, and retreats. That's because spending time with friends who believe in Jesus is fun!

When friends who believe in Jesus gather together, Jesus promises that He is with them too (Matthew 18:19–20)! Isn't that amazing?

When is the last time you got together with friends who know and love Jesus? Maybe today is a good time to call a friend or two and make plans for some fun Christian fellowship!

Thank You, God, for Your gift of good Christian fellowship.

? Want to know more? See August 29, "Is It Okay to Pray Out Loud with Another Person?" and September 20, "Why Does God Want Me to Be Involved in a Church?"

OCTOBER 19

Is It True That Christians Can't Have Any Fun?

But the grace of our Lord was fully given to me. And with that grace came the faith and love that are in Christ Jesus.

—1 TIMOTHY 1:14

Some people have the wrong idea about Christianity. They think it's a religion full of rules about what you can and can't do. They think that Christians can't have any fun.

A funny thing happens when you choose to follow Jesus. You feel good. You have joy. Did you ever feel so happy that you wanted to burst out singing? Or do a cartwheel? That is how it feels when you know deep in your heart that you are trying your best to please God.

To love is to be kind. It's to smile and laugh. It's to think about what is good about other people. It's to enjoy wonderful friendships. It's to live life to the fullest.

Jesus said, "I am come that they might have life, and that they might have it more abundantly" (John 10:10 KJV). The word *abundant* means "plentiful, to the point of overflowing."

With Jesus, life is overflowing with God's love and with fun!

Thank You, God, for sending Jesus so I can live a joyful life.

? Want to know more? See October 18, "What Is Christian Fellowship?"

What Does the Bible Mean When It Says My Body Is the "Temple of God"?

You should know that your body is a temple for the Holy Spirit.
—1 CORINTHIANS 6:19

Through faith in Jesus, God's Holy Spirit lives in the heart of every Christian. This means your body is like a little temple. A *temple* is a structure that welcomes and offers a dwelling place, or home, for God. The apostle Paul said that since we are the Holy Spirit's temples, we are to "honor God with [our] bodies" (1 Corinthians 6:20). That means to respect and love your body and take good care of it. Your human body is very important. That's because God uses your body to get His work done on earth! For example, God uses your mind to think of loving ways to pray. He uses your feet to carry you to people who are lonely, or sick, or sad. He uses your arms to wrap around people who need a hug. He uses your mouth to smile and to speak kind, encouraging words. He uses your hands to gently wipe away another's tears.

Why does God use your body as a temple for His Holy Spirit? To show the world His love.

> *Thank You, God, for the awesome honor of serving as a living, human temple for Your Holy Spirit!*

? Want to know more? See January 17, "Does God Care What My Body Looks Like?" and April 13, "Who Is the Holy Spirit?"

What Does It Mean to "Put on the Armor of God"?

Be strong in the Lord and in his great power. Wear the full armor of God.
—EPHESIANS 6:10–11

Being human isn't always easy. At some point, we all experience times of sadness. We have disappointments and difficult challenges. The good news is that God gives us powerful tools to help us through hard times. Over the years, these spiritual tools have become known as "putting on the armor of God." The apostle Paul described it like this in Ephesians 6:10–18:

- Helmet of *salvation*
- Breastplate of God's *righteousness*
- Shield of *faith*
- Sword of the *Holy Spirit*
- Belt of God's *truth*
- Shoes of the *gospel*
- Supernatural power of *prayer*

How loving of God to give us such powerful spiritual armor. When we put on the full armor of God, we are ready to face and win any battle!

> *Thank You, God, for the amazing gift of Your head-to-toe set of spiritual armor.*

? **Want to know more?** See January 20, "What Are Some of God's Promises for Me?" and September 14, "What Is Saint Patrick's Breastplate Prayer?"

What Does It Mean to Be the "Salt and Light" of the World?

"You are the salt of the earth. . . . You are the light that gives light to the world."
—MATTHEW 5:13–14

Jesus wants us to make a positive difference in the world as God's helpers. So what does Jesus mean when He says we are the "salt of the earth"? Salt is a seasoning. It improves the taste of food. With the love of Jesus, we can improve the world. Salt makes people thirsty. With the love of Jesus, we thirst—and cause others to thirst—to know God better. Salt is used to melt ice. With the love of Jesus, our cold hearts melt with kindness and compassion. Salt is a preservative that helps food stay fresh longer. Thanks to Jesus, we can live forever!

What does Jesus mean when He says we are the "light of the world"? Light shines in the darkness. Light exposes evil and dangers. Light shows people the way to safety and causes living things to grow. The love of Jesus does all these things and more. The bright, shining love of Jesus shows people the way to God (John 14:6).

Thank You, God, for the love of Jesus, living and shining in my heart.

? Want to know more? See April 1, "Why Do We Light Candles on Easter?"; April 15, "How Does the Holy Spirit Help Me?"; and November 30, "What Is an Advent Wreath?"

OCTOBER 23

How Is It Possible to Be Weak and Strong at the Same Time?

I am very happy to brag about my weaknesses.
Then Christ's power can live in me.
—2 CORINTHIANS 12:9

The apostle Paul said he delighted in his weaknesses because "When I am weak, then I am truly strong" (2 Corinthians 12:10). How can this be? Have you ever heard of the Japanese art of *kintsugi*? *Kintsugi*, or "golden joinery," is the art of repairing cracked or broken ceramics with pure gold. Why? To show how something broken and fixed can be even more beautiful and stronger than the original. In *kintsugi* pottery, the shining golden cracks are the focal point. The golden-veined pots and bowls are not only stronger than the original unbroken pieces, they are also considered more beautiful and valuable! Because we are human, we're all broken in some way. We all struggle. But when we confess and give God our brokenness, we open ourselves to His forgiveness and healing. We gain compassion and are able to love others better. We can delight in our weakness, because God turns it to strength—like pure gold!

> *Thank You, God, for how You lovingly transform*
> *my weaknesses to beauty and strength.*

? Want to know more? See July 2, "Who Is the Apostle Paul?"; July 3, "What Is the Thorn in Paul's Flesh?"; and December 7, "How Can Anything Good Come Out of Pain and Suffering?"

What Is a Quiet Time?

*Because you are his sons, God sent the Spirit of his Son into
our hearts, the Spirit who calls out, "Abba, Father."*
—GALATIANS 4:6 NIV

God your heavenly Father is not a legend, myth, or fairy tale. He is
alive and real, and He loves you—and He wants you to know Him! One
way to do this is to set aside some time each day to spend with God—just
the two of you. Some refer to this special, private meeting with God as
a "quiet time."

When I was a little girl, I loved to sit on my father's lap, wrapped in
his big, strong arms. We were very close, and I loved him so, so much.
When he died, I thought my broken heart would never heal. One day,
while praying to God, I cried, "Oh, Daddy, I miss my father so much!"
Daddy? I thought. *Why would I ever call God "Daddy"?* But later I learned
this was how Jesus prayed to God too! *Abba* means "Daddy" or "Papa"
(Mark 14:36).

Now, when I have quiet time with God, I picture myself snuggled all
cozy and warm on my heavenly, *Abba*, Father's lap, wrapped in His big,
strong arms. You can love your quiet times with God too!

> *Thank You, God, for being my loving "Abba,"
> my perfect heavenly Daddy.*

? Want to know more? See February 17, "What Makes Jesus So
Important?" and October 25, "How Can I Make the Most of My
Quiet Times with God?"

How Can I Make the Most of My Quiet Times with God?

"Come with me by yourselves to a quiet place."
—Mark 6:31 NIV

There are no set rules for quiet times with God. The more time you spend with God, the more you'll get to know Him! Maybe start by setting aside ten to fifteen minutes each day to meet with God. The time of day doesn't matter. God is *always* available—every minute of every day! Here are a few tips for making the most of your special time with God:

- Be silent. Try to quiet your thoughts. Listen carefully for God.
- Pray. The more time you spend listening and talking to God, the better you'll get to know Him.
- Read your Bible. You'll be amazed how God can speak to you through the pages of His book!
- Write God a letter. Some people also use a prayer journal to keep track of prayer requests and answers.
- Read a daily devotional.

Thank You, Abba, Daddy, for meeting with me every day.

? **Want to know more?** See August 11, "What Is Prayer?"; August 31, "What Is a Prayer Journal?"; and September 1, "What Should I Do When I Can't Think of What to Pray?"

What Is Tithing?

*"One-tenth of all crops belongs to the Lord. This includes
the crops from fields and the fruit from trees."*
—LEVITICUS 27:30

Tithing is the age-old practice of giving ten percent of your income to God. The word *tithe* means "tenth."

Jesus encouraged religious leaders to tithe (Luke 11:42). And the apostle Paul wrote this to the members of the early church: "On the first day of every week, each one of you should put aside as much money as you can from what you are blessed with" (1 Corinthians 16:2). While tithing is a good guideline for giving, many Christians give away much more than ten percent of their income! God especially loves it when we give happily (2 Corinthians 9:7).

Tithing is a fun way of saying "Thank You!" to God. Do you get five dollars a week for allowance? You might want to give fifty cents of it to God, to show that you love Him. You can give your tithe to your church and other organizations that do good work for God. Talk to your mom and dad about this. They will have good ideas too!

> *God, fill my heart with gratitude, and inspire
> me to be a generous and happy giver!*

What's the Difference Between Fasting and Dieting?

They were all worshiping the Lord and fasting for a certain time.
—Acts 13:2 NCV

Fasting is an age-old practice that Christians use as a way to get closer to God. To *fast* is to not eat, or to eat very little, for a certain length of time. Christians also pray when they fast. Jesus expected His disciples to fast (Matthew 6:16–18).

Some Christians fast and pray to seek God's guidance. Many Christians fast during certain seasons in the church year, such as Lent. Hunger caused by fasting reminds us of others who are hungry all the time. It reminds us to pray.

Fasting and dieting are very different. Dieting is eating certain kinds and amounts of food to lose or control weight. People diet to improve their physical health. People fast to improve their spiritual health.

Most children do not fast or diet because their bodies are still growing and need all the good nutrition they can get. You don't need to fast to get closer to God. You can always read your Bible, pray, and enjoy meaningful quiet times with God.

> *Thank You, God, for giving me so many ways to grow closer to You!*

? Want to know more? See February 16, "What Is Lent?" and October 24, "What Is a Quiet Time?"

Does It Matter to God How Much Time I Spend Online and Watching TV?

Do not be shaped by this world. Instead be changed within by a new way of thinking.

—ROMANS 12:2

Everything you take in with your mouth, eyes, and ears affects you. Your mouth feeds your body, and your eyes and ears feed your mind and soul. Too much junk food can hurt your body, and too much junk entertainment can hurt your mind and soul. Some entertainment is good. Some is not. God wants you to feed your mind and soul with things that are wholesome, healthy, fun, and good. God wants you to become more like Jesus by being "changed within by a new way of thinking" (Romans 12:2). How do you do this? You can read your Bible, pray, and spend time with friends who know and love Jesus. You can watch movies and read books that have positive, faith-filled messages, such as The Chronicles of Narnia, by C. S. Lewis, or a daily devotional like the one you are reading right now!

God, show me how to spend my time today in healthy ways.

? Want to know more? See October 18, "What Is Christian Fellowship?"; October 19, "Is It True That Christians Can't Have Any Fun?"; November 3, "Who Is C. S. Lewis?"; and November 14, "How Does God Want Me to Spend My Time?"

OCTOBER 29

Can I Have Friends Who Aren't Christians?

We are Christ's ambassadors. God is using us to speak to you.
—2 Corinthians 5:20 TLB

Yes, it is possible to be friends with people who don't know Jesus. God loves all His children. God wants us to love everyone too! At the same time, remember that we are easily influenced by others. Good friends can be a good influence, and bad friends can be a bad influence. Jesus had lots of different kinds of friends. Some believed in Him. Some didn't. Some just didn't know what to think! Jesus didn't change when He was with different kinds of people. When people spoke or behaved badly, He didn't join in. He was always true to Himself and His Father God. He was honest and good. He was generous and kind. He was patient and forgiving. Most of all, He was loving. The Bible teaches that we are ambassadors for Jesus. An *ambassador* is an official representative. As Christ's ambassador, the words you say and the way you act make a big impression on others—especially on friends who don't yet know Jesus.

> Thank You, God, that Jesus lives in my heart. I am so honored and happy to be Your earthly ambassador!

? Want to know more? See January 14, "What Is the Kingdom of God?"; October 5, "Is It True to Be a Missionary You Have to Travel Far from Home?"; and November 15, "How Do I Tell a Friend About Jesus?"

OCTOBER 30

What's Wrong with Horoscopes, Fortune-Telling, and Ouija Boards?

Do not let your people practice fortune-telling. . . . Anyone who does these things is detestable to the LORD.
—DEUTERONOMY 18:10, 12 NLT

God created human beings with curiosity. The word *curiosity* means "the desire to know or learn." Curiosity can be healthy and good. But curiosity can also have an unhealthy, dark side. Some people believe occult practices such as astrology, tarot cards, and Ouija boards will give them secret knowledge about the future. The word *occult* means "secret" or "hidden." Other occult practices include fortune-telling, palm reading, numerology, witchcraft, and trying to contact the dead through people known as psychics or mediums. God doesn't want us to put our trust in occult practices. Only He knows what the future will hold. Involvement with the occult leads to confusion, deception, and darkness. It doesn't lead to God. In fact, God *forbids* His children to be involved in any way with the occult! God doesn't want you to be deceived or confused. He wants to give you His good and true answers.

God, please steer me away from any and all occult practices!

? Want to know more? See February 26, "Why Did Jesus Do Miracles?"; April 17, "What Are the Gifts of the Holy Spirit?"; and April 23, "What Is the Holy Spirit's Gift of Prophecy?"

317

What Kind of Holiday Is Halloween?

God is light, and in him there is no darkness at all.
—1 JOHN 1:5

Tomorrow, November 1, is a Christian holiday called All Saints' Day, or All Hallows' Day. *Hallows* is an Old English word for "saints." The word *Halloween*, or *Hallowe'en*, is a shortened version of "All Hallows' Eve," which takes place on October 31. Halloween is *not* a Christian holiday. Halloween began as a Druid festival of the dead in northern Europe. The Druids were *pagans*, or people who had not yet heard the good news of Jesus. Druids believed that on this night, the souls of the dead came and walked with the living. This was a very creepy, dark, and scary thought. The Druids hollowed out turnips and potatoes and put candles inside to symbolize ghostly spirits. They dressed up in costumes to disguise themselves from harmful evil spirits. Even after they became Christians, some people continued these customs and called it Halloween. Over the years, Halloween has become a fun time for parties and trick-or-treating. But remember, Halloween was created by people who did not know God or Jesus. God is never creepy, dark, or scary. God is life and light and love (John 8:12). This is very good news!

Thank You, God, for being the source of all that is loving, beautiful, and good.

? Want to know more? See April 1, "Why Do We Light Candles on Easter?" and November 1, "What Is All Saints' Day?"

NOVEMBER

What Is All Saints' Day?

I [the apostle Paul] am going to Jerusalem in a ministry to the saints.
—ROMANS 15:25 NRSV

All Saints' Day is a Christian holy day that honors all saints, known and unknown, living and dead. The word *saint* means "set apart for God."

Who is a saint? A saint is any person who believes in, loves, and follows Jesus. In God's eternal kingdom, Christian saints also include believers in Jesus who have yet to be born! That's a lot of saints! Some Christian churches have a tradition of making saints official after they have died through a process called *canonization*. The word *canonize* means "to admit to the official list." But you don't need to be canonized to be a saint. In fact, because you believe in Jesus, *you* are a saint! Isn't that awesome?

Some of the best-known saints include the writers of the four Gospels: Matthew, Mark, Luke, and John. Today's Bible verse, written by Saint Paul, is one of the earliest times the word *saint* is used to describe believers.

> *Thank You, God, for calling me to love and follow Jesus.*
> *I am so honored and happy to be Your saint!*

? **Want to know more?** See January 14, "What Is the Kingdom of God?"; September 21, "Why Are There So Many Different Kinds of Churches?"; and November 4, "Who Is Mother Teresa of Calcutta?"

Who Is William Wilberforce?

The [children of God] groaned in their slavery and cried
out, and their cry for help . . . went up to God.
—EXODUS 2:23 NIV

William Wilberforce was an English politician born in 1759. He's famous for being a great leader who helped abolish the slave trade in England. The word *abolish* means "put an end to." William loved Jesus. His Christian faith opened his heart to see that buying and selling humans was pure evil. The slave trade was big business in England, which ran many sugar plantations in the British West Indies colonies. They shipped slaves there from Africa, and it was horrible. Families were split up, shackled, and packed as human cargo at the bottom of dirty ships. Many of them died.

As a boy, William was small and sickly. But as he grew, God blessed William with the gift of *oratory*, or public speaking. When William spoke, people listened. He gave speeches and worked to pass a law ending the slave trade in England in 1807. But slavery was still legal in the West Indies colonies. Still, he never gave up. He never stopped praying. On July 26, 1833, three days before his death, Wilberforce finally heard the good news he had so longed for: the government had finally agreed to pass a law that would end the practice of slavery throughout the whole British Empire! *Hooray!*

Thank You, God, for William Wilberforce!

Who Is C. S. Lewis?

We are children of God. . . . We know that when Christ comes
again, we will be like him. We will see him as he really is.
—1 JOHN 3:2

Clive Staples Lewis was a brilliant scholar, writer, and Christian apologist born in 1898. A Christian *apologist* is someone who makes a case for the truth of Christianity. Using his first-rate knowledge of philosophy, logic, and reason (and inspired by God's Holy Spirit!), he wrote some of the world's most famous books about the truth of Christian faith.

As a teenager, Lewis lost his faith. Later, he earned a scholarship to Oxford University, where he studied literature. Lewis loved to write and share ideas. He formed a group called the Inklings, where authors and friends met regularly to talk. One of Lewis's best friends was fellow professor and writer J. R. R. Tolkien, who loved Jesus. After many long, deep conversations with Tolkien, Lewis rediscovered faith in God and asked Jesus into his heart. His struggle with faith made Lewis one of the greatest Christian apologists of all time! You may know C. S. Lewis for his classic children's books, The Chronicles of Narnia, a collection of exciting faith-filled stories that I highly recommend!

Thank You, God, for C. S. Lewis!

? Want to know more? See November 5, "Who Is J. R. R. Tolkien?" and December 28, "Is It Okay to Question and Sometimes Have Doubts About God?"

Who Is Mother Teresa of Calcutta?

"Whatever you did for one of the least of these brothers and sisters of mine, you did for me."
—MATTHEW 25:40 NIV

Saint Teresa of Calcutta was a Roman Catholic nun born in 1910 who loved Jesus. She devoted her life to serving the sick, dying, and poor. Known as Mother Teresa, she worked for many years in Calcutta, India, where she founded a group of nuns serving the "poorest among the poor." In 1979, Mother Teresa was awarded the Nobel Peace Prize. She chose not to attend the fancy ceremony and gave the award money to the poor. When asked how to increase world peace, she famously replied, "Go home and love your family." Mother Teresa died in 1997. She was canonized in the Roman Catholic Church in 2016, when she officially became Saint Teresa. Today members of her religious *order*, or group, the Missionaries of Charity, continue to serve the sick, dying, homeless, and poorest of the poor around the world. The word *charity* means "love." Mother Teresa believed with all her heart Jesus' teaching that when we help one another, we are also loving and serving Jesus!

Thank You, God, for Mother Teresa!

? Want to know more? See August 4, "Why Did Christians Invent Orphanages and Hospitals?" and November 1, "What Is All Saints' Day?"

Who Is J. R. R. Tolkien?

We have sufferings now. But the sufferings we have now are
nothing compared to the great glory that will be given to us.
—ROMANS 8:18

John Ronald Reuel Tolkien was a brilliant scholar, poet, and author
born in 1892. He wrote wonderful books such as *The Hobbit* and The Lord
of the Rings trilogy. He was also a devout Christian who loved Jesus.

Tolkien was just three years old when his father died, and with the
tragic death of his mother at age twelve, he and his little brother became
orphans. As a young man, Tolkien fought for the English in the terrible
trench warfare of World War I, where nearly all his friends died. Despite
so much sadness and suffering, Tolkien never lost his faith. After the
war, he became a professor of Old English at Oxford University, where
he became best friends with fellow scholar and writer C. S. Lewis. In
their literary group called the Inklings, they talked about their works in
progress. They encouraged each other's writing—and Tolkien encouraged Lewis to renew his relationship with God. When they first met,
Lewis had lost his faith in God. But after many long, deep talks with his
good and faithful friend, Lewis asked Jesus into his heart.

Thank You, God, for J. R. R. Tolkien!

? Want to know more? See November 3, "Who Is C. S. Lewis?";
November 15, "How Do I Tell a Friend About Jesus?"; and
December 19 and 20, "What Is the Christmas Miracle of 1914?
(Parts 1 and 2)."

Who Is Corrie ten Boom?

You are my hiding place. You protect me from my
troubles. You fill me with songs of salvation.
—Psalm 32:7

Cornelia "Corrie" ten Boom was born in 1892 in the Netherlands. She and her family are famous for helping save approximately eight hundred Jews from the Nazi Holocaust of World War II. *Holocaust* means "destruction or slaughter on a mass scale." This was a terrible time in human history, from 1933 to 1945, when Adolf Hitler's Nazi Germany and its allies killed approximately eleven million people, including six million Jews.

The ten Booms were a close-knit family who loved Jesus. They lived above their watch shop on a busy city street. In 1940, German Nazis began hunting down Jewish Dutch citizens. Risking their lives, the ten Booms built a tiny, closet-sized secret room as a hiding place for Jews trying to escape. Corrie also organized a network of secret "safe houses" throughout Holland.

In 1944, the Nazis raided the ten Booms' home and arrested the family, sending them first to prison, and then to terrible Nazi work and concentration camps. Only Corrie survived. After the war she devoted herself to helping Holocaust survivors and sharing the love of Jesus around the world. You can read her amazing story in her book *The Hiding Place*, which I highly recommend!

Thank You, God, for Corrie ten Boom!

Who Is Billy Graham?

Before [people] can believe in the Lord, they must hear about him.
And for them to hear about the Lord, someone must tell them.
—ROMANS 10:14

Born in 1918, in North Carolina, William Franklin "Billy" Graham Jr. is one of the world's best-known Christian evangelists and authors. The word *evangelist* means "bearer of good news." A Christian evangelist shares the good news of Jesus Christ. It's thought that through his radio broadcasts, televised preaching, revivals, and books, Billy Graham has touched more than a billion human hearts with the love of Jesus! Isn't that amazing?

At the time of this writing, Billy Graham is nearly one hundred years old. His body is frail, but his faith is as strong as ever. He reads his Bible and prays every day. He misses his wife, Ruth, who passed away years ago. When he dies, he will be missed by his family and so many people he has helped. But he is not afraid of death. This is because he knows his sins have been forgiven, and his life will continue in heaven with God. When asked how he could be sure about this, he famously replied: "I've read the last page of the Bible. It's all going to turn out all right."

Thank You, God, for Billy Graham!

? **Want to know more?** See December 12, "Will I See My Pet in Heaven?"

Who Is Harriet Tubman?

"This is what the Lord says: Let my people go."
—Exodus 8:1

No one knows the date of Harriet Tubman's birth, because she was born to enslaved parents in Maryland, sometime between 1820 and 1825. This was a terrible time in American history, when slavery was still legal in most southern states.

In 1849, after she escaped slavery and found freedom in Pennsylvania, Harriet Tubman became a leading abolitionist prior to the Civil War. An *abolitionist* works to *abolish*, or put an end to, slavery. Tubman is best known for being "conductor" of the Underground Railroad, a network of secret "safe houses" that led hundreds of people from slavery to freedom in northern states. In fact, Tubman was so good at freeing people, she was nicknamed "Moses."

Her devout Christian faith kept her strong and brave. Tubman worked for the Union Army as a cook and nurse during the Civil War, and eventually she became an armed scout and spy! She was the first woman to lead an armed mission in U.S. military history, freeing more than seven hundred slaves. In 2016, it was decided that she would be the first woman to appear on U.S. money, replacing President Andrew Jackson on a newly designed twenty-dollar bill.

Thank You, God, for Harriet Tubman!

? Want to know more? See May 23, "Who Is Moses?" and November 2, "Who Is William Wilberforce?"

Who Is Fred Rogers? (Part 1)

Let all men see that you are gentle and kind.
—PHILIPPIANS 4:5

Born in Pennsylvania in 1928, Fred Rogers is best known for his beloved children's TV show, *Mister Rogers' Neighborhood*, which ran from 1968 to 2001. This great songwriter, puppeteer, and author loved Jesus with all his heart. In fact, he was an ordained Presbyterian minister! But instead of preaching, Fred wanted to use his gifts to show children God's love. He's still remembered for what he told his young viewers at the end of every TV show: "There's no person in the whole world like you, and I like you just the way you are." This unconditional love is how God feels about all His children—including *you*!

Years ago, I got to meet Fred Rogers. He was just the same as he was on TV—patient, gentle, kind, and soft-spoken. He carried his puppets with him in a brown leather briefcase!

Over the years, Fred Rogers received countless awards, including the Presidential Medal of Freedom. His trademark cardigan sweater is displayed in the Smithsonian museum in Washington, DC, as a "Treasure of American History." But most of all, he's forever treasured for his tender love, concern, and respect for children.

Thank You, God, for Fred Rogers!

? Want to know more? See April 29, "How Can I Discover My God-Given Gifts and Talents?" and November 10, "Who Is Fred Rogers? (Part 2)."

Who Is Fred Rogers? (Part 2)

"God does not see the same way people see. People look at the outside of a person, but the Lord looks at the heart."
—1 SAMUEL 16:7

When I met Fred Rogers, I asked him why he always ended his TV show, *Mister Rogers' Neighborhood*, by looking straight into the camera and saying to children watching: "There's no person in the whole world like you, and I like you just the way you are." Smiling, he told me how when he was a little boy, his favorite person in the whole world was his grandfather, who lived on a big farm surrounded by stone walls. More than anything, Fred wanted to climb those walls. But his mom and aunts always said, "No! You can't climb the stone walls! You'll get dirty! You'll hurt yourself!" But one day Fred's grandpa said to the fussy women, "Leave the boy alone. Let him go." Then he turned to Fred and said, "Come see me when you get back." So Fred climbed the stone walls. He got dirty. He skinned his knee. He tore his pants! When he got back, he thought for sure he was in *big* trouble. But his grandpa didn't scold him. Instead, he looked Fred in the eye and said, "Always remember: There's just one person in the whole world like you—and I like you just the way you are." And then he gave Fred a big hug.

> *Thank You, God, for loving me just the way I am.*

? **Want to know more?** See January 16, "When God Looks at Me, What Does He See?" and July 30, "Does God Stop Loving Me When I Sin?"

Who Is Madeleine L'Engle?

*Beautiful words fill my mind. I am speaking of royal
things. My tongue is like the pen of a skilled writer.*
—Psalm 45:1

Born in New York City in 1918, Madeleine L'Engle is an American author best known for her young adult fiction, especially the book *A Wrinkle in Time*. She also deeply loved Jesus.

L'Engle loved to explore big scientific ideas about the universe, planets, space, and time—and she wove faith and science together in her stories. As a writer, she respected her young readers. She said, "A child will often understand scientific concepts that would baffle an adult. You have to write the book that wants to be written. And if the book will be too difficult for grown-ups, then you write it for children!"

L'Engle received many awards throughout her eighty-eight years of life. In 2013, six years after her death, a crater on the planet Mercury was named in her honor! Isn't that amazing?

If you have not yet read any of Madeleine L'Engle's books, I whole-heartedly recommend that you do! A good place to start is her children's classic, *A Wrinkle in Time*. Happy reading!

Thank You, God, for Madeleine L'Engle!

? Want to know more? See December 11, "Can I Believe in Science and Still Believe in God?"; and December 30, "Is It Really Possible for Mountains and Trees to Sing?"

Who Is Eric Liddell?

So let us run the race that is before us and never give up.
—HEBREWS 12:1

Eric Liddell was a Scottish Olympic athlete who loved Jesus. He ran so fast his nickname was the "Flying Scotsman."

A devout Christian, Liddell became famous in the 1924 Summer Olympic Games when he refused to run on a Sunday. For Liddell, Sunday was the Lord's day—a day set aside for prayer and worship. This disqualified him from the race he was best at. Instead, he had to run a longer race, which *no one* expected him to win. But he did! Liddell gave God the glory for his gold medal. "I believe God made me for a purpose," he grinned, "but He also made me fast."

Liddell later moved to China to be a Christian missionary and teacher. When World War II broke out, Liddell was put in a Japanese internment camp, where he grew sick and weak. But he never lost his faith. He helped and encouraged the elderly and children there, teaching about God's love. Sadly, Liddell died there shortly before the war ended. Liddell knew what it meant to live a powerful Christian life. The early part of his story is told in the excellent 1981 movie *Chariots of Fire*.

Thank You, God, for Eric Liddell!

? Want to know more? See January 14, "What Is the Kingdom of God?"; January 19, "Does God Ever Sleep?"; May 30, "What Are the Ten Commandments? (Part 2)"; and October 5, "Is It True to Be a Missionary You Have to Travel Far from Home?"

What Is a Hypocrite?

"Why do you notice the little piece of dust that is in your brother's eye, but you don't see the big piece of wood that is in your own eye? . . . You are a hypocrite!"
—LUKE 6:41–42

Did you know everyone has a blind spot? Here's a fun test to prove it:

Hold this page about one foot away. Close your left eye and look closely at the cross with your right eye. Slowly move the page toward your face. Keep your right eye focused on the cross. Eventually the spot will disappear. This is your blind spot! Just as our eyes have blind spots, our spirits can too. It can be easy to find fault in others and not so easy to see our own faults. A *hypocrite* is a person who says or thinks he is one way but behaves another way. It's someone who "doesn't practice what he preaches." There's a lot of wisdom in the old saying, "Never judge a man until you've walked a mile in his shoes." Jesus put it this way: "Don't criticize, and then you won't be criticized" (Matthew 7:1 TLB). When you feel tempted to judge or criticize someone, it helps to remember that God loves that person too. Ask God to help you see the person through His loving eyes. You may be surprised at what happens!

Help me, God, to see the good in others!

How Does God Want Me to Spend My Time?

Teach us how short our lives really are so that we may be wise.
—PSALM 90:12

One day at my church, the speaker held up a big jar and filled it with medium-sized rocks. She asked, "Is this jar full?" "Yes!" we all agreed. Then she shook a bowl of pebbles into the jar. They filled the gaps between the rocks. She asked, "Now is it full?" "Yes!" we said. Then she poured a cup of sand into the jar. It filled the tiny spaces. She asked, "*Now* is it full?" "Yes!" we replied, laughing with surprise.

The jar represents our lives, the speaker explained. Rocks are important things such as God, family, friends, church, school, and activities and interests that make life full and happy. Pebbles are less important things such as clothes and possessions. The sand is the small, really unimportant stuff, such as wasting time online and watching junky TV. Guess what? If the sand goes into the jar first, there's no room for the rocks or pebbles! In the same way, if we waste all our time on small stuff, we'll never have time for the good and important things. Because God loves us, He wants us to enjoy full and happy lives. This is possible when we use God's amazing and precious gift of time wisely.

> *Help me, God, to use Your gift of time wisely.*

? Want to know more? See January 1, "Who Invented Time?" and October 28, "Does It Matter to God How Much Time I Spend Online and Watching TV?"

How Do I Tell a Friend About Jesus?

"Don't worry about what you should say. Say the things God gives you to say at that time. It will not really be you speaking. It will be the Holy Spirit."
—MARK 13:11

If you think a friend might want to know more about Jesus, don't be shy. Speak right up! Just speak honestly, from your heart, and the Holy Spirit will take over. You could share: 1) how Jesus helps you every day; 2) how you were introduced to Jesus; and 3) what you love most about Jesus.

If your friend wants to ask Jesus into her heart, here's a simple prayer: *Jesus, I want to know you. I believe You are the Son of God and You died for my sins. Thank You for loving me so much. Now please come live in my heart. Amen.* If your friend prays this prayer, encourage her to share it with a grown-up who loves Jesus.

> *Thank You, God, for giving me just the right words when I talk about Jesus.*

? Want to know more? See April 13, "Who Is the Holy Spirit?"; September 5, "Is It True That God's Holy Spirit Can Help Me When I Pray?"; September 22, "Is It Okay for Me to Invite a Friend to Visit My Church?"; October 29, "Can I Have Friends Who Aren't Christians?"; and November 5, "Who Is J. R. R. Tolkien?"

Why Do People Have to Die?

There is a right time for everything. Everything on earth has its special season. There is a time to be born and a time to die.
—ECCLESIASTES 3:1–2

For human beings, death is part of the natural order of things. This is because all earthly living things, including our human bodies, are mortal. The word *mortal* means "subject to death."

This is not what God originally intended. The Bible teaches that because of the choices made by the first man and woman, Adam and Eve, sin and death came into the world (Romans 5:12). For every person there is "a time to be born and a time to die" (Ecclesiastes 3:2). Still, no one wants to die. Death is sad for the people left behind. Because it's mysterious, the thought of death can be scary.

Thanks to Jesus, you don't have to be sad or scared about death. Because you believe Jesus died for your sins and was raised from the dead, God promises that your sins are forgiven and you will live forever in heaven (John 3:16).

Why would God promise such a wonderful thing? Because He loves you.

Thank You, God, for sending Jesus to overcome sin and death.

? Want to know more? See July 28 and 29, "Who Are Adam and Eve, and How Did Sin Enter the World? (Parts 1 and 2)."

What Will Happen to Me When I Die?

No one has ever imagined what God has prepared for those who love him.
—1 CORINTHIANS 2:9

Death, in some ways, is a lot like birth. Picture an unborn baby, all snug and warm in his mother's womb. For that baby, the thought of being born might be pretty scary.

If the baby could talk, he might say, "What? Are you kidding? You want me to leave my safe, warm world for someplace I know nothing about? *No way!*" He might be sad or scared to go someplace new.

Think how hard it would be to explain to him how wonderful life is on Earth! How could you describe the brilliant colors of a rainbow? The taste of a chocolate ice cream cone? The sound of laughter? The excitement of Christmas Eve?

When your body dies, the Bible says that your soul joins Jesus and God and the angels in a wonderful new world called heaven. Heaven is a world that we, like an unborn baby, can hardly begin to imagine.

But we can try! What do you think heaven will be like?

> *Thank You, God, again, that death is not the end, but a new beginning.*

? Want to know more? See January 14, "What Is the Kingdom of God?"; March 25, "How Is Jesus' Resurrection Body Different from My Body?"; and December 1 and 2, "What Is Heaven Like? (Parts 1 and 2)."

Are There Really Angels? (Part 1)

An angel of the Lord came down from heaven. . . . He was shining as bright as lightning. His clothes were white as snow.
—MATTHEW 28:2–3

Yes, there really are angels. Thousands upon thousands of them (Hebrews 12:22)! The word *angel* means "messenger." The Bible says God created the angels to be His personal messengers on earth (Hebrews 1:14). Here are some more fun facts about these amazing heavenly creatures:

1) Angels worship and praise God (Hebrews 1:6); 2) Angels don't die (Luke 20:36); 3) Angels are often described as beings of light. Because they can be so bright (Matthew 28:3), angels are often pictured with golden halos around their heads. They don't have actual golden halos; 4) Because angels can appear and disappear so quickly, they are often pictured with wings (Judges 6:21; Luke 1:11–12). The Bible does not say they have wings; 5) Angels are very strong and powerful (2 Peter 2:11); and 6) Angels do not marry or have baby angels (Matthew 22:30).

Tomorrow we will learn more about angels, which are as real as you and me.

> *Thank You, God, for angels, Your heavenly messengers!*

Are There Really Angels? (Part 2)

Remember to welcome strangers into your homes. Some people have done this and have welcomed angels without knowing it.

—HEBREWS 13:2

Yesterday we learned how God created the angels—thousands upon thousands of them—to be His personal messengers on Earth. Here are more facts about these amazing heavenly creatures:

1) When angels appear to people, the first thing they often say is, "Don't be afraid!" (Judges 6:23). From this, we can assume that to see one of God's angels is awesome and frightening; 2) Sometimes, if it suits God's purposes, angels can appear as human beings (Hebrews 13:2); 3) In the Bible, two angels are given names: Gabriel and Michael. God sends the angel Gabriel to deliver important messages (Daniel 8:16; 9:21; Luke 1:19, 26). Michael is God's archangel (*ark*-angel) or "top-level" angel, who is a warrior for God (Revelation 12:7); 4) God's angels are watching over us (Hebrews 1:14); and 5) When Jesus returns to Earth in His resurrection body, He will come with many angels (Matthew 16:27).

Thank You, God, for all Your awesome angels busy at work.

? Want to know more? See April 9, "What Is the Second Coming of Christ?"

When I Die, Will I Become an Angel with a Halo and Wings?

But listen, I tell you this secret: We will not all die, but we will all be changed. It will only take a second. We will be changed as quickly as an eye blinks. This will happen when the last trumpet sounds. The trumpet will sound and those who have died will be raised to live forever. And we will all be changed.
—1 CORINTHIANS 15:51–52

Human beings and angels are both created by God. But human beings and angels are two very different kinds of creatures. Human beings have earthly, mortal bodies that die and eternal souls that live forever. Angels are eternal spiritual beings. They don't have bodies that die. Angels are already living with God in heaven.

Human beings do not become angels when their bodies die. Human beings get new bodies, like Jesus' resurrection body. Our resurrection bodies will never die. They are very special bodies designed to join God's holy angels in heaven (1 Corinthians 15:42).

Thank You, God, for Your promise that one day I will receive a new resurrection body and live forever with You and Jesus and all the angels in heaven!

? Want to know more? See March 25, "How Is Jesus' Resurrection Body Different from My Body?" and November 18, "Are There Really Angels? (Part 1)."

Is It True That I Have a Guardian Angel?

*He has put his angels in charge of you. They will
watch over you wherever you go.*

—PSALM 91:11

Jesus deeply loves and respects children. That's because He recognizes that children are born with the gift of faith. For kids, believing in God is as natural as breathing.

One day, people were bringing their children to Jesus to have Him bless them. But the disciples thought this was silly and told the people to go away. Big mistake!

"Don't think these little children are worth nothing," Jesus scolded them. "I tell you that they have angels in heaven who are always with my Father in heaven" (Matthew 18:10).

The Bible also promises that God "has put his angels in charge of you. They will watch over you wherever you go." So, yes, it is true that you have a guardian angel. You may have many!

Why does God command His angels to watch over you? Because He loves you.

Thank You, God, for so lovingly sending Your angels to watch over me!

? Want to know more? See March 8, "Why Does Jesus Love Children So Much?"

Are There Really Demons?

Not death, not life, not angels, not ruling spirits, nothing now, nothing in the future, no powers, nothing above us, nothing below us, or anything else in the whole world will ever be able to separate us from the love of God.
—Romans 8:38–39

Yes, there really are demons.

Human beings live in a physical world. We experience it through our physical senses: sight, touch, hearing, smell, and taste. But we're also surrounded by an invisible spiritual world, where God the Father, Jesus, God's Holy Spirit, and all God's holy angels exist. It is also a world where demons exist (Mark 1:34).

The word *demon* means "evil spirit." Angels are good. Demons are evil. Angels love God and all God's children. Demons hate God and all God's children. The leader of all the demons is Satan, who is a wicked angel. Throughout human history, God and His holy angels have been at war with Satan and his demons (Ephesians 6:12).

The good news is that thanks to Jesus, you don't need to fear Satan or his miserable demons (Romans 8:38–39). Jesus has won the battle of good over evil for all time!

Thank You, God, that nothing can separate me from Your great love.

? Want to know more? See January 14, "What Is the Kingdom of God?"; February 5, "Who Is Jesus?"; and February 18, "Why Did Jesus Come to Earth?"

Is the Devil Real? (Part 1)

How you are fallen from heaven, O Lucifer, son of the morning! How you are cut down to the ground, you who weakened the nations!
—ISAIAH 14:12 NKJV

Yes, the devil is real. Today he is known as Satan.

No one knows for sure how Satan came to be. Many biblical scholars believe he started out as one of God's archangels named Lucifer. Lucifer was the most beautiful and strongest of all God's creatures in heaven. But Lucifer didn't want to obey God. He wanted to be worshipped like God. Lucifer's sinful jealousy turned to anger and hatred. So Lucifer rebelled and took as many as one-third of heaven's angels with him to serve as his demons (Revelation 12:4).

Lucifer is Satan. He tricked Adam and Eve into sinning, and he is still busy causing trouble in the world today. In the Bible, Satan is also called a dragon, a serpent, and the devil (Revelation 12:9).

The word *devil* means "liar." The word *Satan* means "enemy" or "accuser."

Tomorrow we'll learn more about this wicked being. We'll also learn good news about God's all-powerful love!

Thank You, God, for all Your goodness.

? Want to know more? See July 28 and 29, "Who Are Adam and Eve, and How Did Sin Enter the World? (Parts 1 and 2)."

Is the Devil Real? (Part 2)

And the devil, who deceived them, was thrown into the lake of burning sulfur . . . tormented day and night forever and ever.
—Revelation 20:10 NIV

Know this: Satan is nothing more than a furious, wicked angel. Still, Satan and his demons can cause much heartache and misery. Satan is not only evil; he is very cunning and tricky.

Jesus called Satan "a liar" and "the father of lies" (John 8:44). The apostle Peter warned, "Control yourselves and be careful! The devil is your enemy. And he goes around like a roaring lion looking for someone to eat" (1 Peter 5:8). *Yikes!*

The war Satan started between good and evil will continue until the day Jesus returns to earth with God's holy angels (Mark 8:38). Thanks to the Bible, we know how the story ends. God's goodness, truth, justice, and peace *triumph*, or win. Satan and his demons will not go unpunished. In truth, thanks to Jesus, the battle between good and evil has already been won! Even though we struggle with troubles and sin, with Jesus living in our hearts we are "more than conquerors" (Romans 8:37 NIV). This is very good news!

> *Thank You, God, that thanks to Jesus, the war between good and evil has already been won.*

? Want to know more? See April 9, "What Is the Second Coming of Christ?" and December 5, "If God Is All-Loving and All-Powerful, Why Does He Allow Evil to Exist?"

Is Hell Real? (Part 1)

*"Depart from me, you who are cursed, into the eternal
fire prepared for the devil and his angels."*
—MATTHEW 25:41 NIV

Yes, hell is real. Like heaven, hell is a spiritual dimension that exists outside our human experience of matter, time, and space. Like heaven, there are sometimes glimpses of hell on earth. When people commit terrible acts of cruelty and murder, we get a glimpse of hell on earth. Destruction and death caused by natural disasters also give us glimpses of hell. The word *hell* means "the underworld." The Bible teaches that hell is the final dwelling place for Satan, his demons, and the souls of human beings who choose to reject God's love. It's an experience of unending physical pain and torment (Revelation 20:10). But even worse, hell is a place of eternal separation from God and His love. It is a place of unbearable, endless emotional pain. No doubt about it, this is very bad news. But not to worry! Tomorrow we'll learn the answer to the problem of hell. Here's a hint: it's very *good* news!

> *Thank You, God, for Your promise that nothing
> can separate me from Your love.*

? Want to know more? See January 14, "What Is the Kingdom of
God?"; December 1 and 2, "What Is Heaven Like? (Parts 1 and
2)"; and December 5, "If God Is All-Loving and All-Powerful,
Why Does He Allow Evil to Exist?"

Is Hell Real? (Part 2)

God demonstrates his own love for us in this: While
we were still sinners, Christ died for us.
—ROMANS 5:8 NIV

Yesterday we learned that hell is real. This is a problem. But God has given us a solution to the problem of hell, and it's very good news!

When God's Son, Jesus, was on the cross, He suffered for all the sins of everyone in the world. He experienced hell *for* us. His physical pain was terrible. But the emotional pain Jesus suffered was far worse. As Jesus was dying on the cross, the thought of being separated forever from His Father was terrifying. He cried out, "My God, my God, why have you left me alone?" (Matthew 27:46).

But in the end, God did not leave Jesus. God raised Jesus from the dead! Thanks to God's great love, when you die, you will not experience hell. Because God sent His Son, Jesus, to die for your sins, and because you love Jesus, you will one day be with Him in heaven.

Why would God do such a wonderful thing? Because He loves you.

> *Thank You, God, that because You did not*
> *leave Jesus, You will not leave me.*

? **Want to know more?** See March 14, "Why Did Jesus Have to Die?" and March 18 and 19, "What Are the Seven Sayings of Jesus on the Cross? (Parts 1 and 2)."

What Kind of Holiday Is Thanksgiving?

Come into his city with songs of thanksgiving. . . .
Thank him, and praise his name.
—PSALM 100:4

Thanksgiving Day is a national holiday celebrated in America on the fourth Thursday of November. The word *thanksgiving* comes from an Old English word that means "gratitude." Many cultures celebrate similar holidays. That's because God has planted thankfulness as a gift in our hearts.

America's first Thanksgiving was a celebration held by the Pilgrim settlers in 1621, in Plymouth, Massachusetts. The Pilgrims were English Christians seeking religious freedom in the New World. Life was hard, food was scarce, and many died. But the faithful Pilgrims understood that even in hardship, we still have God's gift of thankfulness to make our hearts happy.

In 1863, when America was suffering as never before with the terrible Civil War, President Abraham Lincoln still declared Thanksgiving an official national holiday. He knew what the Pilgrims knew: Thankfulness is a gift from God. Everything we have is a gift from our loving God (James 1:17). One way to feel truly thankful—even during hard times—is to count our blessings.

Thank You, God, for all Your many gifts!

What Does It Mean to Count My Blessings?

*"I will open the windows of heaven for you and
pour out all the blessings you need."*
—MALACHI 3:10

When I was little, I remember my mom saying, "Whenever I'm feeling blue, I count my blessings." What is a blessing? It's anything that fills your heart with delight and gratitude. Of course no one is happy all the time. Because we're human, we all sometimes feel blue, and happiness and joy seem very far away. That's the time to count your blessings. It fills your heart with thankfulness! One good way to count your blessings is to make a list. Here are ten blessings to get you started. Once you make your own list, you might discover that you have many more. Happy counting!

- I'm alive!
- God is real!
- God loves me!
- God has a special, unique purpose for my life!
- Jesus is real!
- God's Holy Spirit is real!
- Angels are real!
- Heaven is real!
- The Bible is true!
- God hears and answers my prayers!

Thank You, God, for all the many blessings!

? **Want to know more?** See January 3, "Who Is God?"; February 5, "Who Is Jesus?"; April 13, "Who Is the Holy Spirit?"; and May 5, "How Do I Know the Bible Is True?"

What Is Advent?

The virgin will be pregnant. She will have a son, and they will
name him "Immanuel." This name means "God is with us."
—MATTHEW 1:23

Perhaps you can feel the excitement in the air. Christmas is coming! Carols and holiday songs are being played on the radio. Stores are decorated with wreaths and colorful lights. It is a season of anticipation. For Christians, there is an even deeper excitement about Christmas and what it means for the world and all the people in it—including *you*!

Advent is the season that captures this deep excitement and marks the beginning of the Christian church year. Advent begins four Sundays before Christmas and ends on Christmas Eve. The word *advent* means "coming" or "arrival."

Advent is a time when Christians remember that God sent His only Son, Jesus, to earth as a human baby (Luke 2:1–20). Advent is a time when Christians prepare their hearts for Christmas and remember God's great love.

Thank You, God, for the season of Advent!
Prepare my heart to celebrate Jesus.

? Want to know more? See February 8, "How Did Jesus Get His Name?"; February 11, "What Is the *Song of Mary*?"; and February 18, "Why Did Jesus Come to Earth?"

What Is an Advent Wreath?

God once said, "Let the light shine out of the darkness!"
—2 CORINTHIANS 4:6

To celebrate the season of Advent, some Christians make a table-top wreath of evergreens with five candles. Since ancient times, holiday wreaths have been made by twisting evergreen branches into a circular shape. Because it has no beginning and no end, the circle symbolizes eternity. The color green stands for God's everlasting life. Candlelight is a symbol of Jesus' victory over the darkness of evil, sin, and death. It's also a symbol of Jesus' love, which shines in our hearts (Romans 5:5).

The Advent wreath has four candles on the outside, three purple and one pink, and a white candle in the middle.

The three purple candles symbolize hope, peace, and love. They are lit on the first, second, and fourth Sundays of Advent. The pink candle symbolizes joy. It's lit on the third Sunday of Advent. The fifth candle is white and stands tall in the middle of the Advent wreath. It symbolizes Jesus, and it is lit on Christmas Day. It's like a birthday candle for Jesus!

As Christmas approaches, thank You, God,
for filling my heart with light!

? **Want to know more?** See April 1, "Why Do We Light Candles on Easter?" and October 22, "What Does It Mean to Be the 'Salt and Light' of the World?"

DECEMBER

What Is Heaven Like? (Part I)

He will wipe away every tear from their eyes. There will be no more
death, sadness, crying, or pain. All the old ways are gone.
—REVELATION 21:4

Heaven is another word for the kingdom of God. Heaven has existed since before the creation of Earth and humans. Heaven is a spiritual dimension that exists mostly outside our human experience of time, matter, and space. Still, every minute, heaven breaks through and touches Earth and its people in ways large and small. Through God's Holy Spirit, we carry heaven in our hearts.

Heaven is home for God the Father, Jesus, God's Holy Spirit, God's angels, and all humans who know and love God. Heaven is *your* eternal home (2 Corinthians 5:1)! Another word for heaven is *paradise*, which comes from a Greek word meaning "garden." The apostle John said one day there will be a "new heaven and new earth" (Revelation 21:1), where God and humans will laugh and sing, eat and drink, work, play, and worship together. The Bible tells us heaven is a wonderful place full of love, peace, forgiveness, and joy. In heaven there is no more death or sadness. And that's just the beginning! Tomorrow we'll learn more.

Thank You, God, for heaven!

? Want to know more? See January 14, "What Is the Kingdom of God?"; April 13, "Who Is the Holy Spirit?"; August 17, "What Is the Lord's Prayer? (Part 3)"; and November 17, "What Will Happen to Me When I Die?"

What Is Heaven Like? (Part 2)

*We know that our body—the tent we live in here on earth—will be
destroyed. But when that happens, God will have a house for us.*
—2 CORINTHIANS 5:1

Here is very exciting news about heaven: God promises that one day,
like Jesus, we will get brand-new heavenly bodies! Here on earth, our
human bodies aren't designed to last forever. Over time they get old and
wear out, get hurt, sick, and die. But our human souls never die. And
in heaven our souls will be wrapped in very special resurrection bodies that will never get sick, never feel pain, and never get old. They are
bodies that will laugh and sing, eat and drink, work and play, love, and
worship God. Best of all, our new heavenly bodies will live forever (1
Peter 1:23)! Isn't that amazing?

Through God's Holy Spirit living in our hearts, we can also glimpse
heaven on earth. Heaven is the way it feels in our hearts when we love
another person. It's the way it feels when we know deep down inside that
we are loved back. How wonderful heaven is (1 Corinthians 2:9)!

*Thank You, God, for the gift of heaven and for
the future gift of my resurrection body!*

? Want to know more? See March 21, "What Is the Resurrection
of Jesus?"; March 22, "Why Is the Resurrection of Jesus So
Important?"; March 23 and 24, "How Can I Know for Sure That
Jesus Really Was Resurrected? (Parts 1 and 2)"; and March 25,
"How Is Jesus' Resurrection Body Different from My Body?"

How Is It Possible for God to Truly Love Billions of Different People?

*"Can a mother forget her little child? . . . Yet even
if that should be, I will not forget you."*
—ISAIAH 49:15 TLB

I asked Dr. Bill Wilson, a world-famous psychiatrist who also loved Jesus, today's question. "Good question!" He grew thoughtful. "When I was training to be a doctor," he said, "I delivered many babies. One thing amazed me. No matter how long a mother is in labor, no matter how painful, the first thing she wants after giving birth is to see and hold her baby. This is because a new mother loves her child instinctively. It doesn't matter if it is her first, second, fifth, or twelfth child." Dr. Wilson smiled. "It's hard to imagine a love so strong. But here's the truth: God's love for us is even stronger! We are His children, and He knows and loves each one of us unconditionally—like a new mother."

How is it possible for God to truly love His billions of children in the world? Because God invented love. In fact, God *is* love (1 John 4:8). As our perfect heavenly Father, He loves each of us with an eternal love that never runs out.

> Thank You, God, for Your endless fountain of love for Your children!

? Want to know more? See January 3, "Who Is God?" and January 4, "If God Is My Creator, How Is He Different from My Parents?"

If God Truly Loves People, Why Do Bad Things Happen?

Now we see as if we are looking into a dark mirror. But at that time, in the future, we shall see clearly.
—1 CORINTHIANS 13:12

Bad things happen because the world is not the way God originally created it. In the Garden of Eden, there was no human pain, suffering, or death. But Adam and Eve chose to sin, and now the world and all the people in it are broken. For now, pain, suffering, and death are part of being human. But God is good. The Bible says, "God is love" (1 John 4:8). God is perfect. We are not. God sees all of human history from heaven, which is outside our experience of time and space. We can only see here and now. For now, there are many things about God we cannot understand. But because we trust God, we can accept His mysteries. One day, God will let us see clearly. But until that day, bad things will happen. Even though bad things still happen, God promises to help you through them. He hears your prayers, He watches over you, He loves you, and He promises that one day you will live with Him forever.

Thank You, God, for hearing my prayers and helping me when bad things happen.

? Want to know more? See January 20, "What Are Some of God's Promises for Me?"; July 28 and 29, "Who Are Adam and Eve, and How Did Sin Enter the World? (Parts 1 and 2)"; and August 3, "What Is Christian Hope?"

If God Is All-Loving and All-Powerful, Why Does He Allow Evil to Exist?

Trust the Lord with all your heart. Don't depend on your own understanding.
—PROVERBS 3:5

There are many things about God that we cannot understand. Today's question is one of God's biggest mysteries. Let's face it. God sure seems to be taking His time fulfilling some of His promises—especially His promise of a "new heaven and a new earth" (Revelation 21:1), where evil no longer exists. But then, in God's kingdom "one day is like a thousand years, and a thousand years is like one day" (2 Peter 3:8)! What we know is God is good. God hates evil. God is not a destroyer. God is a life-giver. God didn't come to Earth in a terrifying show of power. God came as a humble, helpless human baby. Maybe this is because God doesn't want us to run away from Him in fear, but run toward His loving open arms with total trust.

Thank You, God, that there is no question too hard for You!

? Want to know more? See January 14, "What Is the Kingdom of God?"; February 18, "Why Did Jesus Come to Earth?"; August 3, "What Is Christian Hope?"; December 4, "If God Truly Loves People, Why Do Bad Things Happen?"; and December 28, "Is It Okay to Question and Sometimes Have Doubts About God?"

Why Do People Hurt Other People?

"Love your enemies. Pray for those who hurt you."
—Matthew 5:44

Human beings are not perfect. People hurt other people for many reasons. Sometimes they're afraid or sick or sad. Sometimes people hurt others because they've been hurt themselves.

When I was little, I had a beautiful boxer named Roxie. Roxie belonged to another family before us. They used to go away on long trips and lock poor Roxie in their cold, dark basement. Scared and lonely, Roxie hated it!

A few months after Roxie came to live with us, we had to go away on a trip. The minute Roxie saw my suitcase, she looked at me with panicky eyes and ran away! It took my dad an hour to catch her. I loved Roxie, and it hurt my feelings that she ran away. Did it mean she didn't love me? My dad explained that the reason Roxie ran away was because she had been hurt by her other owner. She just didn't want to be hurt again.

There is a lot of wisdom in the old saying: "Be kind. For everyone you meet is carrying a heavy burden." People hurt one another; it is true. People are not perfect. But we can always pray and try to show one another love and kindness (John 13:34–35).

> *God, please help me to be kind and understanding and to pray for others.*

How Can Anything Good Come Out of Pain and Suffering?

[Jesus] had much pain and suffering. . . . But he took
our suffering on him and felt our pain for us.
—ISAIAH 53:3–4

Everyone experiences pain and suffering in life. God doesn't cause pain and suffering. But God can turn it into something beautiful, valuable, and good. Think of a pearl, for instance. A pearl starts as a bit of sand that gets trapped in an oyster. The sand scratches and irritates the oyster, so it reacts by covering the sand with layers of protective coating. Over time, the sand becomes a beautiful pearl! Sometimes we can have a difficult person in our lives. When we cover the person with layers of love and prayers, he doesn't irritate us as much. The person may even become a beautiful friend! The best example of God turning pain and suffering into something beautiful and good is when God resurrected Jesus from His death on the cross. Because Jesus rose from the dead and received a resurrection body that can live forever in heaven, one day we will too! Remember: God can turn *anything* into something beautiful and good.

Thank You, God, that You can turn anything, even pain
and suffering, into something beautiful and good.

? **Want to know more?** See July 3, "What Is the Thorn in Paul's Flesh?"; October 23, "How Is It Possible to Be Weak and Strong at the Same Time?"; and December 13, "How Is It Possible to Experience Joy in Life's Troubles?"

Is It True That Knowing Jesus Is the Only Way to Know God?

*"I am the way. And I am the truth and the life. The
only way to the Father is through me."*

—JOHN 14:6

God is everywhere. Even when people have never heard about Jesus, they can know God as their Creator through the beauty of nature and the miracle of life. That's why thousands of years ago the psalmist David wrote: "The heavens tell the glory of God. And the skies announce what his hands have made" (Psalm 19:1). Isn't that beautiful?

But there's an even deeper way of knowing God: through Jesus. Jesus said, "If you really knew me, then you would know my Father, too" (John 14:7).

Yes, it's true that the only way to know God as our personal loving Daddy, *Abba* or Father, is through knowing His Son, Jesus. Knowing Jesus is God's way for us to understand who He really is. Knowing Jesus is God's way for us to experience firsthand the power of His forgiveness and love (John 3:16; 14:7).

> *Thank You, Father God, for sending Your Son, Jesus, to
> show me who You really are and how much You love
> the world and all the people in it—including me!*

? **Want to know more?** See February 17, "What Makes Jesus So Important?" and February 18, "Why Did Jesus Come to Earth?"

Do People Who Have Never Heard of Jesus Go to Heaven Too?

"I give you a new command: Love each other. You must love each other as I have loved you."
—JOHN 13:34

Not everyone has heard the good news about God's Son, Jesus. Many people lived and died before Jesus was born. Even today, with TV and the Internet, millions of people still haven't heard about Jesus. We know from the Bible that God is perfect in every way—He's loving, wise, fair, and good. God knows the heart of every human. We can trust Him to make the right choice about who does or doesn't go to heaven, including those who have never heard of Jesus. God does *not* want you to worry about who gets to go to heaven. But you can *do* something about it!

You can: 1) Love God and love others; 2) Do your best to live a life that pleases God; 3) Read God's holy Word, the Bible; 4) Share with others the good news about Jesus; 5) Pray for the world and all the people in it . . . Then, when you meet your Father God in heaven, He'll wrap His big, strong arms around you and say, "Well done!" (see Matthew 25:23).

Thank You, dear God, for being wonderful, amazing, and loving!

? Want to know more? See November 15, "How Do I Tell a Friend About Jesus?"

Does God Still Love People Who Choose Not to Believe in Him?

"While the son was still a long way off, his father saw him coming. . . .
So the father ran to him, and hugged and kissed him."
—LUKE 15:20

Yes, God loves all His human children, whether they believe in Him or not. That's because God is a loving Father (Matthew 5:45). Nothing will make God stop loving us. Yet when a person chooses not to believe in Him, it makes God *very* sad.

But God never gives up. Because He is a loving Father, God waits patiently for His children to return to Him. Day and night, He looks for them, watching and waiting (Luke 15:11–32). How happy God is when a lost child returns! The Bible says that angels sing and all of heaven rejoices (Luke 15:10).

Here's good news: it is never too late to come home to God. Never! You can be ten years old or one hundred years old. God is always waiting with open arms for His children to come to Him.

Why? Because God is love (1 John 4:8).

> *Thank You, God, for always welcoming Your*
> *children home—including me!*

? **Want to know more?** See September 29 and 30, "What Is the Amazing Story Behind 'Amazing Grace'? (Parts 1 and 2)."

Can I Believe in Science and Still Believe in God?

*"When the rainbow appears in the clouds, I will see it. Then
I will remember the agreement that continues forever. It is
between me [God] and every living thing on the earth."*
—Genesis 9:16

Yes, you can believe in science and still believe in God. The Bible was
not written by modern-day scientists. In fact, back in the days of the
Bible, science as we know it didn't even exist! People didn't know about
things such as the solar system, or gravity, or atoms, or germs! God
created our universe. Science is the ongoing effort of human beings to
understand how God's creation works. My science teacher friend who
also loves Jesus says, "When I look at a rainbow, science tells me that I
am looking at white light hitting tiny water droplets in the air. But being
a person of faith, I can also say, 'Thank You, God, for creating such a
beautiful rainbow!' I remember how the rainbow is a symbol of God's
love." Science can tell you what life is made of. But science cannot tell
you what life is for. Only God, who loves you, can do that.

Thank You, God, for science!

? Want to know more? See May 3, "How Did We Get the Bible?"; May
5, "How Do I Know the Bible Is True?"; May 10, "Was There Really
a Flood During the Time of Noah?"; and September 27, "Is It True
That an Astronaut Celebrated Communion on the Moon?"

Will I See My Pet in Heaven?

Then wolves will live in peace with lambs. . . .
And a little child will lead them.
—ISAIAH 11:6

The Bible is very clear about our future home in heaven (John 3:16). But when it comes to animals, the Bible is a little less clear. We do know that humans and animals are deeply connected, because we share the same loving Creator God. Our pets are very special creatures, and we are all members of God's family of creation. Like Noah and the animals in the ark, we're all in the same boat!

To love an animal is a good and beautiful thing. What happens to the love we feel for our pets? The Bible says love never ends (1 Corinthians 13:8). It also promises, "No mere man has ever seen, heard or even imagined what wonderful things God has ready for those who love the Lord" (1 Corinthians 2:8–10 TLB). Evangelist Billy Graham says, "God will prepare everything for our perfect happiness in heaven, and if it takes my dog being there, I believe he'll be there."

Will you see your pet in heaven? What do you think?

Thank You, God, for loving Your great, big, beautiful family of creation!

? **Want to know more?** See May 10, "Was There Really a Flood During the Time of Noah?"; November 7, "Who Is Billy Graham?"; and December 1 and 2, "What Is Heaven Like? (Parts 1 and 2)."

How Is It Possible to Experience Joy in Life's Troubles?

You know that [many kinds of troubles] are testing
your faith. And this will give you patience.
—JAMES 1:2–3

In the 1800s, cod was the most popular fish in America. It was nutritious and tasty—but only when fresh! People tried shipping live cod in big saltwater tanks. But when the fish arrived, their long period of inactivity in the tanks made them taste yucky and mushy. One day a catfish slipped into one of the cod tanks. The catfish is the cod's natural enemy. During the trip, he chased the cod. All that swimming made the cod fit, healthy—and *yummy*! From then on, a pesky catfish was included in every shipping tank of cod. Just like the cod, we all have catfish in our lives. The catfish are our troubles! They nip at us and keep us awake at night. But when we turn to God in prayer, our pesky troubles—like catfish—can make us spiritually healthier and stronger! This is because when we talk to God, our faith grows. When our faith grows, we become more trusting and joyful—and better at being God's helpers!

> Thank You, God, for turning my troubles into
> spiritual health and strength.

? Want to know more? See July 3, "What Is the Thorn in Paul's Flesh?"

Who Are the Magi?

After Jesus was born, some wise men from the east came to Jerusalem.
—Matthew 2:1

Traditional Christmas cards, carols, and pageants suggest that the Magi were three wise kings. But the Bible tells a slightly different story!

It is true that the Magi (*may*-jye) were wise men who followed a star on a long journey to Bethlehem. The word *magi* is the plural form of *magus*, a Latin word meaning "sorcerer." But Bible scholars think they were actually educated priests who were not Jewish, but who recognized that Jesus was God's promised *Messiah* or "anointed one."

There were at least two Magi, but there may have been more—perhaps many more! The Bible doesn't mention their names, or any camels either. The Bible doesn't say Jesus was in the manger when they arrived. The Gospel writer Matthew says that Jesus was a "child" at home with His mother (Matthew 2:11). Maybe Jesus was walking and talking, and when the Magi gave Him their gifts of gold, frankincense, and myrrh, He clapped His little hands and laughed with delight! Maybe Mary said, "Now, Jesus. what do you say?" If this happened, I imagine Jesus said, "Thank you!"

Thank You, God, for the good and wise Magi.

? Want to know more? See January 6, "What Is Epiphany?" and December 16, "Was There Really a Star of Bethlehem?"

DECEMBER 15

Why Did the Magi Present Jesus with Gifts of Gold, Frankincense, and Myrrh?

They opened the gifts they brought for him. They gave him treasures of gold, frankincense, and myrrh.
—MATTHEW 2:11

These three costly items were used as gifts to honor powerful kings and *deities*, or pagan gods. Imagine how grateful and yet confused Mary and Joseph must have been by the Magi's arrival at their home with such special gifts. These gifts have deeply prophetic and symbolic meanings:

- *Gold* is a gift for kings, and Jesus is the King of kings (John 18:36; Revelation 1:5).
- *Frankincense* means "high-quality incense." Incense in Jesus' day was burned in the Jewish temple by priests as a symbol of their prayers going up to God (Psalm 141:2). Jesus is our one true Priest (Psalm 110:4).
- *Myrrh* means "bitter." It was burned as incense, too, but was also used in the oil priests used to anoint God's holy prophets. In addition, myrrh was used in preparing bodies for burial. This bitter gift foreshadowed Jesus' suffering and death on the cross (Mark 15:23; John 19:40).

Many years passed before Mary and Joseph understood the deep meaning of these special gifts for Jesus.

Thank You, God, for inspiring the Magi to give such perfect gifts!

Was There Really a Star of Bethlehem?

[The Magi] saw the same star they had seen in the east. It went
before them until it stopped above the place where the child was.
—MATTHEW 2:9–10

Yes, there really was a star of Bethlehem. The Bible tells us that the Magi followed a star to Bethlehem in search of the Messiah.

Was the star of Bethlehem a sparkling meteor? A long-tailed comet? A brilliant supernova? In his book *The Christmas Sky*, astronomer Dr. Franklyn M. Branley suggests that the light in the heavens during Jesus' birth may have been one or more very unusual "wandering stars," or what we now know to be planets!

Like many biblical scholars, Dr. Branley believes that Jesus was probably born not in December, but in the springtime, sometime between 8 BC and 4 BC. Today astronomers know how long it takes each planet to orbit the sun, so they can figure out the position of each planet in the sky at any time in human history. They can figure out precisely which "wandering stars" appeared above the horizon at the time of Jesus' birth! Isn't that amazing?

> *Thank You, God, for the mystery and wonder*
> *of Your beautiful star of Bethlehem.*

? Want to know more? See February 6, "When Was Jesus Born?" and December 25, "Is December 25 Really Jesus' Birthday?"

What Is a Christmas Crèche?

*The shepherds went quickly and found Mary and Joseph. And
the shepherds saw the baby lying in a feeding box.*
—LUKE 2:16–17

One of the most popular decorations at Christmastime is a table-top crèche, or nativity scene. The French word *crèche* (kresh) means "crib," meaning the manger or feeding trough where the newborn baby Jesus lay. The word *nativity* comes from the Latin *nativus*, which means "arisen by birth."

Saint Francis of Assisi, Italy, is credited for creating the first nativity scene in 1223. He used actual people and live animals to re-create the birth of Jesus as recorded in the Gospels of Matthew and Luke. So we can thank Saint Francis for inventing the Christmas pageant too!

The simplest, most basic crèche includes the infant Jesus in a manger; His mother, Mary; and her husband, Joseph. Some nativity scenes also include angels, shepherds, sheep, donkeys, oxen, camels, and Magi. Nativity scenes come in all shapes and sizes. The best thing about them is how they capture our imagination and help us picture and think about the first Christmas when God sent His only Son, Jesus, to be born into the world.

Thank You, God, for the true-life story of Christmas!

? Want to know more? See February 7, "Why Was Jesus Born in a Stable?"

What Does *Gloria in Excelsis Deo* Mean?

All the angels were praising God, saying: "Give glory to God in heaven, and on earth let there be peace to the people who please God."
—LUKE 2:13–14

When I was a little girl, our Christmas crèche included a beautiful hand-painted plaster angel. When I was old enough, my mother let me carefully hang her above the baby Jesus, where she dangled from a silver ribbon—the finishing touch to our nativity scene. She carried a banner that read, "*Gloria in Excelsis Deo.*" I recognized the words from my all-time favorite Christmas carol, "Angels We Have Heard on High." I didn't know what the words meant, but I still felt like my heart would burst with joy whenever I sang them: "*Glo-o-o-o-o-O-o-o-o-o-O-o-o-o-o-O-ri-a, in ex-cel-sis De-o!*" At church, our choir director explained that it was Latin for "Glory to God in the highest!" which is what the angels proclaimed to the shepherds on the night Jesus was born. Here's the first verse for you to sing too!

> *Angels we have heard on high, Sweetly singing o'er the plains.*
> *And the mountains in reply, Echoing their joyous strains.*
> *Gloria, in excelsis Deo! Gloria, in excelsis Deo!*

Glory to God in the highest! Gloria in excelsis Deo!

? **Want to know more?** See November 18 and 19, "Are There Really Angels? (Parts 1 and 2)."

What Is the Christmas Miracle of 1914? (Part 1)

Grace and peace to you from the One who is and was and is coming.
—Revelation 1:4

World War I was a deadly conflict that raged from 1914 to 1918, claiming more than 16 million lives. Worst of all for the soldiers was trench warfare, where they shot at one another from deep trenches dug into the ground. The space between the opposing trenches was known as a no-man's-land.

On Christmas Eve, 1914, where the war was being fought in Flanders, Belgium, a miracle took place. On one side the English and the French hunkered down in their trenches. On the other side, the Germans did the same. It was a bitter cold night.

Then, drifting across no-man's-land, came the sound of German soldiers singing, "*Stille Nacht, Heilige Nacht.*" The others replied with the same tune in English: "Silent Night, Holy Night." Someone raised a sign: YOU NO SHOOT, WE NO SHOOT. The English and French soldiers waved a banner saying, MERRY CHRISTMAS. Before they knew it, they were out of their trenches, celebrating Christmas together.

The Christmas miracle of 1914 showed the love and peace of Jesus breaking through and touching human hearts in a powerful way.

Thank You, God, for Your miracle-working love and peace.

? Want to know more? See November 5, "Who Is J. R. R. Tolkien?"

What Is the Christmas Miracle of 1914? (Part 2)

The angel said to them, "Don't be afraid, because I am bringing you some good news. It will be a joy to all the people."

—LUKE 2:10

Yesterday we learned how a simple Christmas carol invited God's Spirit to halt a raging war—if only for one night and day. *Stille Nacht* ("Silent Night") was written in Austria in 1818. In 1859, a pastor in New York City translated the English version we sing today. As you read part of this beloved hymn, I hope you'll feel God's love and peace in your heart, just as the soldiers in World War I did so many years ago.

Silent night, holy night,
All is calm, all is bright
Round yon virgin mother and
    Child.
Holy infant, so tender and
    mild,
Sleep in heavenly peace,
Sleep in heavenly peace.

Silent night, holy night,
Shepherds quake at the sight;
Glories stream from heaven
    afar,
Heavenly hosts sing Alleluia!
Christ the Savior is born,
Christ the Savior is born!

Thank You, God, that Christ my Savior is born. Alleluia!

Why Do We Give Gifts at Christmas?

"Surely your heavenly Father will give good things to those who ask him."
—MATTHEW 7:9–11

In the days leading up to Christmas, more books, toys, games, clothing, and candy are advertised and sold than any other time of year. Do you have a gift list for others? Giving gifts to family and friends at Christmas is a loving thing to do. Receiving gifts is fun too! But sometimes we can get so excited about Christmas presents that we almost forget the reason we are giving and receiving them.

Yes, it is true that we give gifts to our family, friends, and teachers to show our love and appreciation for them. But at Christmas there is a deeper, even more important reason for gift-giving.

The Bible says that God loves to give good gifts to His human children (Matthew 7:11). We give gifts at Christmas to remind us of God's greatest gift to the world—His Son, Jesus. Gifts help us remember and celebrate God's great generosity and love.

> *God, with every Christmas gift I give and receive,
> help me remember Your loving gift of Jesus!*

? Want to know more? See February 5, "Who Is Jesus?" and March 1, "What Other Things Besides Miracles Did Jesus Do to Show Us What God Is Like?"

Why Do Some People Spell Christmas "Xmas"?

Pilate wrote a sign and put it on the cross. It read: "JESUS OF NAZARETH, THE KING OF THE JEWS." The sign was written in the Jewish language, in Latin, and in Greek.

—JOHN 19:19–20

The word *Xmas* is sometimes used as a short way of spelling "Christmas." In the days of the early church, Greek was a commonly spoken and written language. When Jesus was crucified, the sign attached to the cross was written in three languages: Latin, the language of Jerusalem's Roman rulers; Aramaic, the language of Jesus and the Jews; and Greek, the shared common language of the day. In the Greek alphabet, the cross-shaped letter *X*, or *chi*, is the first letter of the Greek word *Christos*, which means "Christ." In the early church, the Greek letter *chi* was often used as a symbol for Jesus. Some people today think it is disrespectful to use Xmas as a short way of spelling Christmas. But the early Christians wouldn't think so. The letter *X* actually *does* stand for Christ!

> Thank You, God, for Your awesome gift of human language! Whenever I speak or write of You, help me choose my words carefully.

? Want to know more? See May 2, "What Is the Bible?"; May 6 and 7, "What's the Difference Between the Old Testament and the New Testament? (Parts 1 and 2)"; and August 9, "What Is the Secret Message Hiding in the Greek Word for Fish?"

What Is the Difference Between Saint Nicholas and Santa Claus? (Part 1)

A bishop then must be blameless, . . . temperate, sober-minded, of good behavior, [and] hospitable.
—1 TIMOTHY 3:2 NKJV

Saint Nicholas was a real person who was born around AD 270, in modern-day Turkey. Nicholas loved Jesus. He served as a bishop, or leader, in the early Christian church and was known for his kindness, wisdom, and generosity. He died in AD 343, on December 6, which became known as Saint Nicholas Day.

In one famous story, Saint Nicholas gave a gift to a poor man with three daughters. The man loved his daughters, but because he didn't have any money, his daughters couldn't get married. (Back then, it was the custom for the bride's family to give money to the groom's family.) Saint Nicholas threw three bags of gold coins through an open window in the man's house. The bags landed in each daughter's stocking, which the girls had hung above the fireplace to dry. Over time, the legend of Saint Nicholas as a giver of gifts grew famous around the world. Does Saint Nicholas remind you a little bit of Santa Claus?

Thank You, God, for Saint Nicholas!

? Want to know more? See November 1, "What Is All Saints' Day?"

What Is the Difference Between Saint Nicholas and Santa Claus? (Part 2)

Every good action and every perfect gift is from God.
—JAMES 1:17

Yesterday we learned about the real-life Saint Nicholas. He's also the inspiration for Santa Claus! When English settlers arrived in America, they had Dutch neighbors. The Dutch name for Saint Nicholas is *Sinterklaas*. When excited English-speaking children repeated it, it came out sounding like "Santa Claus!"

For centuries, Saint Nicholas was pictured as a tall, thin man in a red robe with a white horse. In 1809, American author Washington Irving wrote a story that described Saint Nicholas as plump and bearded, smoking a clay pipe, and riding a wagon in the sky that was filled with gifts.

In 1823, a newspaper published a poem that came to be known as "The Night Before Christmas." In it, "Saint Nick" had a round belly, twinkling eyes, and a nose like a cherry. He drove a sleigh with eight flying reindeer. In the 1930s, the Coca-Cola company released an advertisement poster featuring Santa in the first ever red Santa suit.

Americans love the legend of Santa Claus. And why not? He's fun! But remember: tomorrow is the day we celebrate Jesus' birthday.

Thank You, God, for Christmas Eve!

Is December 25 Really Jesus' Birthday?

In [Jesus] there was life. That life was light for the people of the world.
—JOHN 1:4–5

No one knows what day Jesus was born. The decision to celebrate Jesus' birth in December came from Constantine the Great (AD 306–337), Rome's first Christian emperor. Life in ancient Rome was hard. People worshipped many gods, including Sol, the sun god. For one week, beginning on December 17, they celebrated a festival called Saturnalia, to welcome back the sun and longer days. They sang and danced and feasted. They decorated trees, a symbol of growth, and they gave gifts to one another. Constantine loved Jesus and decided to replace the festival welcoming the sun god. Instead, they would worship God's Son, Jesus! The first mention of a December 25 Christmas is in AD 336. The word *Christmas* comes from an early English phrase meaning "Mass of Christ." In the Roman church, *mass* means "worship service." Today most Christians celebrate Christmas on December 25.* It's a time to celebrate God's love for all His children—including *you*!

> *Because Eastern Orthodox Christians use a different church calendar, they celebrate Christmas on January 7.

Thank You, God, for Christmas!

? Want to know more? See February 6, "When Was Jesus Born?"; October 12, "How Did the Christian Church Grow Over the Ages? (Part 1)"; and December 16, "Was There Really a Star of Bethlehem?"

What Is the Parable of the Long Spoons?

Jesus said, "Feed my sheep."
—JOHN 21:17 NIV

The parable of the long spoons is a medieval tale about the difference between heaven and hell. It's not from the Bible, but it still contains a spiritual truth in a memorable way. It goes like this:

One day, a student wanted to know the difference between heaven and hell. His wise teacher said, "Follow me, and I will show you."

They took a peek into hell. They saw people sitting at long tables filled with steaming bowls of delicious stew. But the people were nothing but skin and bones! Some were angry. Others were sobbing. All were exhausted and starving. Because their wooden spoons were six feet long, they couldn't bend their arms enough to feed themselves!

Then the student and teacher took a peek into heaven. They saw people sitting at long tables filled with steaming bowls of delicious stew. Their spoons were six feet long too. But the people in heaven were well-fed, healthy, and happy. The difference? In heaven, they reached their long spoons across the table to *feed one another!*

What's the lesson? Love and kindness can transform even the worst situation into something beautiful and good.

> *Thank You, God, for Your heavenly, life-transforming love!*

? **Want to know more?** See July 7, "What Is a Parable?"

DECEMBER 27

What Is the Difference Between an Atheist and an Agnostic?

*But God showed mercy to me because I did not know what I
was doing. I did those things when I did not believe.*
—1 TIMOTHY 1:13

An atheist is someone who believes God doesn't exist. *Atheist* means
"godless" or "without God." An agnostic is someone who believes people
can't know if God exists. *Agnostic* means "incapable of being known."
I can't imagine how sad this makes our loving Father God feel. Even
though atheists and agnostics don't believe in God, God still loves them.
Belief in God and in His Son, Jesus, is a gift that God offers all people.
But like any gift, it must be accepted and opened. So how does a person
get faith? The apostle Paul says, "Faith comes from hearing the Good
News. And people hear the Good News when someone tells them about
Christ" (Romans 10:17). Do you know someone who might want to accept
God's gift of faith? If so, share what you know about God's reality and
love. More precious than gold, belief in God and His Son, Jesus, can
change a person's life forever.

Thank You, God, for Your awesome gift of faith. I joyfully accept!

? Want to know more? See January 29, "What Are God's Promises
for Me When I Need More Faith?"; July 26, "What Is Faith?";
and November 15, "How Do I Tell a Friend About Jesus?"

Is It Okay to Question and Sometimes Have Doubts About God?

I do believe; help me overcome my unbelief!
—MARK 9:24 NIV

Yes, everyone does. **Questioning God** is not unbelief. It's the sign of a healthy, curious mind! God loves it when you're honest and bring Him all your questions and doubts. That's because God knows you inside and out and cares deeply about every detail of your life! When you ask questions and admit your doubts, you're in good company. Many famous believers sometimes felt unsure about God. The apostle Thomas doubted Jesus had risen—until Jesus visited him in His resurrected body! Saint John of the Cross, a sixteenth-century Spanish believer, called his doubt the "dark night of the soul." When Jesus was suffering on the cross, He questioned: "My God, why have you left me alone?" (Mark 15:34). He was in terrible pain and felt totally cut off from His Father. But even then, Jesus never lost His faith and never stopped asking God questions.

> *Thank You, God, that I can come to You anytime, anywhere, with any question.*

? Want to know more? See January 29, "What Are God's Promises for Me When I Need More Faith?"; March 19, "What Are the Seven Sayings of Jesus on the Cross? (Part 2)"; and October 24, "What Is a Quiet Time?"

What Is a Godparent?

*You are . . . fellow citizens with God's people
and also members of his household.*
—EPHESIANS 2:19 NIV

What do you think when you hear the word *godparent*? I always used to think of the fairy godmother in *Sleeping Beauty*! That changed when my best friend asked *me* to be her son's godmother. What an honor! But what did being a godparent mean?

My pastor explained that godparenting goes back to the early Christian church, when believers were persecuted and people lived shorter lives. A godparent is a *steward*, or guardian of faith, for a newly baptized child, helping make sure the child is raised knowing God and Jesus, and is involved in the church. A godparent can pray, give fun faith-building gifts, and remember the anniversary of the godchild's baptism.

As soon as I learned what being a godparent meant, I called my friend back and said, "Yes, yes, yes, I would love to be Joshua's godmother!" I'm going to say a prayer for him right now. While I'm at it, I'll say a prayer for you too!

Thank You, God, for Your loving gifts of godparents and godchildren!

? Want to know more? See July 26, "What Is Faith?"; September 16, "What Is the Most Important Prayer in the World?"; and September 17, "What Is the Church?"

Is It Really Possible for Mountains and Trees to Sing?

Earth, shout for joy, even in your deepest parts! Sing, you mountains,
with thanks to God. Sing, too, you trees in the forest!
—ISAIAH 44:23

The Bible is full of descriptions of God's creation singing His praises—not only humans, but the heavens and our earth, including animals, rivers, oceans, mountains, and trees! How can the earth shout? How can mountains and trees sing? For years I thought this language was simply poetic—beautiful and expressive, not really real. After all, our planet is not "alive." It's made of rock, with a molten lava core. Then, one day, a friend showed me an amazing satellite video of the Earth sped up. I couldn't believe my eyes as I watched the icecaps grow and shrink and deserts turn from brown to green. The time-lapse motion made it look as though our planet was breathing! Earth was *not* just a piece of dead rock; it was alive!

"God is the King of all the earth," the Bible says. "So sing a song of praise to him" (Psalm 47:7). So, yes, it's possible for the Earth to shout and for the mountains and trees to sing!

Thank You, God, for our living, breathing planet Earth.

? Want to know more? See August 7, "Why Is Taking Care of Our Planet Important to Christians?"; November 11, "Who Is Madeleine L'Engle?"; and December 11, "Can I Believe in Science and Still Believe in God?"

What Does Jesus Mean When He Tells Us to Be Perfect?

"You must be perfect, just as your Father in heaven is perfect."
—MATTHEW 5:48

A year has nearly passed, and a new one is almost here! Now's the time for making New Year's resolutions. A *resolution* is a well-intentioned, firm decision to do or improve something. For me, this means to eat less junk food and watch less TV. Wait a minute . . . those are exactly the same resolutions I made last year!

In today's verse, Jesus tells us to be "perfect." *Ugh.* For a long time I wondered, *How could Jesus ask such a thing? How can He forget that because we are human beings, perfection is not possible?* Then I learned that the Greek word commonly translated "perfect" in this passage more accurately means "whole" or "complete." Wow! Suddenly the verse made sense! Jesus is not telling us to be perfect, which is impossible. Jesus is telling us to be *whole and complete*, which—thanks to God's perfect love—*is* possible.

Jesus is making you whole. It doesn't happen overnight; it's a lifelong process (Philippians 2:12–13). Remember this when you're making New Year's resolutions. God bless you on your faith journey over the coming year!

> *Thank You, God, for loving me and making me whole.*

? Want to know more? See February 1, "What Are God's Promises for Me When I Have Failed?"

Index of Questions

Jesus

God's Holy Spirit

The Bible

The Bible: Old Testament

The Bible: New Testament

The Church

Christian Seasons, Holidays, and Traditions

Famous Christians